ROADBLOCKS ON THE JOURNEY OF PSYCHOTHERAPY

ROADBLOCKS ON THE JOURNEY OF PSYCHOTHERAPY

Jane S. Hall, M.S.W.

JASON ARONSON
Lanham • Boulder • New York • Toronto • Oxford

Published in the United States of America
by Jason Aronson
An imprint of Rowman & Littlefield Publishers, Inc.

A wholly owned subsidiary of The Rowman & Littlefield Publishing Group, Inc.
4501 Forbes Boulevard, Suite 200, Lanham, Maryland 20706
www.rowmanlittlefield.com

PO Box 317
Oxford
OX2 9RU, UK

British Library Cataloguing in Publication Information Available

Library of Congress Cataloging-in-Publication Data

Hall, Jane S.
Roadblocks on the journey of psychotherapy / Jane S. Hall.
p. cm.
Includes bibliographical references and index.
ISBN 0-7657-0349-1 (hardcover : alk. paper)
1. Transference (Psychology) 2. Psychotherapist and patient. 3. Psychotherapy. I. Title.

RC489.T73H355 2004
616.89'17—dc22

2004005303

Printed in the United States of America

∞™ The paper used in this publication meets the minimum requirements of American National Standard for Information Sciences—Permanence of Paper for Printed Library Materials, ANSI/NISO Z39.48-1992.

To the patients who are the real teachers.
In memory of Gertrude Blanck

Contents

Acknowledgments

My first thank you goes to Norma Pomerantz for her initial phone calls. "How about another book, Jane." Six months later: "Are you working yet, Jane?" Jason Aronson has been encouraging and patient, as have Jason Proetorius and Jon Sisk at Rowman & Littlefield. Louise Crandall gave me some ideas she thought would be helpful to her for teaching purposes: "A modern-day textbook on the basics" was one idea, so the first four chapters were inspired by her. Arlene Richards has been tremendously encouraging and has read many chapters, enthusiastically and helpfully, and Arnie Richards has straightened me out about some important things. Barbara Stimmel is a wonderful writer and having her editorial advice, sometimes on a moment's notice, has certainly improved the book. Karen Trokan carefully read and helped me rethink two chapters. Ed Eisenberg has been thoughtfully encouraging and Eve Golden, my editor, has been tough and wonderful at the same time.

Teaching and supervising at the New York School for Psychoanalytic Psychotherapy and Psychoanalysis, the New York Freudian Society, and the Metropolitan Institute, as well as in private seminars has continued to shape and improve my teaching skills. Many students shared clinical vignettes and I want to thank them for their generosity: Karen Szurek, Rachel Miller, Janet Bellsey, Laura Cholowsky and Sidney Rosenblatt, Tracy Morgan, and Craig Warn. I was also privileged to present papers and lead workshops at the Southwest Florida (Tampa) Psychoanalytic Society, the NASW in New Jersey, the National Membership Committee on Psychoanalysis, and also in Boca Raton, Florida, and on Staten Island. Meeting the dedicated clinicians and students who attended these symposiums alerted me to all kinds of important clinical concerns in treating patients that I try to address in these pages.

I learned so much from my close friends, Liz McKamy and Arlene Richards, who generously contributed rich clinical material.

On a personal note: my daughter, Devra, a published author, teacher, dear friend, and lovely person pre-edited the whole book. Seeing how she combines her perfectionism with patience has been a revelation and something to emulate. My husband, Jim, has stood by—cheering me on and up when I needed it—making it possible for me to spend the time on this project. His sense of taste, timing, and humor, and his dedication to growing creatively, have always inspired me. And last, but certainly not least, thanks to Django, my dog, who sat by fairly patiently for over two years trying to get a word in, remaining ever affectionate and ready to play during breaks.

Introduction: Perspectives

Once a journey toward self-understanding has begun, impulses to turn back may threaten the process. Even when progress seems to be smooth, the smoothness itself may be masking a struggle against real change. Inner roadblocks on both sides of the couch impede the journey of psychoanalytic psychotherapy, and these roadblocks are what this book is about. Conscious and unconscious resistances, transference fantasies and fears, the wish to avoid anxiety—these are ubiquitous; in fact, they are at the same time the reason for psychotherapy and the means by which it is accomplished. The patient's tendency to cling to the status quo is the major roadblock in treatment and a serious challenge to the quest for self-understanding, knowledge, and growth. When the road becomes dangerous or disappears, it is the therapist who must build bridges, ford rivers, cross deserts, and brave storms, all the while keeping her fearful patient/companion from abandoning the journey. Sometimes it is necessary to sit by the side of the road for a long time until the dangers appear less acute (chapter 8); sometimes the road remains impassable and the journey ends precipitously.

The pressure to repeat the past in the present, including the attachments to pain and the difficulty of letting go of abusive relationships (both internal and external) are enemies of growth and change. These roadblocks (*resistances*) and some of the forms they take will be explored and illustrated in this book.

Psychoanalytically informed psychotherapy is the work of making connections—between past and present, conscious and unconscious, dream and waking life, patient and therapist, fantasy and enactment. In making these connections, both parties cooperate in identifying tears in the fabric of life and sometimes in reweaving them.

The first connection in this work is between patient and therapist. Psychodynamic psychotherapy is a collaborative effort (although it often does not feel that way) to understand and modify behavior and perception, thereby making new choices available and change possible. Without the therapist's commitment to the process and her courage as a guide on this most important journey, the patient's confidence will waver. The therapist needs perseverance, fortitude, the nerve to embrace questions without knowing the answers, and a willingness to explore uncharted territory if she is to convince her patient that she is worthy of trust. Her understanding of, empathy for, and courage in the face of the patient's fear of change, and her ability to recognize, address, and contain the anxieties beneath it, help keep the possibility of travel alive.

The actual psychotherapeutic work begins with the very first phone call. Even the process of making the initial appointment adds a new layer to the structure of fantasy that is already in place. As the patient begins to discover the derivatives of her unconscious and its complex and often destructive forms of expression, the very problems that interfere with functioning in the outside world start to appear in the consulting room with the therapist. Problem relationships, addictive cravings, fears and wishes about dependency, inhibitions, dissatisfactions in general begin to take shape and become manifest within the treatment. The patient begins to see the therapist with less and less objectivity as the patient's expectations, fears, and desires (*the transference*) take center stage. Regardless of how the therapist behaves, the patient may idealize, denigrate, mistrust, love, or hate her. Such transference feelings are usually based on past relationships, and the real crux of psychoanalytically based treatment is the work in and with the transference, for this is where the patient has a chance to observe and examine in safety her deepest feelings. This same transference, however, so important and useful, may also become the most powerful obstacle to change. How does this happen? This book addresses that complex and intriguing question.

Roadblocks on the Journey of Psychotherapy is also about the *therapist's* resistance to the work, and the forms this resistance takes. *Countertransference* (chapter 2) is as powerful a concept as transference. The therapist must constantly scan her own thoughts, fantasies, and behavior for evidence of feelings—hostile, envious, erotic, rageful, controlling, and so on—that she may be acting out in the treatment. Empathy, responsibility, and genuine, benevolent curiosity are important conscious attitudes, but the therapist also needs access to her unconscious ones, to her own anxieties, prejudices, and predilections. These are bound to distract her from time to time, affecting the treatment, and the therapist needs constructive ways to face this inevitability (chapters 2 and 7).

The single error that is most often fatal to the work is to give up what has been called *the therapeutic frame* (Langs, 1976). This frame guarantees the patient a place where judgment is not passed, where reflection is encouraged, and where confidentiality is assured; it provides a consistent time, a therapist who is on time for appointments, who listens attentively, and who remains as abstinent and as neutral as possible. Once the therapist gives up the wish to understand and replaces it by attempting to direct, advise, or control, the treatment is in danger, whether it ends prematurely or not. Flexibility, tact, timing, and common sense, within a well-established and carefully protected therapeutic frame, are the bedrock of any successful psychotherapy. Because each treatment is different, rigidity has no place in this work. However, the concepts of neutrality and abstinence are too valuable to discard. *Abstinence* is defined by Webster's New Collegiate Dictionary (1975) as "voluntary forbearance especially from indulgence of appetite." In psychoanalysis it means the same thing, relating specifically but not exclusively to sexual boundary violations.

To me, *neutrality* means relaxing my propensity to make judgments and accepting instead that any person has many layers, ideas, capacities, affects, and defenses, most of which will never be exposed, even in treatment. Whatever *is* exposed must be greeted with benign curiosity (Sharpe, 1947) and not judgment. Neutrality is not a given, but a stance for the therapist to strive for. It was once thought that the therapist was a "blank screen" or "mirror." As psychoanalytic theory advanced, the idea of neutrality has been challenged as impossible, and sometimes as undesirable as well. I think, however, with many of my colleagues, that these concepts have more of a place than ever in the field of analytic work. It is ironic, for example, that at the same time that abstinence and neutrality are being called obsolete concepts, there are more reported sexual violations in the field of psychoanalysis than ever before. Moreover, the ensuring of boundaries is soothing and sensible when explained to the patient. Not to take sides is another important example of neutrality. We therapists must leave room for the patient to change her perception and her perspective, for if we invest too much in any one view of the patient's past or present, she may feel pressured to perpetuate her story. The steadiness and consistency of that neutrality and abstinence facilitate new experiences for many of our more fragile patients. In fact, patients often need to test the therapeutic frame and its boundaries for long periods of time before they feel safe enough to trust it. Many of our patients need the consistent and caring atmosphere necessary to optimal development, and they require a background of safety and steadiness in which self and object constancy can develop (Sandler, 1960).

Remembering who you are is key in psychodynamic work. However empathic or sympathetic (or shocked or overwhelmed) the therapist may be in this work so filled with transference, countertransference, and resistance, the fact that she is a guide with one purpose will help her stay the course. The clinician's main job is to clear the path so that the journey can continue for as long as it must. The jobs of judge, jury, assistant, crutch, seer, or enabler belong to someone else. The therapist is both a leader and a follower; she is consistent; she maintains confidentiality; she is a "new object" (Loewald,

1960); she does not demand or expect equal time. Her modus operandi must stem at all times from a benign curiosity and respect for the patient's autonomy.

This book is meant for clinicians who want to understand and negotiate the roadblocks that get in the way of a deepening treatment. Awareness of the theory behind technique is indispensable, even though the pathways through the unexplored terrains of psychotherapy are largely intuitive and dependent on unconscious connections the dyad partners make with each other. In all treatments, there are times when one partner (or both) wants to give up. Empathy, will, stamina, and insight may be eroded by fatigue, fear, or hatred. At times like these especially, respect for the patient and respect for the method can save the day. The theories that guide us in our encounters with therapeutic obstacles have been multiplying ever since the early days of psychoanalysis. The therapist has been understood as blank screen, as mirror, as idealized object, as collaborator, and as co-actor. What do these shifts mean? Are they for the benefit of the patient or the therapist? Does familiarity with the history of technique enhance our understanding of present issues and debates? How much should we clinicians focus on the patient's remembered past, style of defense, adaptive capacities, and fantasies? How much should we focus on the "here and now" interaction, with or without tracing it to the past? Such questions are important to explore. Only as we listen to a patient can we learn how to help her, and only as she observes us can she decide if she can use our particular kind of help. The beauty of psychoanalytically informed work is its flexibility How to view and interpret resistance, where to hear and use transference, when to work in the here and now, and when to trace back to the past—these are skills that we use differently, depending on the patient. What I find more and more in my own work is that the patient makes the theory.

Understanding is hard and complex work. Moments of bewilderment and frustration interweave with times of intense pleasure, keeping the treatment alive (when we are lucky) when it seems dead, hopeful when pessimism takes over, and possible when times are bleak.

How I assess, listen, perceive, and connect rests on my intuition, my experience, the work of my own analysis, awareness of my countertransference, and my own individual theory of technique. Familiarity with the vicissitudes of transference, enactment, unconscious fantasy, attachment, individuation, object relations, depressive and paranoid positions, drive and defense—all help me get my bearings when I'm lost. My focus on listening, resonating, and keeping myself at the service of the patient's journey of self-understanding is another intangible that helps me stay in touch with how we are progressing, digressing, and regressing along the way.

Chapter 1, "Transference," and chapter 2, "Countertransference," explore these concepts and how they affect treatment. The recognition and interpretation of "here and now" transference manifestations are illustrated, as are when and how to connect them to the past (*genetic interpretation*). The use of reconstruction and the reasons for letting transference phenomena build are discussed. Transference as resistance is explained and illustrated, as is resistance to the awareness of transference. Case material illustrates the early interpretation of transference and how it can pave the way to deeper work by engaging the patient in the use of this powerful tool. Most examples illustrate more than one aspect of transference and so are somewhat interchangeable. Resistance to the awareness of transference, for instance, may also present itself as hidden transference, negative transference, and enactment.

"Tracking Transference," chapter 3, gives clinical illustrations of the use of the transference and discusses how to hear it and make it useful to the patient.

Chapter 4, "Inner Roadblocks," briefly sketches the history of the concept of resistance. It demonstrates the understanding of resistances as messages that express unconscious fears and fantasies and provides information about resistances. It discusses examples of acting out and enactment. When roadblocks of this kind occur, turning them into bridges by putting activity into words and then connecting the words to feelings becomes the major task of therapy.

The most formidable block to psychoanalytic work with abused patients is the patient's attachment to the abuser and her representatives in the patient's inner and outer worlds. The tenacity of the need to repeat the sadomasochistic approach to life can be modified only by intensive work. The patient's fear of letting go of the abuser threatens the treatment because the internalized abuser is now an integral part of the patient. This is a fact that has to be reckoned with by the therapist. Chapter 5, "Attachment to Abuse," explains this roadblock and considers both the patient's fear of giving up the internalized abusive object and the way this fear can frustrate the therapist. Manifestations of sadomasochistic attachments within the therapy are a constant threat to therapeutic work.

Sometimes an analytic dyad may skirt or avoid a patient's rage (Hall, 1998). This avoidance can grow into a major obstacle. Chapter 6, "The Many Faces of Rage," shows the lengths to which people may go in their efforts to camouflage, deny, and bury murderous rage, and how important it is that the therapist helps unearth it—and withstand it. How to spot derivatives of disguised rage, how to use the countertransference, and how to recognize *projective identification* are illustrated. As unconscious fantasies and feelings of rage and envy are expressed in words, a shift in the work takes place. The deadness in the treatment characteristic of denied anger ebbs as murderous wishes emerge. Sterile verbal exchange becomes fruitful again. Rage as a defense against loving feelings is also explored.

Chapter 7, "Professional Dilemmas," looks at the ways therapists may be deflected from their therapeutic aims and at other distractions such as interruptions and conscious and unconscious reactions to patients. Psychotherapists are often asked, "How can you do that? Isn't it *depressing*?" What are the answers to those questions? How necessary is the therapist's own therapy? What happens when either party becomes ill? This chapter describes in some detail the experiences of pressure, frustration, and hope of the therapist over the course of treatment.

"Stalemates and Beyond," chapter 8, provides examples of some therapies that ended prematurely. Patients frequently threaten to "quit," or they provoke the therapist into ending treatment. What should a therapist do in the face of these extreme resistances? Isolation of affect, the perverse transference, and regression in treatment are examined. These roadblocks may affect the therapist deeply and may cause countertransference reactions severe enough to damage a treatment. This chapter raises questions about if, when, and how to end a treatment.

"Light at the End of the Tunnel," chapter 9, looks at the pretermination period from both sides of the couch. Depression or depressive states, sadness, anxiety, recurrence of symptoms, and silence are some of the hallmarks of this phase, along with signs of increasing wellness and joy. How long the termination phase should be, when and how the date should be set, how to handle the last meeting, and the uniqueness of the experience for both of the therapeutic partners are explored.

Roadblocks on the Journey of Psychotherapy is a sequel to *Deepening the Treatment* (Hall, 1998). Like its predecessor, it addresses some of the common issues that therapists must understand and learn to contend with in constructive ways—ways that will clarify the therapeutic process and facilitate the journey to self-knowledge. The two books share some themes; in them, as in psychotherapeutic work, certain themes come up again and again. I encourage clinicians to explore, search, wonder, and connect. There are no absolute answers—only the deepening connection between patient and therapist that, when the work goes well, eventually alters the lenses through which both explorers see the world.

TRAVEL TIPS

The rules of the road are not meant to constrain, but to keep the travelers safe.

- Benevolent curiosity is the compass.
- The therapist's walking shoes are consistency and reliability.
- Setting appropriate boundaries are her gifts.
- Her walking stick is patience.
- Trust is her destination.
- Countertransference is her radar.
- Neutrality is her life vest.
- Humor saves the day.

❖ CHAPTER 1 ❖

Transference: Its Ubiquity and Utility

> . . . the history itself, a patchwork of seeing and not seeing, a collage of knowing and not knowing, a full cloth made up of many intricate, differently colored tatters. Family chronology defies consciousness. Things happen that we don't know about, and by happening affect the very molecules of our own perception. And so we do not see the prism, all we see are the bends in the light that make the faces of our loved ones seem at times much too beautiful, and at other times, much, much less than pretty.
>
> —Nomi Eve

> Transference is not simply a defense or a displacement of libidinal energy onto the analyst, as Freud proposed at different points in his attempt to grapple with what he was seeing clinically. It is also not simply the activation of an old representation lying in wait. Indeed, transference is not really about "transfer" at all—it is about a continual construction and reconstruction of thoughts, feelings, wishes, fears, patterns of relating, and ways of regulating affect in the context of new relationship experiences that can be understood only in the context of old ones . . . in the deeply intimate, authority-laden situation that constitutes psychoanalytic forms of treatment.
>
> —Drew Westen and Glen O. Gabbard

Transference is ubiquitous. Our perceptions of the present are based on how past relationships and experiences have been internalized, and on the fantasies that organize them. Transference is the most powerful concept in psychoanalytic work, and it is the lens through which everyday life is seen by patient and therapist both. The purpose of psychoanalytic work is to adjust the lenses—our defenses—thereby allowing old and new pictures to be seen with less distortion and from different angles. Transference is the superimposition of unconscious fantasies, anxieties, and object worlds onto everyday life. It drives us to do what we do, see what we see, and be who we are. It explains why we like some people and dislike others, why three people witnessing a crime will observe it differently, and why each of us has a unique way of perceiving, reacting, and relating to the world. The task of psychoanalytic work is to deepen self-knowledge by connecting outside with inside and past with present. Understanding what motivates us by examining the relationship between patient and therapist in the treatment leads to deeper and more satisfying relationships.

I had a patient, for example, who could not hold a job. Laura experienced every boss she ever had as unfair and demanding and would either quit after a few months or be fired for her antagonistic attitude. As the treatment progressed, problems with authority came alive in the transference. It was I who was the bossy and stubborn one. I have policies about paying for missed sessions and sticking to scheduled times. Laura understood these policies and had agreed to them before we began our work. But after several months she began challenging me. "How can you demand so much money?" she'd ask. "Why can't I stay as long as I want to? You're just like my sister, bossing me around all the time." As we explored these feelings, Laura began to understand the history of her relationship with her sister and why she had needed to provoke her in every way possible. Over time, this insight helped Laura understand how she repeated the past in the present—with me and with her bosses. There are more examples of work with the transference in chapter 3.

Transference is both the motor and the main roadblock in psychoanalytic work. It is the therapist's best friend and her worst enemy. It is both pervasive and elusive, often hard to see precisely because it is so encompassing and so well rationalized. The quality of our attachments from infancy through adulthood, along with our innate endowments—self and object representations, unconscious fantasies, and anxieties of loving and losing—create the templates of all our later relationships and experiences. The way experience is perceived in a developing person is influenced by stimuli from both outside and in, and a patient's view of her psychotherapist (and of others) tends to be molded both by her needs and by her expectations. Change and growth occur when the patient can in the present relate to, and experience with, the therapist the loving and hateful emotions that have their origin in the past. It often takes a long time before the patient can see that the therapist is not in fact the dreaded father or the spiteful sister or the disappointing mother, and that these figures themselves were perhaps not as dreaded or spiteful or disappointing as they seemed. But over time, the patient's readiness to let go of or modify her transference distortions makes growth possible.

The concept of transference has encompassed a number of different ideas over time: that transference is a displacement of libidinal energy on to the analyst, which is why patients fall in love with their analysts (Freud, 1914); that the negative transference must be exposed, lest important angry feelings be hidden beneath a façade of cooperation and compliance (Reich, 1933–34); that transference is the use of the analyst as a self–object, that the analyst is perceived and needed as part of the self (Kohut, 1971); that transference is the total psychotherapy situation, that everything that occurs in treatment is a reference to feelings about the therapist (Josephs, 1985); and that transference is an ego function (Bird, 1972). As Bird wrote,

> Transference, in my view, is a very special mental quality that has never been satisfactorily explained. . . . I am particularly taken with the as yet unexplored idea that transference is a universal mental function which may well be the basis of all human relationships. I even suspect it as being one of the mind's main agencies for giving birth to new ideas, and new life to old ones. In these several respects, transference would seem to me to assume characteristics of a major ego function. (Bird, 1972, p. 267)

This chapter, and the two that follow it, elucidate what we mean when we refer to transference, what lies beneath it, and how its exploration leads to growth. Clinical vignettes will illustrate:

- Recognizing, tolerating, understanding, and interpreting transference
- Letting the transference build
- Using the here and now aspects of transference
- Connecting present manifestations of transference to the past

WHAT DOES UNCONSCIOUS FANTASY HAVE TO DO WITH TRANSFERENCE?

Psychoanalytic theories on fantasy posit that certain wishes from childhood become fixated and structuralized and continue to press for a persistent demand for gratification or actualization. These demands and wishes are thought to become fantasy formations that impose themselves on the way we perceive reality. In fact, this is why we all have our own pictures of reality. Reality is always distorted to some degree by such unconscious fantasies (Arlow, 1969). When a person comes to treatment, the therapist is cast in a role or roles that reflect the person's fantasized needs and their attendant anxieties. The data of perception are organized and responded to in ways that actualize the unconscious fantasy system.

In a brief discussion of the developmental stages of life, I will give examples of ubiquitous unconscious fantasies that can emerge in derivative form within the transference during psychoanalytic work. The fantasies that accompany ego and psychosexual development are registered by and stored in the unconscious. In some ways, the unconscious can be likened to the hard drive of a computer, in that nothing is lost. What happens, we think, is that new information fed to the mind/brain/computer may mask, cover over, or blend with the original data, requiring experts to retrieve it, if necessary and when possible (Camelio, 2002). We can posit that, in people, early feelings and fantasies are embedded in the brain and blend with newer ones as the child matures. These memory constellations are organized by screen memories—that is, memories that screen out traumatic or overstimulating events. Most memories act as organizers of what happened before and after them, and in the case of painful experiences, this capacity can be enlisted in the interests of self-protection (Greenacre, 1969). An adult who chooses an object willing to repeat past traumas (as in sadomasochistic relationships, for example) is perpetuating a familiar, although painful, past. In their work, a psychoanalytically based therapist and her patient aim to review the past from the vantage point of the present, using the new relationship that occurs in treatment as a lens (Loewald, 1960). This is a new relationship because the therapist is neutral, benevolently curious, empathic, and consistent. This kind of relationship *is* new to most people, who may have never been listened to before. Its novelty does not mean that the patient drops her need to play out the past in the present with the therapist, but the therapist does not respond according to the patient's transference needs. For instance, the therapist does not respond in kind to a patient's angry, provocative, or insulting remarks. The therapist's benign curiosity and steadiness, her empathy, and the insight she shares offer the patient a space in which to review perceptions, to grow, and to form new attachments. But to the extent that the patient is frightened of change, it may not be easy for her to make use of this space. Powerful anxieties—about separation, loss of the love object or of the superego's love, and fears of castration impede the work.

Freud (1914) believed that repression and symptoms hid and disguised early traumatic memories and fantasies, and he expected that memories would emerge in the analysis through the patient's free association. However, remembering is often too painful, and at those times people use defenses such as denial, dissociation, fragmentation, psychosis, and disavowal to protect themselves from it. Therefore, retrieving memory is no longer the thrust of psychoanalytic work for most theoreticians and clinicians—it has been replaced, by and large, by the search for an affective, emotional understanding of how and why the present is experienced in the unique ways that it is. When an adult revisits, with the therapist, a traumatic childhood, a tremendous burden—the burden of loneliness—is lightened.

UNCONSCIOUS FANTASY

What is unconscious fantasy? How can it be recognized if it is unconscious? How does it inform the transference? Are primitive fantasies accessible? Sandler and Sandler write:

> Man lives simultaneously in two societies—one we know as people in the real external world, and the other [we know] in a phantom world of unconscious fantasy in which the objects are created, updated, and

> recreated, and subjectively reexperienced in relation to the self. We interact with our objects in both these worlds and spend much of our waking life trying to modify ourselves and our environments so that the discrepancy between the two is minimized. From these attempts flow transference, projection, rationalization, and many other familiar everyday phenomena. (Sandler and Sandler, 1998, p. 88)

Unconscious fantasies often appear in derivative form. A patient's initial compliance and unawareness of envy may hide from the therapist-as-parent an intense oedipal fantasy; similarly, a masochistic person may suffer from guilt over a fantasy of oedipal victory. Someone obsessed with cleanliness may be hiding a strong impulse to smear feces, and will eventually include the therapist in the fantasy by casting her as a rigid authority figure. A delinquent who lands in prison may crave boundaries, and her jailer becomes a father or mother whose conditions of love are clear and whose punishments are predictable. Although they are vastly different, the rules of prison life and the rules of therapy both provide structures within which fantasies can be played out. Acting up in prison guarantees punishment. Acting out in treatment opens a door to understanding. These simple generalizations are meant to illustrate that unconscious motives drive behavior.

A DEVELOPMENTAL DETOUR AND THE FANTASIES OF EARLY LIFE

The quality of attachment experienced by a baby and its mother is thought to influence the baby's future development (Fonagy, 2000). It is also thought that in early infancy the baby does not differentiate between self and other (Mahler et al., 1975). The texture of attachment between mother and baby, the mother's attunement, the baby's innate endowment—all these influence how differentiation is accomplished. Will it be smooth and safe or rough and traumatic? Will the baby be optimally encouraged to become a self? Whatever the combination of safety, attunement, roughness, and trauma, this attachment period prepares the baby for the negotiation of all further developmental steps.

In infancy, primitive wishes to eat up, swallow, suck, spit out—to merge with the maternal object and to reject her when she is frustrating—are probably reflected in the characteristic baby behavior of putting things in the mouth and spitting them out. In the treatment of an adult, similar interests might be portrayed by a rejection of the therapist's food (interpretations) or by extreme dependency (sucking the therapist dry). The transference picture may be one in which the patient wants more and more or takes in the therapist's words only to chew them up and spit them out. Chattering patients and patients who bring food to session clue the therapist to a needy, hungry transference and the ubiquitous fantasy "I will eat you up." The sayings "You're good enough to eat," "I could eat you up," and "You're delicious" refer to this early, primitive wish. Some eating disorders can be seen as a compromise between the wish to swallow up the object and the wish to spit it out.

Anal interests and the tasks of separation fill the two-year-old mind. Scatological humor and play and the newfound ability to say "no" are hallmarks of this stage of development, when a separate object, along with the difference between the sexes, is first acknowledged. The foundation of awareness of a separate object begins in the earliest phase of development when the infant is frustrated by an unavailable breast or bottle. How and when the baby is toilet trained affects the struggle between letting go and holding in. A strict, impatient mother may instill compliance based on fear, whereas a calm, patient, rewarding mother will have a smoother outcome. A mother who waits until the child seems ready to use the potty helps preserve the child's sense of control. These are basic generalizations, but power struggles left over from early childhood may make for difficult roadblocks in psychotherapy. Some ubiquitous fantasies—"I am omnipotent"; "*No* is my biggest weapon"; "A baby is born through the anus"; "I *will* make a mess"; "I won't let go of my shit"; "My shit is valuable"—are attempts to bear the loss of omnipotence.

In treatment, such anal fantasies may be expressed in the transference: "I won't pay you"; "I'll be here when I want to be"; "You'll have to prod me to talk." Adult wishes to smear that stem from childhood wishes may be hidden by reaction formations, including driven neatness, pseudokindness, extreme disorganization, and exaggerated sharing. Defiance may show in the transference as procrastination, stubbornness, the holding back of material, failure to pay therapy fees in a timely manner, and often, compliance and negative transference, all for the benefit of the therapist/anal-phase parent. On the other side of the coin, some patients need to impress on their therapists that they are *not* made of shit—their version of "valuable." The patient performs, drops names, and tries to impress and fascinate the therapist. Dramas such as these may be enacted on an enormous—and in the case of famous patients, often public—stage, to the great excitement of both therapist and patient.

Transitional objects and transitional phenomena as discussed by Winnicott (1971) are important in the developing child; they help navigate the rigors of separation and the mastery of the me/not me dilemma. These phenomena, too, may be reflected in the transference. A patient may hold on to a bill or a cancelled check to minimize or even deny separation from the therapist. One patient left a small packet of Kleenex in my medicine cabinet for over a year. Symbolically, she was always in the office. In everyday life, we all maintain mementos or rituals that allow us to think we can hold onto someone. Art, religion, fashion, and literature can all be seen as allaying the anxiety of separateness.

The phallic/oedipal child wants to compete and talks about mommy or daddy going away—dying—so that she can be the exclusive partner of the preferred parent. This oedipal wish can also be thought of as a defense against the realities of individuation. The child experiences herself standing alone in the oedipal threesome and longs to recapture the safety of the mother–child dyad. In therapy, the patient may express envy and jealousy. She competes with the therapist by showing off and/or worrying about the therapist's envy. She may resent others in the therapist's life and yearn for an exclusive relationship with her. Or, rather than competing with the therapist, she may sabotage her—try to make her fail, specifically in her therapeutic endeavors. The possibility of equaling or surpassing the therapist is a threatening one, as it raises the possibility that the therapist—the parent in the transference—in retaliation might leave. The therapist who can endure such competitive fantasies shows that a relationship can survive them and that, therefore, both parties can, too. The transference/countertransference arena—the connection between the dyad—is where all battles and celebrations take place, and the therapist's countertransference (chapter 2) can be used as a barometer of the patient's transference.

With the current focus on early attachment and on the separation/individuation stages, interest in the oedipal drama has lost some ground in psychoanalytic thought. The intense wish for the exclusive relationship with mother or father that involves fantasies of destroying the other parent need renewed attention (Loewald, 1979). Issues of self-esteem, the need for praise, competition in any arena are all influenced by oedipal wishes to conquer and by attendant fears of conquering. The transference aspect is clearest when the patient tries to defeat the analyst, either through failure to improve or by achieving goals that she believes are unwelcome to the analyst. But like all other transference manifestations, these need to be interpreted, understood, and resolved at the end of a successful treatment when both patient and therapist can recognize each other as equals.

Children's Stories and Transference

Developmental fantasies and fears common to us all are portrayed in children's stories. *Peter Rabbit* contains many themes: the temptations and risks of disobedience, the absent mother, eating someone else's food, the connection between assertion and danger, the fear of loss, and the hope of return. In *Snow White*, Prince Charming can be seen as the wished-for oedipal father, the woodsman might be the henpecked but concerned father, while the wicked stepmother can be thought of as an embodiment of Snow White's own projected envy, or as the bad oedipal mother's destructive envy of her beautiful daughter. The poison apple can connote the bad breast. *Bambi* is notorious, and important, for being one of the few stories for young children that deal explicitly with the death of the mother. *Winnie the Pooh* is about animals who, despite their differences, get along and have adventures together. Only in times of danger is Christopher Robin, the only human, called upon. The ability to touch base with the parent is referred to by Mahler et al. (1975) as refueling and crucial to the child in negotiating the rapprochement phase. This is a hallmark of separation/individuation, when separation anxiety is paramount. In psychoanalytic psychotherapy, the therapist listens with an ear for themes that may be variations of these early anxieties and wishes, and she looks for her own place in the transference, whether it is as Mrs. Rabbit or Christopher Robin or Snow White's mother.

Normal experiences of loss and pain leave children feeling helpless; fantasies of omnipotence help them tolerate these feelings. Superman, Batman, Wonder Woman, and Charlotte with her amazing web are some well-known heroes and heroines.

> Andrew, a thirty-year-old computer programmer, was addicted to Superman comic books. He was ashamed of this and didn't tell his therapist for months. When he did, he burst into tears. "How can I read this stuff? What's wrong with me? I hide this from my wife." Associating to Superman, Andrew began to see how unbearable were his feelings of impotence around his brother's death. His identification with Superman was eventually understood to be a compensation for the guilt and despair he felt, as well as a wish to rescue. Clark Kent represented the ten-year-old self that he was when his brother died, and of course Superman was who he longed to be. Expressing these feelings and experiencing the empathy he longed for in treatment let Andrew see that his need to be super was based on the fantasy that he should have saved his brother.

Exploration is a major theme in these books filled as they are with daring and safety, with loss and return, with the victory of good over evil. The presence of a rescuing figure is a constant; in chapter 5, "Attachment to Abuse," I elaborate some further developments of this theme that are common to abused children.

Fantasies such as these, from all stages of life, connect, overlap, and interweave, creating the fabric of our lives. It is important to remember that phases of development are never neatly organized and that the mind is always at work trying to resolve the difficulties and dangers of growing up and being grown up.

The inevitability of overstimulation and frustration in childhood leads to varying degrees of rage. The anxieties that surround the knowledge of the difference between the sexes and the idea of being a separate individual may at times feel overwhelming, and the solutions or compromises that we come to in dealing with them reflect our ability to be cruel as well as loving. Both sadism and masochism are normal developmental attitudes that begin in the oral phase of psychosexual development, when biting and sucking are major modes of connection. An adorable child is a cruel child as well, and this conjunction remains true throughout life. Sadomasochistic fantasies are ubiquitous outcomes of childhood—no matter how smoothly development may occur.

The personal and universal fantasies of patient and therapist may intertwine, resulting in enactment. "The word enactment suggests an action whose purpose, force, and intention are raised to high intensity. That intensity gives concreteness and actuality to its impact on the implicit other person in the field of action. It is an act, the intention of which is to persuade, or to force the other into a reciprocal action. The message is carried in words, silence, action, and particularly non-verbal communications" (McLaughlin and Johan, 1992). When an enactment is interpreted, understanding becomes possible and growth may occur. The therapist working with regressed patients cannot help but be affected. Her own conflicts, no matter how well resolved, are awakened to some degree; this may make her better able to identify with her patient, but the setup of therapy itself also revives power struggles, thus inviting sadomasochistic interactions that can be analyzed.

Children's Games and How They Recur in the Transference

The following familiar games and fantasies reflect some of the wishes and fears proper to the developmental stages and incorporate ways of dealing with the anxieties characteristic of them:

Peek-a-boo—*Are you still there? Did I swallow you up? I made you disappear. I made you come back. I am powerful.* Peek-a-boo addresses oral and differentiation issues and helps build a sense of object constancy. A reflection in therapy might be a patient who tests the therapist's reliability by missing a number of sessions and then returning for a scheduled appointment without calling to see if the therapist is still waiting.

Hide and seek and treasure hunts—*Have I lost a part of myself? Are my feces me? Where are they? Where are you? I will find you. Can you find me?* These are more sophisticated games, with both anal and separation roots. They address the fears and mastery strivings that are the two sides of separation anxiety and that show in therapy in patients' reactions, for instance, to their therapists' absences over weekends and vacations: "Will she be there waiting for me? Can I get angry at her without her leaving me? Will she find me if I don't show up?"

Musical chairs—*Will there be a place for me? I must grab for one. Will this be fun even if I lose?* Musical chairs explores the rivalries and anxieties of the phallic/oedipal phase, inviting aggressive and manipulative contests that prepare the child/patient for victory—and disappointment. It also has sibling rivalry roots for some children, who struggle to master the fear that mother does not "have enough to go around." Some patients worry whether the therapist, with all her other patients, will remember their stories and associations. "How do you remember everything I tell you?" asked one patient who grew up in a large family.

Ring around the rosy—*Will we all fall down or will I be the only one? Will it hurt? How will we get up? What happens if I let go?* This game addresses regression and resilience in all phases, as well as the anxieties of losing control and the thrills of gaining it. Just think of the five-year-old who has mastered toilet training until the new baby comes home or the four-year-old who climbs into the crib. We all regress at times of anxiety and stress. Fran came to session after a fight with her boyfriend. As she retold what happened, she became enraged and then panicked, thinking that she would be alone. Her crying and screaming alarmed the therapist, but as the therapist learned,

Fran needed to let these feelings out in a safe place with a safe person. The therapist must learn to tolerate the patient's expression of strong emotions in treatment (Hall, 1998). When the session was over, Fran composed herself and called later to say she was feeling much better. Support groups such as Alcoholics Anonymous (AA) and Adult Children of Alcoholics (ACOA) are examples of how falling down can be followed by getting up.

Giant steps—*I want to move ahead. Do I have to say "May I"?* The increasingly separate child negotiates issues of autonomy, obedience, and impulse control, as do psychotherapy patients. In most treatments, negotiations over the frame and the boundaries provide important chances to rework early issues with authority and autonomy that delineate "giant steps" in development. Carol was outraged when her therapist charged her for a missed session, although this policy had been discussed and agreed to in the consultation phase. Suddenly, she could not understand why she should pay when she wasn't there. The therapist listened to Carol's anger and then explained once more that Carol was responsible for her sessions whether she was there or not. The therapist is obligated to pay for rent, electricity, and telephone whether the patient is present or not. Carol kept refusing to pay, and the therapist kept including the fee for the missed session in her monthly bills. A year later, Carol paid for the missed session, saying: "It took me a long time to understand that you have needs and a life separate from mine. At first, I couldn't tolerate that idea, but painful as it is, I see it now." Another example involving impulse control would be the patient who brings food to a session. Here, the therapist may ask the patient to wait until the session is over. If the patient asks why, the therapist may explain that the eating is distracting to both parties. For some patients it is a giant step to realize the "we" in treatment and in life. Patients can express their autonomy in many ways within the frame. They can be late, go on vacation when they choose as long as they pay, even quit. It must be remembered that the patient hires (and fires) the therapist.

These and other childhood concerns are symbolized, sublimated, and reflected in our games as children and in our daily routines as adults, but they remain present for us in the primitive levels of the conscious and unconscious, addressing and expressing the anxiety and excitement of life's developmental stages.

All of these fantasies and more are played out in psychoanalytic treatment—whether once or five times a week. In fact, one reason that people choose a less-intense form of treatment (or no treatment at all) is their attachment to their unconscious fantasy life. The therapist represents a threat to the ambivalent comfort of the status quo. This major roadblock may prevent travel.

TRANSFERENCE AND TECHNIQUE

Developmental Hurdles Reworked in Transference

To her children, mother is both nurturer and demanding object, both queen and witch. Wishes to preserve her and destroy her conflict with one another. Father is knight in shining armor, but also rival and castrator. He attracts his own share of conflicted feelings, but his presence can help the child overcome the symbiotic pull toward the mother (Loewald, 1951). Siblings are both competitors and companions. As the therapist may stand in for all of these characters at different times, an intense drama unfolds in treatment.

And many other fantasies populate unconscious life as well, some of the wish-fulfilling type and some of the mastery type, some primitive and some sophisticated. Some other universal fantasies include the phallic woman fantasy (Bak, 1968), which addresses the fear of castration by assigning a penis to everyone; the fantasy of oedipal victory (Loewald, 1979), of having mother or father to oneself; the fantasy of the an imaginary companion (Bach, 1971), which provides a friend at times of loneliness and helps the child through the anxieties of the anal stage of development.

By the time a child reaches school age, these fantasies are overt enough to be played out in games and stories. The development of the superego, the new intellectual capacities of the ego, new interests such as reading, writing, and arithmetic, and developing motor skills help the child express them in play and relationships. For instance:

> Teddy was devastated by the death of his father when he was six. He put his anger at his loss, and anxiety about it, into action on the school playground, where he played soccer with his peers. This gave vent to his aggression and helped him ward off his sense of helplessness. As a teenager, he excelled in soccer, and when he grew up, he chose a profession where his competitiveness was constructive, but where a fear of loss was ever-present; he became a stockbroker. He learned to tolerate feelings of loss by manufacturing masterable opportunities in which he could be both aggressive and anxious, and he held on to this solution by leading a competitive life—thus avoiding his sense of helplessness. When he finally encountered a situation in which he could not succeed, however, he became depressed, and sought therapy. Mourning his early loss could no longer be avoided.

Children turn at all developmental stages to fantasy—in games, in fairy tales, in movies—to learn to articulate universal themes of birth, death, murder, jealousy, envy, greed, magic, and merger. In treatment, the therapist can tune in to the hidden unconscious by attending to the patient's story lines, as well as the contents of a session, the patient's affect and action, and her own feelings.

Transference Roles

The therapist fulfills many transference roles: comforter, lover, punisher, teacher, victim, and more. The wish for oedipal success and the fear that goes with it may be played out with the therapist, as are the wishes to be anally penetrated and the oral wishes to be nurtured. Patients hold on to fantasies of grandeur and omnipotence, especially if they have suffered childhood abuse. The capacity to recognize and resolve transference wishes eventually gives the patient new choices. Becoming an independent adult requires that early impossible wishes for power and security be replaced by realistic pleasure in achievement and the capacity to handle anxiety.

What Awareness of Transference/ Countertransference Achieves, and How

Psychoanalytic work sets out to enhance perception and promote growth by examining pictures of early-formed self and object representations as they appear in the present and anxieties as they are externalized in treatment and in everyday life. It is a form of treatment that can soften dangerous introjections, allowing more constructive new ones to develop. It is an arena in which old scripts can be observed and brought to life in the "here and now" of the transference. To facilitate this, to elicit the free expression of such transference manifestations, the therapist tries to be as nonjudgmental and as benignly curious as possible. Beginning therapists often have difficulty hearing transference manifestations and are sometimes heard to say, "there is no transference. Nothing the patient says has to do with me." However, the very fact of making an appointment and walking into a therapist's office implies a strong transference in itself. Fantasies about therapy, first impressions, wishes for cure, and fear of talking are all transference manifestations to be understood. The therapist's first impression of the patient has transference aspects, too, and as Rothstein (1994) points out, "If I find myself thinking about differential diagnoses rather than considering a patient's sensitivity, I assume that I am responding to some transference trend that evokes unpleasure in me" (p. 683). He goes on to warn that the analyst's countertransference may provoke an overly negative diagnosis of the patient and thus preclude analytic work. Whether this is countertransference or the therapist's transference to the patient is a question that Rothstein does not answer. I include it here because I believe that some manifestations of apparent countertransference are more properly treated as transference on the therapist's part. Either way, the therapist must look inside herself to explore her own feelings.

> All feelings and reactions of the analyst concerning the patient are *prima-facie* evidence of the analyst's transference. . . . [E]very feeling of warmth, pity, sadness, anger, hope, excitement, even interest; every

> feeling of coldness, indifference, disinterest, boredom, impatience, discouragement; and every absence of feeling, should be assumed to contain significant elements of the analyst's transference as focused on the patient. This would mean, essentially, that everything arising in the analyst about his patient is assumed to be part of the substance of analysis, that nothing represents merely the analyst's "real" reaction to his patients, and that especially when something seems most real it can be counted on to contain important aspects of the analyst's transference. (Bird, 1972, p. 299)

Countertransference will be discussed in chapter 3.

The treatment situation is set up to ensure the therapist's consistency and reliability, thus allowing the patient a sense of safety and steadiness. The therapist's benign reflection of and benevolent curiosity about what she sees helps the therapeutic partners progress in their attempt to understand how the present reflects the past, how the past affects the present, and how the patient and therapist affect each other. As this is understood, the patient becomes freer to express affect, to see beneath the surface, to make connections heretofore impossible, and to resume development (Loewald, 1960). Long periods of time are usually required for this resumption to occur. The ego is strengthened as the superego becomes more loving, and the drive derivatives are tamed, neutralized, or redirected. Self and object representations are modified and reparations are made as forgiveness and gratitude become possible.

Letting the Transference Phenomenon Build

The avoidance of transference understanding is a potential roadblock on both sides of the couch. This is not to say that we therapists should pounce on every manifestation of transference. On the contrary, letting the feelings build is an important therapeutic skill. I have heard patients say, "It always has to be about you!" Some say it sarcastically, knowing that the therapist is correct in a transference interpretation; others are truly not ready to hear about the therapist as separate; and some are embarrassed. There is a fine line between avoiding mention of the transference and letting it build. But when a patient says that her mind is blank, the therapist can say: "You are having thoughts that are uncomfortable to say. Perhaps they are about me" (Greenacre, 1956). Often the patient will respond with, "As a matter of fact, I was just thinking about your office (or your clothes, or the bill, etc.)." Some patients are startled when the therapist mentions herself. But there are two people in the room, and unless the patient is seriously disturbed, mention of this fact can move the treatment along. For instance, the therapist may ask, "Do you think that my lateness today might be a reason for your silence?" or "Last time I gave you the bill. . . . Are there feelings about that?" or "My vacation is coming up next week and I wonder if that is connected to your being late this week." Tact and timing are required, however. A very narcissistic patient, unaware of "the other," may feel too hurt by a transference interpretation to be able to make use of it. In such cases, the therapist waits until there are signs of readiness, as in the following example.

> After six months of therapy, Bill started making comments about the therapist's lobby. He asked if the lighting was different. As a matter of fact, it was different, but it was the first comment he had made about the therapist's surrounds. More questions about the waiting room and the new bookcase (which was not new) alerted the therapist to the fact that Bill was getting ready to think about her, and she commented: "Perhaps you have a question about me." Bill answered that he had been wondering how long the therapist had been in practice. His fantasy that she was just starting out was explored. Bill was saying that he was starting out and that he hoped the therapist and he had something in common.

Awareness of displaced feelings (anger expressed toward the teacher that really belongs to the mother, for example) is useful, as it provides fuel for the trip of self-understanding. Resistance to awareness of the transference is a problem that arises in many nonreflective, unpsychologically minded patients. Sometimes the therapist can illustrate how *she* reflects, thus offering a patient who may never have been exposed to reflecting a hidden new resource. This may take a long time, and many therapists get discouraged. The therapist's roadblock in such instances may be her own resistance to the patient's transference derivatives or her tuning into her own countertransference. Her own treatment is the best way to understand these concepts. Listening for and hearing transference and countertransference manifestations is a highly developed skill that increases with practice.

Dr. R worked at a clinic where she saw many patients once a week. Deepening the work was not a goal for her until she began her own treatment and realized that more frequent sessions were helpful to her. I think that the therapist's own therapy is what truly prepares her to do this work. Class work and supervision are important, but her own experience of transference and resistance is crucial to understanding and recognizing it in the work with her patients.

EARLY INTERPRETATION OF TRANSFERENCE

Sometimes the therapist makes a transference interpretation early in treatment (Gill and Muslim, 1976):

> At the beginning of his treatment, Mr. A talked about a woman he met frequently on the way to therapy. He was interested in her, but intimidated by what he described as her aloofness. He elaborated on his fantasy about the woman and how such aloofness made him angry and hurt. He brought this situation up, along with similar reactions to a new coworker. The therapist said: "I wonder if you think these feelings are connected to thoughts you've had about me?" At first, Mr. A said that he hadn't known his thoughts about the therapist were relevant to his problems, but then he wondered if the therapist was aloof and if he could work with her.

This early transference interpretation opened the door to Mr. A's perceptions and fantasies about the therapist and others, and let him experience how important his reflections were.

> *As treatment progressed, aloofness became a multidetermined theme. Mr. A and his therapist speculated that he had experienced his mother's depression, along with his own lack of early gratification, as his fault. His*

low self-esteem, combined with the rage and sadness about his neglect, was projected onto women and showed up in the transference where negative expectations were difficult to give up or resolve. Mr. A's internal representation of his mother and his fantasy that he had caused her depression seemed too important to let go of. This way he avoided the pain of his helplessness as a child who in fact could do nothing about his mother's unavailability. As Mr. A began to understand the dynamics of his situation, and to internalize the therapist as a responsive, caring, steady object, his perception of women started to change.

Analytic work cannot occur without reflection. When the therapist discovers with the patient the familiar patterns that occur both in and out of the treatment, they can begin to explore the purposes and reasons for these patterns. Repetition in the transference wards off the dangers of the unknown, which may be felt to threaten whatever measure of safety has already been achieved. An old song is comforting; to learn a new one is challenging. Old friends are predictable and share common experiences; new acquaintances become old friends only after periods of negotiation and testing. Repeating also allows for:

- Soothing
- Mastery
- Avoidance of the unknown
- Attachment to past objects
- Denial of reality
- Living out fantasy

Acting Out the Transference/ Repeating the Past in the Present

Sam missed several sessions without calling. He was also consistently late until his therapist engaged him in wondering about it.

Sam: Oh, I'm never on time for anything. Please don't take it personally. Everyone gets annoyed with me, but after a while they expect it.

Therapist: How does it affect you?

Sam: Well, sometimes I miss out, like at a meeting, but someone usually will fill me in on what happened. Or getting home late for dinner—my wife gets furious. My tennis partner has just about given up on me because the court time is expensive and I just can't manage to get there on time.

Therapist: You focus on how the others feel—what about your feelings?

Sam: I feel awful but I just can't help it. It's a habit I can't seem to break.

Therapist: I think if we explore the habit we should gain some understanding.

Sam proceeded to talk about his feelings about lateness, and he began to realize that he got a kind of pleasure at the idea of others waiting for him. It made him feel important and noticed. "Anyone can be on time and they're taken for granted. No one ever knows what to expect from me. Sure, they get angry but anger is a reaction–it's satisfying in some weird way."

As Sam spoke of his feelings and fantasies, he began to come to his hours on time. He realized that the therapist was really listening to him, and he began to emulate her benign curiosity about his patterns. It evolved that when he was a child, no one had had the time to keep track of Sam. With working parents and six siblings, he got attention only when he stood out. His favored way of standing out was to be late. When he stayed away from home, his mother responded. Sometimes she went out looking for him, and once she called the police. Being late to school also guaranteed attention. The teachers were always sending notes to his mother. When he skipped school, his mother had to visit the principal, and for a while she paid more attention to Sam.

As treatment progressed, Sam gained access to the emotions that his lateness covered. Rage, loneliness, despair, and low self-esteem were experienced in the transference with the therapist. Periods of coming to sessions on time were often followed by periods of lateness, especially around times of separation. The roadblock of Sam's lateness diminished as the therapeutic journey proceeded. Understanding and analyzing the resistance paved the way for insight and change. Sam found that by recognizing and verbalizing his anger and his wish to feel special, his need to act diminished. Projecting his rage onto others was no longer necessary as he accepted it as his own.

> The road to understanding and change was far longer and more complicated than it sounds, however. Along the way, Sam realized that his wife was having an affair. He became depressed and threatened to stop therapy. The material he was frightened to face had to do with the abandonment he had felt as a child when his mother suffered from postpartum depression after the birth of a younger sibling. After Sam saw the role he played in his wife's infidelity and how this was a replay of losing his mother's attention, Sam and his wife began a dialogue that strengthened their marriage.

It is not at all unusual in psychoanalytic work to see a repetition of childhood trauma. But in this case, the repetition provided a door to the past. An enduring connection between patient and therapist is the key to opening the door. The connection in Sam's case took years to build. It was tested repeatedly—first with the lateness, then with fee issues, and finally, under the strain of a marital crisis, with a threat to quit. The therapist showed Sam how and why he treated the therapist as he treated his mother. His perception of the present clearly resonated with his past experience. His fear that the therapist would overlook him was connected to his mother's real inattention and to her depression.

Enactment

Enactment and *acting out* are terms often used interchangeably. Both concepts involve the camouflaging or expression of thoughts and feelings in indirect ways. The way to differentiate the two concepts is to think of the former as involving the dyad and the latter as something done by the patient. However, the patient's acting out often colors the therapist's countertransference, and this leads, in many cases, to enactment. A consistently late patient is saying something to the therapist, but if this message is not deciphered, the therapist may be affected. Whatever she does—interprets, beseeches, ignores—threatens to become an enactment. The two parties are co-acting or enacting something from their pasts. The interaction in the present is a valid starting place: "Let's figure out the lateness."

The pressure to repeat and the need to see the therapist as part of the self or an object of the past is powerful. Many therapies fail because the pull of transference is strong enough to coerce the therapist out of her benevolently curious stance. For long periods of time, the patient's need to cling to the original inner object makes the transference feel irresolvable, and sometimes it is. To gratify early needs, the patient entices, cajoles, bores, bullies, seduces, and threatens the therapist into becoming like the original objects (chapter 8). The therapist's ability to explain/interpret the pull and not give in to it is her contribution to the journey (chapters 5 and 6). Still, it is impossible to do this perfectly or even consistently, and this is why there are enactments in treatment.

Sandler (1976) proposed the term *role-responsiveness* as an aspect of countertransference. He believed that the patient tries to actualize the self–object interaction of fantasy into the therapeutic situation with the analyst. This is accomplished, he thought, through the unconscious manipulation of the analyst, who through her own role-responsiveness enacts with the patient. These enactments are valuable to explore. Something as apparently trivial as handing a patient a tissue may be an enactment, because it can mean more than just the good manners it would be in a social setting. For example, it may mean the therapist, in unconscious response to the patient's fear or anxiety, is covering up her patient's feelings with an act of kindness. The offer of a tissue could convey, *"Don't cry, your pain is too much for me to handle,"* or *"Let me help you deny your pain,"* or *"Don't feel sad."* Or it could mean, *"Stop your sniveling—you don't know what real pain is,"* or *"I don't want to feel vulnerable to your tears,"* or *"This reminds me of my mother, whose tears made me feel impotent,"* or *"I will take care of you."* Most therapists keep tissues in the office and patients usually help themselves—so the therapist who offers a tissue might learn about her countertransference (or role-responsiveness) by reflecting on her offer. An enactment such as this could be viewed as co-transference, because both parties are responding to the other's fantasy as well as their own. Enactment is not just one incident—it can go on for long periods of time—but when the therapist makes the space to step back and observe the situation, her perspective changes and the enactment can be interpreted. Enactment involves both parties in the dyad; acting out, in which the therapist's analytic perspective is not lost, is much easier to spot. Both acting out and enactment occur in every treatment, and both are important clues to the unconscious.

> Henry came to therapy hesitantly. He was in pain, yet he was not sure what a therapist could do about it. An affluent lawyer with an expensive lifestyle including a domineering wife and spoiled children, he hated his work and was miserable with the situation. The therapist, a novice who was working on his tendency to tiptoe, knew that Henry needed more than once-weekly treatment, but he was afraid to say this. Perhaps the therapist was responding to Henry's own hesitation. Every week, Henry questioned how treatment could help. He felt trapped in his life and did not see a way out. His childhood was described as uneventful—he had parents who were not expressive but were "nice people," and he had a sibling born nine months after him. This younger sibling had a congenital deformity that required his mother's constant attention, leaving Henry a minimum amount of time with her. In treatment, Henry felt no confidence in the therapist's ability to tolerate his pain, rage, and neediness. Both patient and therapist were anxious about committing to more-intensive treatment and played it out by avoiding the transference message: "Are you strong enough for me? Do you have time for me?" Realistically, the therapist had no extra hours to offer Henry, but beneath the reality he was unsure of his ability to work with him. The enactment continued until the therapist made up his mind that he could treat Henry and arranged time for another session. The enactment was echoing Henry's distrust of the therapy by making time the issue.

When patients make time an issue, therapists tend to view that as resistance. But therapists can exhibit resistance, too—and resistance on both sides of the couch can add up to enactment. In my experience, the conscious resistance of "not enough time" resolves itself once patient and therapist decide to work together. The therapist's honesty and truthfulness with the patient is important. "I understand how difficult it is for you to get here, but we will get bogged down if eventually the treatment doesn't deepen. That's hard to do on a once-a-week basis—so perhaps you can mull it over." Another approach is to analyze the resistance (Bernstein, 1983). The therapist might say something like, "You are having feelings that you would rather avoid, and coming here more often could make that more difficult." Wading into therapy is an option, and some patients need to test the waters for a long period of time.

Another patient, Ray, was a brilliant but obnoxious out-of-work lawyer. His one saving grace was a sense of humor that allowed him to connect with the therapist. Ray's stubborn refusal to pay for missed sessions was rationalized in myriad ways that eventually caused the therapist to become angry. The enactment involved Ray's need for punishment, and the therapist felt like punishing him. Enactments such as this are common in therapy with sadomasochistic patients who provoke the therapist to retaliate. Eventually, and over time, Ray's therapist brought up the transference/countertransference enactment:

Therapist: "You and I are caught in a struggle. You provoke me to feel angry and then you try to make me laugh. What does this mean to you?"
Ray: "I always do that—I joke my way out of trouble. I love to make people laugh."
Therapist: "Do you also like getting into trouble?"
Ray: "Sometimes. . . . I like to get a rise out of you."

Ray began to connect with the feeling that he should be appreciated not for money but for his entertaining ways. He began to feel grief and longing beneath his obnoxious ways of relating. As the treatment deepened, Ray saw how devastated he was by the lack of attention his family gave him—unless he entertained. "Why can't you be entertained?" he asked his therapist. He eventually remembered that after the death of his brother when Ray was fifteen, his father suddenly expected him to earn a living and told him that jokes did not buy bread. In other words, "grow up."

Listening for Transference Messages

"My boss is unfair." "My teacher is critical." "My wife is cold." "My law partner is greedy." "The movie was horrible." "The food was wonderful." "The newspaper lies to us." These comments, seemingly concerned with external events or people, are often clues to the patient's thoughts about the therapist. Listening for such statements helps the therapist think about transference messages. "Your doorman is so cute, and I think he likes me" is a message that the patient is warming up to the therapist. "Your doorman ignored me today" can alert the therapist to having missed something in the material in the last session. The treatment hour often begins with the doorman, or the receptionist at the clinic, or the cabdriver on the way to a session. Flirting, ignoring, joking, informing—all these exchanges are meant for the therapist, but often they are acted out and not reported.

More subtle and harder to decipher as transference messages are the patient's characteristic modes of relating to life in general. Sardonic, sarcastic, pessimistic patients are usually guarding against intimacy and leave the therapist feeling out in the cold. Sometimes the therapist has to wave a flag to alert the patient to his thoughts about her, as when one therapist, who had a broken leg that a patient never commented on, finally spoke up:

Therapist: I've been limping around on crutches for weeks and you never commented or asked me what happened.

Patient: It's really none of my business. We're here to talk about me, not you, anyway.

Therapist: Your reactions or nonreactions to me are ways of expressing yourself. Ignoring these ways is ignoring you.

Tuning in to the Transference

If the therapist trains herself to listen for transference manifestations, she will hear them. The first moment of a session is often easiest to translate in terms of transference. The way a patient walks in has transference significance, and the first thing she says or doesn't say is transference-laden. Manner of eye contact, position on the chair or couch, style and content of speaking or not speaking, way of dress, body language, odor, signs of anxiety (chewing gum, fidgeting, stuttering), seductive mannerisms—all of these are messages to the therapist that are underlain by fantasy. Each patient has a unique way of expressing herself, and it will take the therapist varying amounts of time to tune in to the unconscious messages her patient gives.

The therapist's perception also deals with the distractions—the "static" of the moment. One patient who used the couch informed the therapist that she thought she had head lice. The analyst, instead of listening to the transference message ("I will contaminate you") was completely distracted, wondering what to do to protect her other patients. Another patient wore heavy perfume that made the analyst very uncomfortable. Here, the message ("I cover up my smell") was overwhelmed by the odor.

Without a consistent schedule and structure for treatment, it is practically impossible for the dyad to explore the transferences and countertransferences in any great depth. In any given session, questions are raised and hints are dropped, but without timely follow-up the leads disappear. Some patients work well in once-a-week therapy, especially when there is a specific issue or problem, but more often consistency is improved by more than one-a-week sessions (Hall, 1998).

Where Is the Transference?

Everything that goes on between a patient and a therapist is an expression of transference (Joseph, 1985). Whatever the patient chooses to bring into the consulting room has a transference message. Laments or outrage about current affairs, movies seen, the weather, the person in the waiting room, a news item are all references to the dyad. On September 11, 2001, and for days after the terrorist attack on the World Trade Center, patients reacted uniquely. Trauma in the present sets off memories of past trauma and the ways with which it was dealt, also touching patients' own aggressive fantasies. Mary stayed away from discussing her reaction, using denial and avoidance as defenses: "It has nothing to do with me." Joe could barely contain his outrage and spoke of nothing else for weeks. "How could those bastards do this? We have to retaliate." Lois became fearful of going outside and cancelled several sessions. All of these people had been subject to trauma in childhood. Their rage at these early circumstances was evoked by the terrorism and the helplessness they felt. In some cases, the idea of leaving treatment (that is, leaving the therapist) came up. Transference messages had to do with:

- How could you let this happen? (anger)
- Why can't you make it better? (wish for the therapist to be omnipotent)
- Do you still want to see me? My problems seem so small. (guilt)
- How can I worry or focus on my problems when others are suffering so much more? (testing)
- Are you shaken—are you OK? (can you face my rage?)
- Maybe this country deserves to be punished. (identification with the aggressor)

CO-TRANSFERENCE (OR THE THERAPEUTIC CONNECTION)

Different individuals register upset in vastly different ways. Whatever the patient sees on the journey of psychotherapy touches off something in the therapist, and the combined perceptions of the two create a picture they both can look at. When Carol talks about a book she has read and asks, "Have you read it?" the therapist may think:

Sounds interesting, I might read it.
Carol wants to give me something.
Carol wishes to hold on to me by sharing a book.
There must be something in the book that Carol wants me to know.
I'll think of her when I'm reading the book.
She wants to be with me when I'm out of the office—maybe reading in bed.
She wants more time than the session permits.
Carol wants to take a detour around what's really on her mind.

The list goes on and on, but in terms of transference the therapist's job is to understand the message that in this case seemed to be:

I want more time.
I want to fill up your time so you won't be involved with others.
I don't want to put that into words.
I want to influence your life.
I want to share with you.
I want the focus off me.
I want you to read and not interact with your family.
I want you to know something that I can't tell you.

Both Carol and the therapist know that this is not a reading group. Yet they are both tempted to let it become one—just for a minute. Whether or not the therapist answers Carol's question, there is still opportunity for reflection, because that is what therapist and patient do—reflect and decipher.

Hidden Transference

Bonnie comes into the office on a rainy day and asks if it's OK to put her wet feet on the couch—a reasonable and pertinent question, but (since Bonnie knows there's a cover on the couch) one also laden with transference meaning. The therapist nods and listens to further material that includes the new puppy ruining the carpet and her sister—her life in a mess—who called to borrow money. More about her resentment toward this sister, three years older, still without a job. Still so needy. Silence. Thinks about asking the sister to stay with the dog when she goes on vacation next month. Silence. The therapist, hearing a change in Bonnie's voice says, "Your voice changed just now." Bonnie starts to cry and tells the therapist how upset she is about missing sessions and having to pay. Her tone changes from sadness to anger: "It's not fair." The therapist wonders if Bonnie is embarrassed by her own neediness about missing her time and covers it with anger. She also wonders if Bonnie wants to regress like her sister and her dog. Bonnie's fantasy had to do with being taken care of, babied, and nurtured. She disapproved of her own neediness, envied her sister, and identified secretly with her puppy. When, whether, and how to interpret these underlying messages depends on Bonnie's resilience, the length of time in treatment, her grasp of the concept of displacement, and her capacity to reflect. As it turned out, in this case, Bonnie made most of the connections herself.

It helps to remember that every patient we meet has some version of reality, shaped by her fantasy life, that is being portrayed in the transference. The fantasy life is a product of instinctual desires, anxieties, internal object relations, innate endowment, and the perceived past; its accessibility depends on the superego. The therapist works with the patient's superego from the beginning by listening with benevolent curiosity instead of with a judgmental attitude. The patient eventually identifies with this attitude, becoming less self-critical and more curious.

Transference covers the whole of our psychological ground. The patient who is experiencing a *positive transference*, seemingly cooperative and anxious to please, will reveal her envy and hatred as the work progresses. The patient who balks, questions, and begins grudgingly or with hostility will uncover her wishes to depend and to be loved and loving as time goes by. These are generalizations, but they are meant to suggest that as human beings we have all experienced everything: all the psychosexual stages of development, the vicissitudes of the separation-individuation process, sadism, masochism, the need to connect, the need for space, the need to be soothed, and the need to stand alone. All of these needs, phases, and modes of affect may be revealed over the psychotherapeutic journey. The therapist must be prepared for everything from the patient. Idealization, (fantasized) murder, disdain, scorn, and love must all be welcomed in the transference because the therapist is the only object ready and willing to withstand and understand the onslaught of the patient's emotional world.

Holding on to the Past in the Transference (Transference as Resistance)

The greatest aid to psychotherapy, and its greatest obstacle, is the transference. To the degree that the patient becomes able to experience the therapist as an independent and separate person, the transference resolves. There is never complete resolution, however, and there always remain remnants of the past and pulls from unconscious fantasy, especially in times of stress.

With abused or neglected patients, the goal of therapy is modification of basic identifications (Shengold, 1989), but therapeutic work, even with severely damaged patients (Hall, 1998), can improve functioning and the quality of object relating, enriching both travelers. As the therapist resonates with the patient's regressions and progressions, she revisits her own conflicts and reworks and reviews her own past, so continuing her own growth. The therapist offers a new experience. In a successful therapy, as hard as the patient may try to turn it into an old experience, she cannot fully succeed. Success is relative, however, and sometimes the therapist may never know just how much her patient has grown. I remember so many of the patients I have seen over the years with respect for the work we've done, even if treatment ended precipitously, and I have a feeling that they remember, too.

❖ CHAPTER 2 ❖

Countertransference

> From the very first moment of the initial interview to the end of a long course of psychoanalysis the unconscious exchange between analysand and analyst, and the analysis of the relationship between transference and countertransference, lie at the heart of the psychoanalytic work.
>
> —Peter Wegner

Transference is the vital force in psychoanalytic work, and that means that countertransference is, too. You can't have one without the other. Whenever two people meet, they register feelings, opinions, and reactions all based on their personal perception, their psychic reality. These reactions can be seen as transference reactions. Comparing perceptions with friends of a stranger at a party shows that each perceiver has different ideas. When therapist and patient meet—even before they meet—they have preconceived ideas about each other. And once the first session is underway, all kinds of feelings and messages are being conveyed beneath the words.

To the degree that the therapist resists awareness of her own countertransference—to the extent that she ignores it—she will resist understanding the patient's expression of transference, and enactment, or a missed opportunity for interpretation, will occur. Countertransference, the therapist's reaction to the patient, is the term for how the therapist resonates with and reacts to the patient. Each therapist will hear a patient with different ears. Her attention is filtered through her own unconscious associations as well as her patient's and involves the therapist's character in general and her frame of mind on that particular day. When a case is presented in a seminar, listeners will pick up on different aspects of the material. Their own associations to the material will vary—and although the treating therapist may have a longer-range view of the patient, the immediate reactions of others can point out blind spots.

The psychoanalytic concept of countertransference has undergone change as clinical theory has developed. In the early days of psychoanalytic thinking, reviewed by Etchegoyen (1991) and Sandler et al. (1992), it was looked upon as an obstacle to treatment. Any feelings the therapist had when treating a patient that were not neutral and objective were viewed as signs of blind spots. Freud suggested that the positions of abstinence and neutrality would protect the analyst from getting emotionally involved with the patient, but eventually realizing how unavoidable this was, he first recommended self-analysis and then, in 1912, training analysis. When he saw that even this was inadequate, he suggested reanalysis for the analyst about every five years.

This attitude, that countertransference was an impediment, was challenged by Paula Heimann (1950). She understood countertransference as a projection of the patient's inner world and saw it as one of the most valuable tools in psychoanalytic work. This view was debated in a series of papers by A. Reich (1951, 1960), who recognized the inevitability of countertransference, but considered it to interfere with the analyst's understanding.

Today, due to longer analytic work, advances in the theory of psychoanalytic technique, and the influence of Winnicott and the British object relations school, countertransference is recognized as ever present and, if not ignored, as a major asset to the therapy. By tuning in to her own feelings and associations, the therapist is able to sense the patient's unconscious motives and messages. Not only is she seen through the lens of her patient's transference, but also she herself can hear the patient through the lens of her own personal transference and the countertransference evoked by the patient. She is also a receptacle of the patient's projected inner objects and feelings. These projections, along with the therapist's own internal world, add up to countertransference. Both transference and countertransference phenomena can become roadblocks if not recognized. Primitive fantasies, translated though they may be into more palatable ones, are ever present. Wishes to merge and murder, to love and hate, are represented by unconscious and conscious fantasies in both patient and therapist. Anxieties are constantly stirred up and defended against. The therapist's own analysis helps her understand some of what the patient experiences. The road, though not the same, is familiar. The concept of enactment (when both parties are reliving an unconscious fantasy together) is not only a roadblock, but also, when discovered, a most valuable tool in analytic understanding. Actually, one can see the whole treatment as enactment of the wish to be rescued and the wish to rescue. Countertransference is the analyst's contribution to the process when she is aware of it.

This progress in thinking about countertransference has been enormously helpful with the so-called widening scope patients. Patients who use primitive defenses such as splitting and projective identification, and who have a propensity for acting out, can benefit from psychoanalysis, but such patients often evoke extreme feelings in the therapist. The induced feelings of countertransference may help the therapist to understand what the patient is feeling. In the United States, analysts are writing openly and informatively about the necessity of using countertransference; outstanding examples are Jacobs (1991), Smith (1999), Renick (1993), and Ogden (1989). Before these theoreticians/clinicians began speaking out, we looked to some British and South American analysts to understand their use of countertransference and projective identification.

The rigidity that once characterized psychoanalytic work has given way to a more humane approach. The stereotypical *New Yorker* cartoon persists in portraying the analyst as a balding male with notepad and pen uttering words of wisdom, or remaining silent. This view is becoming obsolete and being replaced by a vision of two people working together, using the products of their own transferences to create a healing connection. Both parties in the analytic dyad change and grow during the process, whether it is called psychoanalytic psychotherapy or psychoanalysis and whether it is a time-limited venture or a long-term one. When two people meet regularly over a period of time, they change, if only as a function of the fact that they pay attention to each other, listen to each other, fantasize about each other, in a steady, consistent way. The concept and use of transference/countertransference has evolved from a path to a superhighway, from listening to a patient's associations as melody to enriching that melody by the harmony and counterpoint of the listener. A sketch becomes a rich tapestry and a story line becomes a multilayered piece of literature or an engrossing story. As psychoanalytic thinkers are more and more open to listening to their patients with a newly appreciated and legitimated freedom, complex textures, along with dissonances and sophisticated rhythms, are heard.

> Mrs. T has been in analysis for twenty years. During this time, she married, had a child, and flourished in many work-oriented ways. An early trauma resulted in a grandiose fantasy that she had caused a tragedy, and that grandiosity prohibits her from real closeness to anyone. She believes unconsciously (but more and more consciously) that she is above everyone, has dangerous powers, and must stand apart. In the transference/countertransference paradigm, she avoids real closeness with the analyst, who feels shut out, pushed away, and kept at arm's length. Mrs. T includes the analyst in her outside life by giving details, names, incidents, problems, but both parties in this twentieth year are aware of a feeling of distance brought on by the fear of closeness. It has been traced back to the original trauma, which is encapsulated in the grandiose fantasy of her being separate from everyone, and the struggle emerges: will Mrs. T do the work to alter, fight, and free herself from her fantasy? Is she able to change this characteristic mode of protecting herself from the closeness she yearns for? The analyst's countertransference has included feelings of failure, sorrow, rage, empathy, and a wish to give up, and her awareness of these feelings is fed back to the patient. It becomes a useful tool. Also operative is the fear that both parties must someday separate and the anxiety about connection speaks to that fear. Character change and characteristic defenses can be measured by degrees. But growth, in most cases, is what we can see.

The shift away from thinking of treatment in terms of a one-person psychology and toward a two-person view has had a major influence on technique: the recognition and use of countertransference and *self-disclosure* (the analyst's sharing material of her own with the patient) changes the technique of permitting the patient to fantasize about the therapist. With very fragile patients who do not understand the value of their own fantasies, the therapist may say something like, *"I realize my telling you where I'm going on vacation is very important to you, but if you can work with it first, I will tell you where I'm going."* The therapist's intent is to show her patient that fantasy promotes growth and that fact often prohibits the chance to wonder.

The analytic community is raising questions about the analyst's authority and discussing the pros and cons of a more collaborative atmosphere. It is comforting to some therapists to see the dyad as two equals on the playing field, but the fact is that the therapist is defined by her job and prepared for it by her own analytic work and study. How else could she tolerate her patient's loving, rageful, erotic, envious, spiteful, and idealizing feelings? If the therapist took such feelings personally she would reprimand, perhaps gratify, turn away, or react with intolerance and perhaps sympathy at best, or even become a friend—that is, she would step out of her role. So spotting and interpreting transference, countertransference, and enactment is essential.

Hannah, a beautiful twenty-three-year-old from a wealthy and educated family, came into treatment in response to a friend's concern. She too was worried that she was courting danger with her new lifestyle and accepted a referral to a psychotherapist. Hannah had quit college and was supporting herself as a stripper. Her parents, busy professionals who traveled frequently, knew nothing about her new life and assumed that she was still in school. The life of stripping opened up new opportunities and new dangers: porn movies, escort services, prostitution, and drugs. (Modeling was not an option for Hannah because of a physical imperfection.) Hannah's intelligence and judgment had worked to help her avoid danger thus far, but she knew that her lifestyle put her in jeopardy. Men propositioned her, followed her home, offered her jewelry and other luxuries. She was not interested in these temptations, but eventually she found herself attracted to one man. John seemed different from the others—quiet, attentive, refined, and handsome. She began dating him and depending on him for companionship. Their sexual life went from passionate to kinky to sadomasochistic within several months. Drug use escalated from marijuana to cocaine. Hannah used her weekly therapy sessions to "confess her sins" and to cry about her "downward spiral." Her therapist told her that she needed more sessions to help her understand what was happening.

This therapist was psychoanalytically trained and a male. Hannah experienced his suggestion as seductive, and he felt seductive. She wanted to be rescued, and he wanted to rescue. A repetition of Hannah's life was occurring in treatment. The therapist's observing ego led him eventually to understand that an enactment was occurring around his appropriate recommendation. When he became aware of the enactment, he interpreted it. Although Hannah felt rebuffed and injured, her own working ego—her common sense—permitted her to entertain the idea that fantasies of seduction and rescue were precluding the real help she needed. The interpretation of the enactment gave Hannah a sense of security and trust in her therapist that permitted her to increase her sessions. The sexualized transference that emerged stirred erotic feelings in the analyst. He used his awareness of them to understand and then explain to Hannah that her fears of intimacy were covered and defended against by sexualizing her feelings. (This is not to say that analysts' sexual feelings are always projective identifications or induced countertransference. What is crucial is for the analyst to analyze these erotic feelings.)

The purpose of this vignette is to illustrate how far analytic theory has come since 1951 (A. Reich), when countertransference was seen as an impediment that the analyst was encouraged to master and control, often by seeking more analysis. This attitude inhibited those in training; although countertransference is a normal, unavoidable, and useful reaction in analytic work, trainees in those days surely kept it to themselves.

Among the reactions to patients that may fall under the heading of countertransference are:

- Drowsiness
- Boredom
- Anger and impatience
- Sadomasochistic enactment
- Fear of losing the patient
- Fear of working with a patient
- Erotic feelings

- Rigidity
- Envy and insecurity
- Overidentification

Many other reactive feelings of the therapist can lead to enactment. Sometimes she may not become aware of a transference enactment until after the session has ended—and sometimes it may take even longer than that. And it must be considered that, strictly speaking, enactment in its broadest sense is ever present. A clue that transference or countertransference is ready to be recognized is the patient's appearance in the analyst's dreams (or the analyst's appearance in the patient's dreams).

DROWSINESS

Drowsiness is a powerful feeling, on both sides of the couch. Patients fall asleep and so do therapists. This seems to have nothing to do with being tired; it can happen any time. Therapists with whom I have discussed this phenomenon see no correlation with time of day, lack of sleep, or even conscious boredom. The drowsiness has been attributed by some therapists to the patient's lack of affect or tone of voice, or even to the content of the hour. My experience is less traceable to any one of these factors but more connected to an unconscious dialogue, which if brought to consciousness allows one's alertness to return. Some questions I ponder are:

- Is the patient trying to numb me or deaden me?
- Is drowsiness a defense against unbearable anger, anxiety, or empathy—mine or the patient's?
- Is my drowsiness a result of a narcissistic attack by the patient, who is saying, in effect, "you don't exist"?

Sometimes roadblocks (defenses) are meant to be left alone. If a road is in serious disrepair and is truly impassable, inner roadblocks on both sides of the couch must be evaluated. Forging ahead may not always be appropriate; there are times when sitting by the side of the road can be more productive.

Ms. O began working with Mr. F, age twenty-five, at the community mental health center once a week. When she first presented the case in a yearly seminar, she reported being upset by the patient's refusal to talk and her increasing frustration, boredom, and occasional sleepiness. Mr. F lived an isolated life in his mother's house. His only activity was coming to treatment. Before that, he had stayed at home. Week after week, Ms. O tried to draw him out, but to no avail. He had no interests, nothing to relate. Ms. O felt inept. She thought she should know some technique that would make her patient better. She also found it difficult to sit in silence. Sometimes she would talk—trying to engage Mr. F—much of the time, she just sat there quietly. The quality of the silence seemed to vary. Sometimes, after a break in treatment, it felt hostile. Other times, the silence felt soothing. At times, Ms. O felt angry. But very gradually, almost imperceptibly, Mr. F began telling the therapist small things. When he began to talk, Ms. O was amazed and listened to whatever Mr. F told her. She had been tired of getting nowhere and had begun to lose interest in the case, but it seems that her patience had paid off.

Sitting by the side of the road for a long time is hard work, but Ms. O returned to the seminar the following year smiling—as if a miracle had happened. Mr. F was opening up—relating to her—and functioning on a higher level. The members of the seminar were truly moved. Ms. O had experienced different feelings, from empathy to curiosity, to impatience, boredom, anger, and relief. The class wondered if these feelings were induced countertransference, projective identification, or enactments. We never found out—but we felt that all three applied.

BOREDOM

Boredom followed the therapist's initial interest in the following case.

Mrs. M, in analysis for several years, went through a period of talking about her work life in detail, naming all the people she worked with and many of the technical and political problems that filled her life. As she went on and on, the therapist became bored and drowsy to the point that she could not pay attention. One day, it dawned on the therapist that Mrs. M was excluding her. When she realized this, she interpreted the enactment to Mrs. M. "You are shutting me out of your world and it reminds me of how you said you could never remember how you felt about your parents' closed door. I think you're keeping me out of the bedroom." The work changed as Mrs. M dealt with her envy of the therapist's life without her, and this evolved into other threesomes she had difficulty with. Interpretation of the enactment (the therapist had been colluding in order to avoid stirring up her own oedipal jealousy) permitted the work to regain its momentum. Before the enactment was interpreted, there had been other oedipal themes in sessions. The therapist had intuitively (and unconsciously) let this material crescendo into the enactment so the interpretation would be emotionally meaningful and not intellectual.

ANGER AND IMPATIENCE

Anger as a countertransference issue includes such manifestations as mild to intense frustration, annoyance, sarcasm, losing one's cool, and condescension. It is an active feeling, in direct response either to the patient or to a feeling that the therapist's expectations are not being met. The work may remind the therapist of her own trauma or conflict. Work with masochistic patients almost always evokes the therapist's anger and sadism. Time after time, the patient arranges to be hurt, treated badly, overlooked, or ignored by the people in his life and eventually by the therapist. Such patients are highly adept at putting themselves in the line of fire, and when the patient cannot recognize a pattern that is clear to the therapist, the therapist feels exasperated. The more she interprets, the worse it seems to get. It can take long periods of time, working in the transference/countertransference of treatment, on outside relationships and situations, on connecting behavior to the past and to internal objects, before things begin to shift. This difficult work requires the intensity of analysis, in my experience. And such analysis can fail.

The patient's arrogance and sadism may also be roadblocks for the therapist who, when repeatedly taunted, may lose her patience and become sarcastic.

The following vignette, presented in a case seminar, took place after ten sessions of individual therapy conducted every other week and right before the therapist went away on a two-week summer vacation. The therapist tells us:

> Due to an unexpected phone call from a patient in crisis, I am, for the first time ever, two minutes late. There is suddenly a sharp knocking at the door and I know who it is. I speak, with the door closed, telling Bob, "I will be with you in just one minute." When he enters the room, he lies down on the couch, and begins with a long silence. I wait. My silence becomes too much and Bob's frustration boils over.

Therapist: You seem angry at my lateness—can you tell me about it?

Bob [ignoring question]: I think you would just let me talk about whatever I wanted to in here. Do you even take notes? [Turns to look at me from the couch] Do you? I mean, I could talk about fucking bowling in here for 50 minutes and you wouldn't stop me, and isn't it your job to help me by asking questions, saying something relevant, directing me to things you have thought about based on what I have said in previous sessions? What am I paying you for? I am just giving you this money and everything is staying the same. And you do nothing.

Therapist [all of this was said with a great deal of hostility and the feelings induced in me were of shame and fraudulence]: Well, what should I be directing your attention to?

Bob: See! There you go again. I have to tell you what to say. This is ridiculous. I mean, I can just talk to myself.

Therapist: Well, if you think talking to yourself would be more helpful than speaking to me, why do you think you come here?

Bob: Well, I come here because I enjoy talking, but you are supposed to do something with what I say and I am really questioning your ability to be effective. [Vituperatively] I want to know if you take notes? Do you? Or are you just sitting there and doing nothing, because that is what it feels like most of the time.

Therapist: I wonder if some of your anger has to do with my going on vacation for two weeks and my lateness today.

Bob: God! That is ridiculous. I can't believe you would even think that my not seeing you for two weeks or whatever would make a bit of difference or that I would have feelings about that! I only see you every other week as it is, so it is no big deal. It is so predictable . . . your comment.

Therapist: Should I be thinking of myself as incompetent?

Bob: You should just do something. I don't care how you think of yourself.

Therapist: It sounds like I am really screwing up your treatment. Do you know what you would like me to do?

Bob: That is up to you.

Therapist: Would you like me to pick a topic for you to discuss?

Bob: Frankly, yes.

Therapist: And how would that be helpful?

Bob: God! Another ridiculous and waste-of-time question. I feel like you are not even here, you are just sitting back there doing nothing.

Therapist: Well, without telling me what to say or do, do you know what your aversion is to giving me those instructions?

Bob: You are the professional, damn it, and I want you to be in charge.

Therapist: Should I share with you the thought that is coming to my mind?

Bob [pleadingly and full of frustration]: Yes, already.

Therapist: I am wondering how am I supposed to help a person who has one foot in and one foot out the door.

Bob: What?

Therapist: You heard me. You are asking for some guidance, right? Well, I need to ask for your help. What should I do with a patient who has had one foot out the door since the moment he walked in here eight months ago? Every-other-week appointments make it difficult for both of us. [This has been discussed.]

Bob: You are talking about me?

Therapist: Yes.

Bob: Well, you are supposed to help me figure out why I commit so half-assedly to things

Therapist: Well, that sounds like a ripe area of exploration. Should we explore it?

Bob: Of course I had to think it up.

Therapist: Well, there are other things that interest me and that I would enjoy talking about. Should we pursue my interests? I don't mind.

Bob: That is ridiculous.

Therapist: Are you calling the New York Mets ridiculous?

Bob [outraged]: You want to talk about the Mets?

Therapist: Well, if I get to set the agenda in here, which seems to be what you are asking for, I am willing to comply. Do you follow the Mets?

Bob: I want to talk about why I do everything halfway for Christsakes. My marriage, my work, my everything.

Therapist: Halfway here too?

Bob: What do you mean by that?

Therapist: Any guesses?

Bob: Well, I guess I want you to be in charge here so that I don't have to take any responsibility.

Therapist: Look, I don't mind if we do everything my way, but do you know what that gets you?

Bob: You are impossible.

Therapist: I am a tyrant.

Bob: Yes, you are. But if I put it all on you I can get annoyed, I guess, with you for things going on in my life. I blame you.

Therapist: Well, you should. I haven't figured out a way to get you interested in why you are the way that you are, what is the history of your different ways of feeling and thinking and acting, where you got certain ideas you have about yourself, love relationships, work.

Bob: Well, I would rather come in here and talk about Maria or my boss or Maria's parents rather than how I think about things and all of that.

Therapist: How come?

Bob: Because I want everyone else to be the fall guy; it is my m.o. And I get to hide out.

Therapist: So, Bob, I have a question. You are an intelligent, well-educated man. How come you think it is that you have only a sketchy idea of what you want to do with your life?

The seminar members had different comments about the vignette. Most centered on Bob's knocking on the door impatiently. Some participants felt that every-other-week appointments were frustrating him and that the therapist's lateness was like salt in the wound. When questioned about why Bob was being seen every other week and using the couch, the therapist explained that this was the way she was trained to work—but she agreed that another approach might be more effective. The major focus was on the countertransference, and participants felt that the therapist was setting up or adding to Bob's frustration and then losing her patience instead of firmly interpreting Bob's resistance. One member suggested saying: "Bob, you are frustrated because we have not figured out what prevents you from coming here at least once a week." The therapist's guilt mentioned in the vignette was a clue that she questioned her training. She was really caught in a dilemma and it was difficult for her to examine her treatment philosophy.

A therapist's ability to remain constant, consistent, and steady is tested over and over again. This ability grows over time, but the therapist who never loses her "cool" or her equilibrium is a myth. As illustrated by this therapist and Bob, both parties may express impatience and frustration through sarcasm and anger. Beneath the words are feelings of wanting to connect, but not knowing how. Each party blames the other, and only they can really figure out what keeps them squabbling. One seminar member wondered if the therapist and Bob were sexually attracted to each other and trying to avoid these feelings. Another member felt the fear of intimacy was the basic problem.

SADOMASOCHISTIC ENACTMENT

Characterological sadomasochism is difficult to work with, because it always gets enacted in treatment. Mr. M, who will be discussed in detail in chapter 8, never did change. He used his sadomasochism to torture his therapist and others in his life. Every time he showed ability to work in depth, he withdrew, cancelling or being late for sessions. Even when he became aware of his sadistic side, he used it to punish himself. The countertransference proved most difficult, as the therapist enacted both the sadistic and the masochistic roles. Neither revisiting her own sadomasochistic conflicts in treatment, seeking consultation, nor studying the literature seemed to affect what had become a stalemate. After many years of spinning their wheels four times a week, the therapist ended the treatment. She had both lost her patience and made a rational recognition of the point of diminishing returns.

> Mr. M returned to therapy after a break of almost a year—he sounded desperate and, whether due to caring, empathy, sadomasochism, grandiose fantasies of cure, murderous rage, or just plain curiosity on both sides of the couch, the treatment resumed. The therapist hoped that the once-a-week treatment he could afford would tame her expectations and therefore help her react less to Mr. M's provocations. Mr. M seemed to have no capacity for empathy, remorse, or responsibility, except on a surface level. The therapist wondered whether those feelings were denied, repressed, or missing. Depth of feeling was either strongly guarded against or deeply buried by fear of narcissistic injury or powerful unconscious guilt. The therapeutic connection was sadomasochistic most of the time. At times, the patient seemed to soften, and at those times the therapist could feel empathic. Benevolent curiosity kept the treatment alive. It seemed possible that Mr. M was an imposter—fooling himself into believing that he was innocent of cruel fantasies. Although he could pay lip service to his ability to hurt others, more than momentary recognition of his cruelty and lack of empathy was experienced as a major narcissistic injury. He projected the rage he had buried so deeply onto the therapist and others in his life—disappointing everyone, including his children. Killing people's hopes, including his own, was the basis of his lifestyle.

FEAR OF LOSING THE PATIENT

When the therapist acts on her fear of losing the patient without exploring it, chances are the patient will leave.

> Mrs. T asked Dr. Z to reschedule her Thursday hour to Friday. The therapist agreed for he wanted to please Mrs. T, but then he forgot to show up. Mrs. T cancelled her Monday hour and Dr. Z forgot this, too, and sat waiting for forty-five minutes. Dr. Z was not a forgetful man. He did have trouble refusing his patient's requests, and he relied on a strict schedule. His forgetfulness was a compromise formation between wanting to please his patients and wanting to please himself. He said yes and meant no. His supervisor spotted the pattern and Dr. Z brought it up in his own treatment. Resolving his own conflict permitted him to work more effectively. In this case, the countertransference had to do with Dr. Z's own inner life—and so was not induced.

Sometimes patients switch appointment times and then forget. In one case, it turned out that the patient was not comfortable with the therapist's flexibility. "If you change my hour so easily how can I trust you to say no to my sexual demands?" she said.

The therapist's fear of losing a patient is, in many cases, less based in reality than in fantasy. Beginning therapists lack confidence, and that plays into this fear. The therapist's ability to tune in is compromised by the worry about the patient's leaving. This is a countertransference dilemma, because the therapist is projecting her own fear onto the treatment situation. The patient has her own fear to deal with and will usually stay with the therapist who worries less and listens more. After all, the patient has come to treatment for a reason and needs the therapist to do her part of the work.

When a patient threatens to harm herself, however, the therapist rightly worries, and this is a reaction that she must discuss with the patient. Of course this is not only countertransference—it is justified concern—but because it takes place in treatment, more can be learned by thinking about who represents whom and by thinking about what the situation means.

- Can you tell me about wanting to hurt yourself?
- Perhaps my worrying about you is important—no one seems to have cared before.
- We must consider what would make you feel safer right now.

- ACOA and AA are very supportive groups, and it would help to get a meeting list for times when you feel impulsive. These groups meet twenty-four hours a day.
- I am in touch with my tape three times a day and I can call you if you leave a message.
- Let's set up an appointment for tomorrow.
- Threatening to hurt yourself is rage that you're directing inward. I think you're very angry with me.

These interventions, and others along these lines, let the patient know you are concerned and offer some structure. The therapist takes suicide threats seriously; with the patient's knowledge, she may decide to call a family member or friend or, in the last resort, take the patient to the nearest emergency room. I once worked at an agency where some therapists had contracts with patients who tended to act out self-destructively. The patient signed an agreement that he would call before acting. In extreme cases, a phone number and even a plan for hospitalization feels more personal and effective. At the risk of being repetitive, each person who crosses your threshold is an individual and requires made-to-order interventions.

The temptation to categorize troubled patients as borderline or difficult or impossible is great because the countertransference is often intense and naming a problem is easier than solving it. Each therapist does the best she can, and if labeling helps her, she will label. However, benevolent curiosity seems to be diminished by labels. In cases where the therapist is more comfortable with categorizing, it is still important to remember that offering the patient a chance to understand why and how she got to where she is requires the therapist's respect and the ability not to know. The question of the self-destructive patient's anger (in general or at the therapist) must be raised. The therapist's job is to help the patient help herself. A patient who is afraid of losing control will often induce the therapist to take charge. With Mr. M, the therapist was struck, time and again over many years, with his hatred and need for revenge. Explanations, interpretations, and confrontations made intellectual sense to him, but his commitment to revenge and his fear of closeness was too strong. Sometimes there are no answers. (See Mrs. Quincy in chapter 7 of Hall, 1998.)

FEAR OF WORKING WITH A PATIENT

Dr. D told of the following dilemma: An adult woman with several children was being sued for custody by her ex-husband, who claimed that she was manic–depressive. Because she enjoyed the manic periods, she refused medication, thus giving the judge great pause. Mrs. P came to a psychiatrist in hopes of enlisting his help in her court battle. At the end of her fourth session—while the psychiatrist was still assessing the situation—Mrs. P asked if people really used the couch. In the transference, she was saying: "Can I use the couch? I know these custody issues are the tip of the iceberg." The psychiatrist, who was also an analyst, had to decide whether to embark on what was sure to be a difficult, dangerous journey. In the countertransference, he had mixed feelings that were fueled both by his rescue wishes and by his fears of an interminable treatment. The deciding factor would be the analyst's assessment of Mrs. P's strength and the patient's motivation and willingness to commit to the hard work that analysis requires.

EROTIC FEELINGS

Another difficult roadblock is the erotic transference/countertransference. Sometimes the therapist forgets that the erotic feelings, intense as they may be on either side of the couch, are transference and countertransference phenomena and not to be taken personally. The same holds true with positive and negative transference. Holding on to the fact that the transference is a fantasy state allows the therapist to see its defensive aspect. A wish to connect sexually with the therapist denies a painful reality—their separateness. Sexualizing the transference by flirting, or being seductive in therapy, is a defensive move that can ward off dependency, hate, or any other feeling or wish the patient is afraid of facing. Saying to a patient "You're flirting right now" might wound the patient's narcissism, but to ignore it would be equally injurious. A question about the action or a connection to something earlier in the session that is being avoided could be one solution. Erotic feelings are an important part of life and are normal and natural moments in treatment.

Mr. E had a history of visiting massage parlors and occasionally dominatrixes. He had difficulty feeling intimate with his wife, and this behavior seemed to help. One day, the therapist found herself having erotic feelings about Mr. E. (Whether or not these feelings were the therapist's own fantasies based on her own sexual attraction, she had to concern herself with the transference/countertransference meanings of her reaction.) It turned out that Mr. E had succeeded in projecting his wishes onto the therapist. She could not say that she did not enjoy feeling aroused by Mr. E, but she knew that her job was to understand with the patient what was going on. The next time it happened, the therapist asked Mr. E what he was thinking about. After a pause, he said, "You are like my dominatrix. I want you to beat me and to tell me what to do like she does. That's what my mother did when I was a teenager. I thought she had a penis—and that someday she would show herself to be a man. I could give in by being a girl and we could be together." This material might not have emerged if the therapist had not become aware of her feelings. Mr. E's words did relieve the therapist of her distraction, and they deepened both parties' understanding of Mr. E's dynamics and fantasy world. Further treatment revealed that Mr. E's mother subtly encouraged him to become homosexual. He did not, but his perverse tendencies could be seen as a compromise formation. Sometimes a patient's erotic transference is not just defensive, but a sign of improvement. It might be seen as a step on the way to intimacy. I think that the same enactment would have occurred had the therapist been a male.

When the therapist tunes into her own reactions, she is bound to decipher them in relation to the patient and to herself. Erotic transferences are most difficult to interpret, and over the years some therapists succumb to their patient's seductions. This is very unfortunate for many reasons, but the most important one is that it is a betrayal of the patient. When a therapist feels tempted to overstep the boundaries, she must seek help, whether from an analyst, a supervisor, or a colleague—no matter how hard it is to reveal the erotic countertransference (Gabbard et al., 2000).

RIGIDITY

Another type of countertransference becomes visible in a therapist's rigidity. It is understandable that, especially in the beginning of the therapist's career, the stances of abstinence and neutrality are adhered to in a strict way, especially if the case is being supervised. Or the opposite may occur: the therapist may be so worried about keeping a patient that she may bend the frame inappropriately. Both problems ease with experience and can be corrected.

> Tom, a college student, was in analysis at a reduced fee with an analyst in training. One day in the first year of treatment, Tom, on his way to the couch, asked Dr. U if he could borrow five dollars as he had left his wallet at home. Dr. U became flustered. She thought that her supervisor would disapprove if she agreed to the loan, but at the same time she was afraid of the patient's anger. "Analysts are not supposed to gratify," she said to herself. She did not loan Tom the five dollars. Tom never came back.

Years later, Dr. U discussed this case in a seminar about kindness in psychoanalysis and how rigid abstinence can interfere with treatment. In this seminar, she used the term "sticking to one's analytic guns," a phrase that she felt caricatured the analytic stance used when she was in training. Members of the seminar felt the refusal and the term "analytic guns" both implied a hostile attitude toward the patient. Even more important, it is a countertransference problem. It emerged that Dr. U never mentioned what preceded Tom's request. What led up to it? Was there a vacation coming up? Had the prior session been the impetus for forgetting the wallet? Was the request an attempt to feel taken care of? Why was Dr. U avoiding the patient's feelings? Was it in fact Dr. U's own anger that she feared? Dr. U blamed the classical theory and its focus on abstinence and neutrality for her action. She was able to see that her refusal to loan the five dollars and especially the manner in which she did it (silence) was a result of her anger at having to accept this low-fee, nonverbal patient from the clinic.

Analytic tact and timing are talents that evolve through practice. They cannot be legislated by one theory or another. Good therapists take into consideration the patient's capacity to use interpretation at any given moment. Age-old questions about what to do when the patient acts out (asking for a loan at the beginning or end of an hour, not paying in a timely manner, refusing to talk, consistently being late) must be translated in the most appropriate ways possible. The analyst's countertransference always has a great effect on whatever she does at a given time in treatment with a specific patient. Had Dr. U said, "OK, but let's talk about it" to Tom, something may have been learned. She may have just said, "Can we talk about this?" or "Tell me about what happened."

It can be easily surmised that Tom was indeed angry with Dr. U for what he must have perceived as her coldness, and Dr. U was annoyed by the low fee she accepted as part of the training requirement. Had Dr. U taken her countertransference into account by discussing it with her supervisor or her analyst, she might have avoided the enactment that led to the abrupt end of treatment.

Just as the therapist pays attention to the patient's transference, she must examine her own reactions—from her very first impressions and throughout the treatment. Whether she calls them countertransference, enactment, co-transference, or transference, the therapist is responsible for using her feelings to enhance the treatment. In the case of Tom and Dr. U, it seems that both parties were clearly upset with each other and that an enactment ensued. But Dr. U's anger at the training institute was also a factor that she seems not to have dealt with in her own analysis.

ENVY AND INSECURITY

To be on the receiving end of a patient's intense envy may feel devastating to a therapist. It is meant to devastate. Envy often begins as an unconscious communication between patient and therapist. It is not that the patient says, "I envy you. I want what I think you have." But before these wishes reach consciousness they may be acted out by failure, envying others, and subtly or overtly demeaning the therapist's work. A negative therapeutic reaction often precedes the patient's awareness of her envious rage. The working through of envy can be like a volcano. The fire begins deep in the earth and takes its time before it erupts. The therapist's clue is a countertransferential uneasiness that can prepare her for the real heat. This uneasiness of expected attack awakens the therapist's own unresolved envy and helps her understand what the patient is going through.

> After some years of treatment, Mrs. W was preparing for her law boards. A classmate who was also in therapy felt very sure that she would pass easily. Mrs. W, whose insecurity masked her fantasy about being better than everyone else, went into a tailspin of anxiety. During each session, she talked about how well her classmate, Eva, was doing and how shaky she herself felt. "Eva's therapist must give her something I don't get from you." Mrs. W's therapist began to feel uneasy. She started wondering if indeed the other therapist was better. Only when she tuned in to this countertransference could she fully recognize how envy played a role. Mrs. W was really saying, "You are better than me. You have something magic (maybe a penis) that you're not giving me." The therapist could empathize with this feeling by tuning in to her own not completely resolved envy. As this theme entered the transference, Mrs. W's envy of her classmate diminished and she began to value her own talent and competence. Before this enactment, Mrs. W had never felt her envy directly in the treatment. When the therapist became aware of her own envy, the road was cleared for further travel.

It is normal, at the beginning of many treatments, that the patient is seduced by fantasies of cure and that the analyst is seduced by fantasies of making a real difference in her patient's life. These fantasies must be replaced (or at least joined) by the reality of how very frightening, tedious, and provocative this work can be (see Barbara in chapter 5). The grandiose fantasies of both patient and analyst must be tamed by sober concern about present dilemmas and the hope of modifying them; ideas of rescue and being rescued can become the most difficult roadblock in treatment. Unfortunately, many treatments end with the idealization of and identification with the therapist intact (Greenacre, 1966). This is most evident in training analyses where the analysand becomes a disciple of the analyst, carrying his or her work forward.

OVERIDENTIFICATION

Overidentification as a countertransference dilemma is not necessarily unconscious. When the therapist has lost a loved one in the recent past, before mourning is sufficiently resolved, it may be impossible to work with a patient suffering a parallel loss. The same holds true in the case of illness, as discussed in chapter 7. In a treatment that is already under way, the therapist who feels emotionally overburdened and overidentified will want professional support.

TOLERATING THE COUNTERTRANSFERENCE

Carpy (1989) discusses the therapist's reactions to patients who provoke powerful feelings. A woman in once-a-week analysis succeeded in frustrating her analyst by ignoring his interpretations consistently and by veiled questions about his ability. She persisted in denying that her feelings were connected to symptoms of an obsessive, phobic nature. The patient, Carpy says, "got under his skin" and induced him to make "critical" comments. He explains:

> The analyst's acting out allows the patient to see, consciously or unconsciously, that she is affecting the analyst and inducing strong feelings in him, and it allows her to observe him attempting to deal with these feelings; . . . it allows the patient to see that the analyst is affected by what is being projected, is struggling to tolerate it, . . . is struggling to maintain his analytic stance without grossly acting out. . . . [I]t is through this process that the patient is able gradually to re-introject

> the previously intolerable aspects of himself . . . and is also able to tolerate them, which he has observed in the analyst. (p. 292)

Carpy goes on to explain that it is this interaction, not interpretation, that produces change in the patient's psychic structure. The analyst's capacity to tolerate the patient's projections allows the patient to see tolerance in action—as a baby can sense both his mother's frustration and her bearing of it.

Countertransference can be a roadblock but it can also move mountains.

❖ CHAPTER 3 ❖

Tracking Transference: Connecting Now and Then

> My stress will be on the idea of transference as a framework, in which something is always going on, where there is always movement and activity. Freud's ideas developed from seeing transference as an obstacle, to seeing it as an essential tool of the analytic process, observing how the patient's relations to their original objects were transferred, with all their richness, to the person of the analyst.
>
> —Betty Joseph

The question of where to direct transference interpretations is an old one. Early in the history of psychoanalytic theory, genetic interpretations were in favor. The analyst connected the patient's productions, actions, and reactions to her past, giving her a look at her repressed unconscious, or at early childhood memories: "I remind you of your mother/father/sister" and so forth. Genetic interpretation will always have a place in psychoanalytic work, but the idea of working in the "here and now" transference—the transference alive in the present between analyst and patient—has gained favor. Such genetic interpretations as "Your thought that I am controlling reminds you of your mother during toilet training" or "The curiosity you felt in the waiting room has to do with what went on in your parents' bedroom," while probably correct, could be offered and accepted intellectually, thus bypassing the feelings involved. However, a transference interpretation ("You are angry at me for having a schedule of payments") invites the patient to explore his feelings in the present with the therapist. A patient might say: "You just care about the money; I want to pay you when I feel like it—not when you tell me to. You are bossy and controlling and I hate that and you—but logically I know you must be paid on time, so why do I get so angry?" If the analyst knows the patient's childhood history, he might connect the patient's feelings to the past. It is sometimes difficult for a patient to hate a dead parent—but hate in the transference and countertransference is not uncommon. Only after the patient experiences intense feelings with the analyst as stand-in does the connection make emotional sense. It is even more useful when it is the patient who can make the connections to his past.

To use the transference, the therapist must think about the following:

- Hearing the material with an ear to its transference meaning
- Hearing the fantasies that emerge in disguised or displaced form
- Hearing resistance to recognizing transference
- Bringing material into the transference situation
- When transference is resistance
- Transference in the here and now
- What is being enacted and when to interpret it
- How the transference is used in psychotherapy, as opposed to psychoanalysis

These considerations help the therapist keep the analytic work in perspective. They remind her that nothing happens in treatment (or in life) that does not resonate with the past. Keeping track of what goes on in the present—recognizing it within the psychotherapy session—informs therapist and patient about what is being repeated. The ways that an adult patient sees and interacts with the therapist (and vice versa) make up the co-transferences that exist in any treatment, whether sessions take place once or five times a week.

Just as every patient and every therapeutic dyad is different, so is the use of transference different in every treatment. It is sometimes argued that transference interpretations fall on deaf ears when a patient cannot see the difference between self and object and that pointing out the difference may be injurious (Kohut, 1971). While I agree that some patients may not yet be ready to feel empathy for another, I believe that the therapist must keep the concepts of transference and countertransference in mind at all times. Sometimes, we may speak to the patient as though we are not separate—I think of

Kohut's mirror transference here—but we must remember at all times that this is a therapeutic expedient and not a reality. When the patient does express feelings to the therapist—be they love, hate, adoration, or denigration—these feelings must not be taken personally—even the nice ones. The constant awareness that one is a transference object is what makes this work possible. The patient and the therapist are real human beings who develop a unique relationship, but most of the script in the drama was written in the past. As it is played out in the present, the therapist's interpretations invite the patient to revise the script based on new objects and experiences. Long periods of time may go by before the patient acknowledges the therapist as separate—but this does not mean that the patient is completely unaware of the other, even in psychosis.

HEARING THE TRANSFERENCE AND ANALYZING THE NEGATIVE TRANSFERENCE

Sara was adopted as a baby. When she was four, her parents told her this; it went smoothly, and Sara seemed to understand. As an adolescent, Sara went through a fairly normal rebellious stage and decided that she wanted to find her real mother, but she was told by her adopted mother that her birth mother was dead. When she started therapy at age thirty-two on the recommendation of her daughter's therapist, she seemed willing and eager to explore her child's problems and her role in them. She was a pleasant, cooperative, insightful person, and it took some time for the therapist to see her strong need to control. As treatment unfolded, it became clear that beneath the competent, cooperative, pleasant demeanor was a frightened, angry woman with poor self-esteem. The transference shifted from a compliant one to a belligerent one. Sara's material indicated that the therapist was representing the lost mother, and this provided important clues. The fantasy emerged that Sara's real mother was indeed alive but did not want to see her.

Sara [angrily]: I can't connect with you anymore [after two years of twice-a-week treatment]—you don't seem to listen and, anyway, I have nothing to say. I think that after all this time I should have changed, but I'm still distant from my daughter, she still has problems, and she's still in therapy. I want to end this therapy.

Therapist: I have noticed how you push me away [the therapist has felt sleepy in recent sessions], and it seems like you're getting ready to feel your anger. By leaving, you will protect me from it.

Sara [crying]: You know I hate feeling anger—why bother?—and perhaps you'll leave me if I show you. My birth mother probably hated the crying, needy baby and left me.

Therapist: What's happening now has so much to do with your fantasies about the adoption and your feelings about how your mother could have let you be adopted. Right now, I seem to be standing in for her.

Sara: I do hate you. How can you take a week off? You are leaving me—just like she did. How do I know you'll come back? She never came back—how could she have left me? And here I am, a crying, clinging baby and you'll leave me.

This session was a turning point in therapy. The transference manifestation (therapist as abandoning mother) and the countertransference manifestation (Sara's distancing, which caused the therapist to get sleepy) were interpreted, opening the door for deeper feelings to emerge.

The negative transference was interpreted. The therapist saw who she was in the drama. The psychotherapy was consistent and constant, providing a secure stage for the emerging drama. A few months later, Sara increased the frequency of her sessions and began using the couch. The treatment continued to deepen.

USING TRANSFERENCE IN ONCE- OR TWICE-A-WEEK TREATMENT

The belief that four- or five-times-a-week treatment is a requirement for transference work does not hold up. Although it is easier to work in consecutive sessions, experience shows us that what goes on in the dyad is based on transference, and that even in once-a-week treatment recognition of transference contributes to growth. Even in so-called supportive treatment (in reality, all treatment is basically supportive) connecting present perceptions and feelings to past experience helps the patient feel understood. For instance: "I think you feel extra sad today because it is the anniversary of your father's death and it coincides with our separation next week. Two losses are a lot to deal with." The therapist's empathic recognition is both supportive and integrative in that it accepts the patient's mood and explains it as well. The therapist's main task in making such a connection is to avoid condescension. I usually prefer to preface a connection with "I think" or "it seems" rather than saying "you are" because that makes clear that I am sharing my own perception—I believe that most interpretations are offerings, not declarations. There are times, of course, when the therapist is sure of a connection and declares rather than offers.

> After five years of work, Brian still refused to see any connection between his feelings of anger and the therapist's vacations. Yet every July he balked or became sullen before the August break. One day, the therapist, who had been trying to interest Brian in connecting his mood and her vacation, said: "Brian, I have been doing this work for many years, and with you for five years. You will have to take my word for it that the vacation break is indeed connected to your negative mood. Your unwillingness to consider this is your way of telling me that you're angry." Not so amazingly, Brian cried. He had been given permission to express the dependency needs that he had been hiding beneath his stoic facade.

9/11 AND WHAT IT UNEARTHED

> Carla came in for her regular weekly session on the afternoon of 9/11. She commented on how horrible the WTC attacks were and how badly she felt for the victims and their families. Then she went on to talk about her problems with Robert, her husband of two years, and how the marriage was deteriorating—mostly due to her abrupt mood swings. This had been her reason for

seeking therapy, and she had been focusing on it for the past months. She and the therapist had talked about her unstable childhood, her moody, sometimes volatile mother, and how this past relationship made it impossible for her really to trust anyone. Carla loved her husband and had been able to use her fear of closeness with him to explore her pervasive inability to trust. Robert was a loving, considerate mate, and she knew it. But her intellectual knowledge of what a good man he was made her feel worse about herself for not being able to appreciate him fully. Naturally, this situation was being repeated in the transference.

Weeks and then months went by, and the therapist noted to herself that Carla never again mentioned 9/11. The therapist's ears perked up when it did come up some six months later while Carla was talking about a friend who was still very upset.

Therapist: Have you had any more thoughts or feelings about the event?

Carla: No, I really haven't. It surprises me and makes me feel different from my friends and family, who are all involved in some way—volunteering and so forth. It's not that I don't feel sorry—but I feel detached.

Therapist: I wonder if your detached feelings about 9/11 are connected to your distant feelings with Robert—and with me, in our sessions.

Carla [interested]: As a matter of fact, I'm always this way—I feel like I'm on the fringes of everything. I'm never really involved emotionally—like a part of me is always the onlooker, the outsider with no emotion. Instead of reacting to what's already happened, I worry about the next time. In fact, I obsess about the future and pass up on feeling in the present.

Therapist: I think this is the way you protect yourself from the real despair, fear, and longing you felt for your mother, who would turn on you without warning. You learned to seal off or deny the moment of pain and direct your thoughts to the possibilities of future upsets. I think your trouble feeling close to me is related.

Carla: I hate to talk about my childhood. My mother was scary—I hated to go home after school—and I guess the more I hated her, the more she hated me. How can I have children? I'll just repeat the pattern.

Therapist: That's why you came here—to break the pattern.

How the repercussions of 9/11 manifested themselves was unique to each patient. My experience supervising and working with patients leads me to believe that some patients who suffered early trauma were so well defended by avoidance, denial, dissociation, and depersonalization that their reactions were buried as the earlier traumas had been buried. The patients who were aware that they had little reaction to 9/11 and were curious why had an opportunity to revisit early fears—and to understand how the early trauma deprived them of the full experience of life. Early maltreatment causes screens, walls, and curtains that prevent trust and therefore closeness. Those who have suffered from early maltreatment often develop a stoicism that protects them from feeling anxiety and deprives them of the richness of life. Anxiety is often contained by phobic reactions, psychosomatic pain, or reclusiveness.

Bill, a sixty-year-old businessman, immersed himself in volunteer work, contributed to 9/11 funds, and talked about the tragedy constantly. He wanted to rescue people, and this wish distracted him from his family. His first grandchild was born on 9/11, and he had little time to visit with the child or celebrate the occasion. He was obsessed with his rescue activities.

Tuesday session–

Bill: I had a dream: I was at the beach—it was thundering—there was lightning. I was afraid. An elephant walked by, and then I saw a clown. It turned into an outdoor circus. I ran away.

Therapist: Thoughts about it?

Bill [fidgeting and becoming visibly agitated]: I think of an amusement park—Coney Island [excuses himself to use the bathroom].

Bill: I can't swim. I'm embarrassed. I made sure my kids were taught to swim—it's so important. Someone could drown. [Transference message: I'm embarrassed to tell you—I want to impress you by my volunteer work—I want you to think I'm a good person.]

Thursday session–

Bill: That dream has haunted me. I'm sorry I told you. Opening a can of worms.

Therapist: Hmm.

Bill: I never told you, but my cousin drowned when I was six. I was the closest one at the beach and I couldn't move. I called for help, but it was too late. [sobbing] I never think about that. In fact, my children don't even know.

Therapist: Keeping that buried has caused you more pain—you blamed yourself for something you could do nothing about.

Bill: My uncle and aunt moved away after that—I thought it was my fault that they hardly ever kept in touch.

Therapist: It is possible that this early tragedy is connected to your need to rescue today to the extent that you still have not seen your grandson.

Bill: I'm not comfortable with babies. [silence] They are so helpless—I might hurt him somehow. Don't you think my work is important? [Transference message: I fear that you will judge me—like my aunt and uncle who moved away.] I feel guilty and powerless—seeing the baby drown was paralyzing. My parents tried to comfort me, but they were so upset and I felt lost. [Will you understand my guilt or will you leave me alone?]

Tuesday Session–

Bill: Karen [wife] put her foot down. We're visiting the baby tonight. I have a fund-raising dinner tonight. We fought. She says I'm ignoring my family because of my involvement in 9/11.

Therapist: Can you see her point?

Bill: Yes. But I feel paralyzed.

Therapist: You felt paralyzed when your baby cousin drowned. This grandchild is evoking old memories of that day—your attempts to rescue everyone today is a kind of atonement for your imagined sin of not saving your cousin. And you're worried that you'll lose my full attention like you lost you parents' attention that day.

Thursday session–

Bill: I visited Pete [the grandson] last night. I got very emotional and actually cried when I held him. It felt so good—I hope it lasts. I also signed up for swimming lessons at the gym—I won't need you anymore. [Transference message: I've accomplished my mission here and hope it lasts. Now I can leave feeling good about myself and understanding how that trauma affected me and my whole life. If it doesn't last, will you be here?]

Present-day catastrophe can unearth early childhood trauma, whether shock trauma or strain trauma (Kris, 1956). In these and other cases, the shock of 9/11 afforded an opportunity to revisit and rework the early pain and guilt always present in childhood trauma. The helpless child often assumes responsibility in an attempt to feel less helpless. Carla felt responsible for her mother's moods. Although she hated them, in order to feel some control, she responded by provoking her mother in different ways, making her mother even moodier. By alienating her husband and pushing her therapist away, Carla was reliving the past. As she worked in therapy, she began to see both intellectually and emotionally how she defended herself. She alternated between being a "good, pleasing" patient and a cold, distant patient. The therapist was surprised at the changes and thrown off balance. Carla was letting the therapist see what she had lived through as a child. Back then, she had withdrawn into fantasy and doll play. She had done well in school and camp, but had never felt close to anyone. By softening these defenses and internalizing the therapist as a new object, she inched toward closeness.

Bill's was a case of shock trauma. It was a one-time-only event that he had suppressed. The fact that his aunt and uncle moved away and lost contact with him intensified his guilt. Luckily, his parents were loving and steady. Bill developed into a loving husband and father and a community-minded man. When 9/11 and the birth of his first grandson coincided, he sought therapy because he knew he was out of control. Short-term treatment helped him resolve old and new wounds.

EMERGING FANTASIES

When a person first calls or makes arrangements to see a therapist, she has something in mind. Whether she is forced into therapy (as in a rehab program) or is in psychic pain and is self-motivated, there exists a fantasy. This fantasy will determine the transference/countertransference that evolves. One's perception of the world is based on past experience, ego strength, unconscious fantasy, drive derivatives, innate capacities, selective identifications, good and bad parenting, genetics, disposition, and such things as nourishment, comfort or discomfort, trauma, and resilience.

Jill's mother died when she was three. Her father remarried quickly. The parents ignored the children's emotional needs and Jill and her brother Tom bonded together, constructing their own comforting, private world. When Jill was eleven, Tom introduced her to sex. When she was eighteen, he died in a car accident. Jill went to a counselor at college and stayed in counseling for four years. Her attachment to the counselor helped her finish school and then law school. Jill's intelligence, psychological mindedness, and ability to identify with her counselor were the prelude to the intensive psychotherapy she began when, at age thirty-two, her life was on the verge of falling apart. The precipitating event was that a man in the law firm asked her out. Jill was panic stricken and became physically ill. Wise enough to realize that her illness was brought on by the idea of dating Hal, she began twice-a-week psychoanalytic work. Jill's first three years in treatment were spent reconstructing her past and discussing her present. The traumatic loss of her mother was seemingly dealt with by substituting her older brother as caretaker. Jill did not tell the therapist about her sexual relationship with her brother for three years. When she did, guilt, shame, and tremendous loss emerged. The work of mourning was exhausting for both therapist and Jill. The unconscious fantasy of herself as killer, and of therapist as judge and executioner, took shape in the transference. By facing her anxieties and seeing that she could live through them, Jill deepened the

> treatment by coming more frequently and using the couch. This brief summary is meant to illustrate the emergence of the unconscious fantasy: "I kill those who get close." Her fantasy of cure was conscious, however. Confessing her crime would relieve her of her pervasive guilt and lead to the punishment she deserved. For many years, therapy was experienced as reform school.

Types of anxiety are omnipresent and defended against throughout life. Wishes to devour, merge, castrate, and murder are projected onto the other, and only when such wishes are owned in words does anxiety diminish. Most people choose to live with the balance they have achieved, for even when it is dysfunctional or pathological it has been adaptive in some ways. So when a person comes to therapy, she is understandably wary of losing her balance. Jill was already losing hers. Consciously, she hoped for redemption—a hope that lays the foundation for the emergence of a positive transference. Unconsciously, she wanted punishment. This fear appears in the negative transference.

A BAD START: THE EFFICACY OF EARLY TRANSFERENCE EXPLORATION

The very idea that change is necessary goes against one's narcissistic love of self. Whether or not a patient and therapist connect is a complex question based on both parties' unconscious communication, conscious perception, timing, realistic factors, and gut feelings. The patient's wish to destroy may be acted out before therapy by never making it to first appointment or, when treatment has begun, deciding not to continue. A therapist's wish to cure may blind her to helping her patient understand what motivates her (Hall, 1998; Sharpe, 1947). The understanding of how and why one carries conflict wherever one goes and in whatever situations one creates is of paramount importance. Understanding with a patient why she feels injured, frightened, or angry at the recognition of another person in the room is an important goal with narcissistic patients. Such emotional and intellectual understanding strengthens the ego and the capacity to differentiate self and object. The therapist's ego strength is often loaned to the patient—until she can make it her own. In such cases, it is not always possible, or even useful, to interpret transference manifestations, but keeping track of them is important and enlightening for the therapist.

> Miss B was given my name by her idealized supervisor. She waited a few months before calling and had difficulty setting up an appointment time. When she got to my building, she went to the office next door. I found her there twenty minutes after she was due. She apologized for going to the wrong office and thanked me for finding her.
>
> Why did I look for her? Realistically, I knew that there were other office suites on the way to mine. I had alerted the doorman that I was expecting a new person so that he would show her the way to my office. When Miss B had not arrived after twenty minutes, I went to check with the doorman and discovered that she had walked into a neighboring office, even though the doors were marked. I wanted a new patient and wanted to spend the consultation time fruitfully. All these thoughts and the action I took were my agenda based on my transference wishes (transference because I pictured her lost and needing to be found). Her needs—not to be found, to be late, not to begin therapy, to hide—were overridden by mine. A battle had begun even before we started.
>
> During the abbreviated session that followed, Miss B told me that she had been in couples treatment with her boyfriend, who was independently wealthy and paid for everything. "After all," she said, "I'm in school." There were certain things she was unwilling to talk about—specifically, her brother and that her wanting to have her own therapy would upset her boyfriend and their couples therapist.
>
> The consultation proved awkward, and as it drew to a close she opened her appointment book, could not find time for a second meeting, and said she would call me when her schedule was clear. Miss B called a month later and left a message informing me that unless I could negotiate the fee she would begin shopping around for another therapist and asked me to leave my address on her tape as she had lost my bill. I returned the call, leaving my address.

The old rule "always interpret the negative transference" is still pertinent when the patient is on the way to quitting. At such times, the therapist can say something such as: "It may have to do with thoughts about me; it could be helpful to explore them." "I gave you the bill last time—any feelings about that?" "The vacation break is coming up. Could that be connected to why you think of leaving now?" Had I helped Miss B to explore her feelings about going to the wrong office and about being found, she might have made another appointment.

RESISTANCE TO THE AWARENESS OF TRANSFERENCE

"Why would I have feelings about you?" a patient asks after two years of twice-a-week therapy. "You're a therapist and your job is to keep me out of trouble and to help me find a husband. It has nothing to do with you." Such statements are common. A relational approach would show the patient that there is indeed something going on right now in the room and that keeping the analyst so far away has meaning. This approach has merit and is worth pursuing, but if a patient is adamant it would appear to be intrusive for the therapist to insist. Another approach might be to wait for a sign, in either content or change in affect, that the therapist could explore with the patient: "You mention in your dream that a faceless man was lurking in the shadows and that you were afraid. I wonder if the faceless man you're afraid of is me." This intervention uses the patient's material and the reality of the analyst's face being covered by a beard to inquire about the transference fear. It is offered with benign curiosity, and although the patient might not say "Aha!" she considers the connection. If a patient rejects an interpretation, this does not mean that it went unheard. The therapist must share her observations and interpretations over and over again in different ways with most patients. In this way, it will gradually become clear to both patient and therapist whether the interpretation is a correct one that the patient needs time to absorb, or whether the interpretation is off target and needs to be reconsidered.

When a patient gives strong cues that the transference is off limits, the therapist can still use the material to make connections to the past or to the outside present: "What you say about your roommate reminds me of what you said about your sister-in-law." Benign connections pave the way for transference interpretation.

Each dyad traverses the transference terrain differently, as each patient is different with regard to the structure of the ego, the strength of the drives, the quality of the superego, the degree of narcissism, the capacity for object relations, and as each therapist is different in terms of training, inherent patience, flexibility, anxiety, experience, and so on. The length of treatment, and the co-transferences that develop are usually results of these combinations. In the case of Mr. C, who was about to get fired for lateness, an exploration of the situation revealed that he was deliberately taunting his boss because the boss had refused him a raise. Unconsciously, losing his job would mean losing his therapy, something he longed for and dreaded. A negative transference based partly on an unavailable father was in place but not acknowledged. The therapist had recently returned from summer vacation, and Mr. C wanted to stop therapy. What can the therapist say? Loss and retaliation stand out in the material.

"This is really important—it all sounds tied in, and I think we can figure out how."

"Wanting to quit is connected to getting fired."

"It sounds as though you would like to fire me."

"Your boss let you down and my being away probably felt as though I don't appreciate you, either."

BRINGING MATERIAL INTO THE TRANSFERENCE

Richard came to a clinic rather than face a jail sentence. He had been arrested for drug possession and the judge gave him the choice of treatment or jail. To assume that Richard chose the lesser of two evils would be a mistake. Actually, his behavior turned out to be a cry for help. An amphetamine addict, Richard had become desperate. His initial transference fantasy was multilayered. His wish to seduce the therapist defended against the experience of his psychic pain. His functioning was deteriorating, and his reputation as a successful actor was in jeopardy. His attempts to help himself had failed, and seeking help was embarrassing to him. The idea that a woman therapist could be of help was an alien one. His mother was an extremely intrusive woman who adored her famous son and experienced him as an extension of herself. Richard experienced conflicting wishes to separate and to merge, to face his rage and to keep it buried for fear of losing the object's love.

While he wanted the same adoration from the therapist, he also wished for something different. One fantasy was that once she learned who he was she would become another sycophant who would applaud him, thus protecting his status quo. He behaved in a charming and seductive manner and was surprised when the therapist kept the sessions to the allotted time no matter how late he was. When the therapist would not discuss her private life, and when she tried to help him understand why he brought jokes and gossip, Richard was upset and surprised.

The therapist's neutral, abstinent, interested stance laid the groundwork for in-depth work. *Neutral* meant not judging Richard, and *abstinent* meant not telling him about her private life. Richard's charm, along with his many vignettes about famous people, allowed the therapist to understand his conviction that acceptance and love depended on his ability to entertain. His health and well-being had never come first with his parents; only his fame mattered. It took him years to trust that love and acceptance did not depend on performance. In fact, when Richard had a relapse in the third year of treatment, the therapist insisted that he hospitalize himself. He was deeply touched when he saw that the therapist's interest was not monetary but that her concern was his health.

As Richard over the years began to understand his attachment to his mother, he developed the ability to see that the two of them were different—were individuals. This was difficult and frightening, especially because his mother was incapable of acknowledging their separateness. First, he began to experience his anger at their mutual dependency.

Richard: She called last night when I got home—2 A.M. Her apartment faces mine, and she can see when I turn the light on. I can't believe she waits up for me. We talked about the opening [a movie], and I told her all about who was there, and who I sat with, and where I went after. [Teasingly] Don't you want to know? There were lots of stars—DeNiro, Minelli, Sarandon, etc. You don't seem turned on. My mother wants to hear it over and over again. Finally, I hung up.

Therapist: You feel that, like your mother, I want to be fed in order to be interested in you.

Richard: How could you be interested or even listen to me otherwise? What would I say?

Therapist: What comes to mind?

Richard [after several minutes of silence]: I can't believe you want to know. I'm thinking of what to do tonight. I have nothing planned . . . could go to the baths . . . could stay home and feel awful. What do you do? Are you married, have a man friend? [Starts to tease again] Come on, tell me. Maybe you're gay, too.

Therapist: You start to tease me in order to shift away from your loneliness.

The bulk of this work took place in the transference, where separations were the occasions for acting out. Richard would regress in various ways, keeping his feelings under cover. Spite, envy, and self-destructive behavior shielded him from his longing and neediness. The acting diminished when the therapist interpreted it as retaliation directed toward her for leaving on vacation. Richard learned eventually, by reliving in the treatment his dangerous and destructive relationship with his mother, that survival was possible. Loewald speaks of the analyst as a mature object:

> The patient, in order to attain structural changes in his ego organization, needs the relationship with a consistently mature object. This, of course, does not mean that during the course of the analysis the analyst is experienced by the patient always or most of the time as a mature object. (Loewald, 1960, p. 20)

Richard teased the therapist constantly. For Valentine's Day, he brought a chocolate tool kit. "Fix me" was one message. He was also repeating the teasing he grew up with and letting the therapist know that he felt safer in child's play. Taking himself seriously was to be avoided. His jokes and anecdotes were funny, and it was difficult not to laugh. His therapist told him this and what she thought it meant—"Your wish to entertain me and make me laugh keeps us away from the real pain that you want me to fix and that's so hard to reach"—and gradually he became more thoughtful and reflective. Content interpretations would have to wait until the resistance was interpreted.

THE DEMAND FOR CONCRETE ADVICE

When we step back far enough, we can see the transference picture even, and especially, when there seem to be no signs of transference. The presentation of a problem is a clue in itself.

Mr. Q presented a problem. His girlfriend of many years was giving him an ultimatum. Either he would leave his wife or she would leave him: a concrete dilemma for which he wanted advice. His few friends differed in their opinions, and he came to the therapist for objective counsel. His wish for another opinion said a lot. Why not make up his own mind? Why not weigh his friends' opinions? Why seek a female therapist? What was his transference fantasy of cure?

After hearing something about his family (alcoholic mother, distant father, retarded brother) the therapist began to understand his loneliness. Mr. Q preferred seeing himself as weak and ineffectual to taking an independent step. He believed it was safer to avoid the rage—particularly at women—that made him so anxious. He came for advice, and if he couldn't get it, why continue therapy? Feelings were uncomfortable and got in his way. The therapist explained that she could not give advice, but that she could help him to get to know himself, and then he would know what to do based on his own feelings. Mr. Q came in the following week and asked how therapy worked. He had been thinking about the therapist and he was curious.

Mr. Q: You seem interested in me—but maybe it's based on money. How do I know?
Therapist: What's your gut feeling?
Mr. Q: Good. Now what?
Therapist: Whatever comes to mind.

Both parties felt hopeful.

Increasing sessions allowed Mr. Q to see that anxiety was tolerable and that the therapist was not frightened. The initial transference was positive and it evolved into an idealistic one. Wishes to depend, to be cared for and about, were revealed and served to cover his rage at feelings of abandonment. He began to see that his threat to abandon his wife or his girlfriend was protecting him from facing his own feelings of abandonment by his mother at age four. Identification with the aggressor was his preferred defense against feelings of rejection and low self-esteem. As he began to understand this, Mr. Q began to open up to his wife, and she began her own treatment. When the therapist finally dropped from her pedestal, after a vacation, Mr. Q experienced his feelings in the treatment, with therapist as abandoning mother.

Mr. Q: I was not going to come back here. I got so depressed—fought with my family—started seeing my girlfriend. How could you leave me? Where were you—what happened? I was feeling better and now I'm nowhere. Worse. What good are you? It's like when my mother left. Who needs this? [Silence.] I guess I felt this way when Mom left, furious and scared.

USING THE "HERE AND NOW" TRANSFERENCE

Ben, a wealthy lawyer, is late for his session. He blames the cab driver for taking the long way. He should have spoken up, but the driver was an older man and Ben did not wish to express anger to an old, less successful man.

His therapist, also an older man, heard the message as a transference reference to himself, with roots in Ben's experience of an ailing father. Ben had been angry the day before because the session time was up and he was just getting to a dream. The therapist was aware that Ben had waited until the last minute of the previous session to tell his dream and felt trapped into interrupting him.

Therapist: I think your anger at the driver is meant for me. I ended yesterday's session and there wasn't time for your dream.

Ben was able to realize that he had not left his office in time for the session and that his anger at the driver was unjustified.

Ben: Yes, I am annoyed at you. You never give me extra time when I feel I need it. You have to end because there is someone waiting. Well, I have important appointments, too, and I couldn't leave the office just for you. If I could have longer sessions, this wouldn't take so long.

This "here and now" interpretation could have included genetic material by using Ben's anger at the cab driver/father who was ineffectual and never made time for him. The therapist could have made a reconstruction showing Ben that his disappointment with his father led him to expect disappointment in the present. The analyst chose to wait, because the father was not in the material and because the affect pointed to the analyst.

CONNECTING THE TRANSFERENCE TO THE PAST (GENETIC INTERPRETATION)

Mrs. S, in treatment for many years, called five minutes before her Thursday appointment to say that she was attending a meeting and would not be in. A national holiday on Monday meant that she would miss that appointment as well. Tuesday, she came in and reported a frightening dream: "I missed today's appointment and was in a panic." She had also panicked over the weekend. The Thursday cancellation had been hostile—she had wanted me to wait and to be annoyed and disappointed. The acting out of hostility caused anxiety because it was unconscious. She was able to rationalize her choice to attend the meeting for a while, but as her anger became more palpable she became frightened of losing me.

In the Tuesday session, she acknowledged her curiosity about what I had been doing over the holiday. As she populated my life with people other than herself, she felt rage. How could I spend time away from her, away from my chair, in the outside world? Envy and jealousy, along with yearning and loss, were expressed in words rather than in action. Thoughts of her mother having a baby when she was two and memories of a bossy sister who felt entitled and an unavailable father flooded the treatment.

Once Mrs. S expressed her anger to me verbally, her access to the past increased. The experience of neediness and envy, although painful to remember and feel in the present, gave her the insight she needed to grow. She mourned the omnipotent fantasy that she was the only one—a compensatory fantasy that served to deny her inner loneliness. As she mourned, she also felt a different kind of connection to me and to others. The energy once spent on denying separateness was available for new object relatedness. A competitive rivalry surfaced, and oedipal wishes and disappointments became the focus, with the analyst representing mother and then father.

ENACTMENT, TRANSFERENCE, COUNTERTRANSFERENCE AS NECESSARY ROADBLOCKS

A week after the therapist returned from vacation, Mrs. R called to cancel her session and to ask for a different hour. The therapist could not accommodate and left a message saying so. When Ms. R still hadn't paid her bill three weeks after it was due, the therapist brought it up:

Therapist: You haven't paid me, yet.

Ms. R: I haven't looked at the bill, yet—did you charge me for my cancelled session?

Therapist: Yes.

Ms. R: How come you can go away for two weeks and I can't take off one day without being charged?

Therapist: You know this is how I work—and it seems there's more behind your anger.

Ms. R: It isn't equitable. [Continues to argue, then falls silent.]

Therapist: I think this is more about my being able to leave you.

Ms. R: I don't care about that—but how come I can't take off when I want to?

Therapist: It makes you feel powerless that I can go away and leave you.

Ms. R remains silent for five minutes.

Therapist [feeling the anger): Now you're leaving me so that I will feel abandoned as you did when I was away.

Ms. R: Yes! Now you're the powerless one. You have to sit here for forty-five minutes.

Therapist: Yes, you do have power. [Tension lifts and the session is over.]

How is this transference? The patient relived her whole life in these minutes. Injured physically in childhood, she was at the mercy of doctors and nurses for a year. Feeling powerless to control the painful circumstances, she became an angry, entitled girl who never allowed herself to feel her sadness. This stoicism saw her through some very rough times, and it stayed with her. Closeness threatened to bring up her neediness and rage. She experienced her wishes to depend as intolerable, but they broke through when the therapist went away. Only after years of work in treatment did she begin to function in her job and with friends. The therapist's ability to last it out with Ms. R was tested time after time—and Ms. R's power over the therapist was acted out for years. This enactment of Ms. R's rage and the therapist's impatience created a platform from which to interpret. The therapist often felt trapped, as Ms. R had as an injured child. Transference, countertransference, enactment, and projective identification were roadblocks that had to be overcome. There were no quick answers. Time allowed both parties to survive and to trust.

TRANSFERENCE AND COUNTERTRANSFERENCE AS RESISTANCE

Ben (the angry lawyer mentioned earlier) is chronically late. He listens to the therapist's interpretations and agrees with the connections offered, but to no avail. His lateness eventually becomes a roadblock, because there is never enough time to settle in to the work of analyzing the resistance on a feeling level. The work neither deepens nor broadens. Ben and his therapist are stuck, enacting the transference. The question for the therapist now becomes the evoked countertransference. Is the therapist in his growing frustration reenacting Ben's relationship with father or mother? Is Ben saying "I can make you impotent by being late and not letting your work succeed?" Is he saying this from a place of revenge? Envy? Anxiety? Is he clinging to the original pleasure he may have experienced in the anal phase of development when he stubbornly held in his feces? How did his caretakers respond to his early refusal to do his "job," as they called it? Was he punished? Was this the beginning of a sadomasochistic character style? Did his parents cajole and reward, giving him power to get special treatment, indulgences, and attention he might have lost had he been acquiescent? Did he retain his feces to symbolize his fantasy of carrying a baby as his mother did (she was pregnant when Ben was two and a half)? He was constipated throughout his childhood. Was he mimicking her pregnancy to identify with, and thus hold on to, her? Did losing his feces represent separation and castration? The idea of losing a part of himself may have been traumatic. Was he afraid to explore his resistance? The old song—his lateness was comfortable. He knew how to sing it.

How the therapist reacts to this roadblock will be a crucial factor in determining the future of the work. Will there be a future? Will the therapist give up out of frustration, anger, or rage? Ben is projecting his own rage on to the therapist, who is now feeling as Ben may have felt when forced to produce. The therapist is feeling a role-responsiveness (Sandler, 1976) in Ben's drama, and feeling alone and impotent, as Ben and his parents must have felt.

What can the therapist do in such cases? Sometimes nothing works and therapy ends prematurely. The therapist may have given his all (interpretation, confrontation, clarification, patience), and because of the recalcitrance of the problem, or the secondary gains it affords, or the pleasure the patient takes in his sadomasochistic character style, the journey ends.

But the therapist must also consider the patient's position and time of life. Ben was planning to marry. He had a difficult and time-consuming job, and these pressures along with his financial situation made therapy seem impossible to him. The therapist must respect the patient's felt reality—even though he may see the resistance involved.

When the therapist is in the midst of a sadomasochistic battle or a power struggle, it becomes almost impossible to see beyond it. This is a powerful co-transference dilemma. All therapists are susceptible to this swampy terrain, this tremendous pull to the sadomasochistic stage of development. The allure of the swamp is ubiquitous. Every baby wants to play with its shit. A full diaper feels warm and soothing. It is the quicksand that must be avoided and a roadblock that may be permanent. Such sadomasochistic transferences are good examples of transference as resistance.

Every day, examples of sadomasochistic fantasy enactments occur in the workplace, at home, and at school, and in politics, creative endeavors, and religion. Wishes for revenge and power, stubborn refusal to go by the rules, wishes to mess up, and feelings of helplessness are universal human feelings that never go away. The best we can do is to modify and tame these wishes with feelings of empathy, respect for autonomy, recognition of and respect for the other, and love. This is not to say that the therapist is always empathic and patient. Frustration and anger at a patient are sometimes expressed—and sometimes this expression of anger gets through the roadblock, and sometimes it makes the roadblock worse.

At times such as this the transference is clearly resistance. But it is also the way Ben has found to stay connected to his father. Anal struggles with the therapist, the boss, and others are charged with energy. The tension has become so familiar and so important to Ben that he can't give it up. Ben has lost sight of the therapist as a therapist. His therapist is now his father—not in a psychotic transference, but as a defense against loss and all that it implies.

In fact, Ben and his therapist did not finish their journey, then. But ten years later—when Ben was fifty—they decided to try again. Ben's father had died, his son was an adolescent, and Ben's awareness of his own fathering potential rested on his ability to resolve issues he had up until then avoided.

TRANSFERENCE BEFORE BEGINNING TREATMENT (FANTASIES OF CURE)

Transference is present and palpable before the first phone call. It is a common experience for a therapist to be told about a referral but never hear from the person. It is also common to receive a phone message from a prospective patient, with no follow-up. It is common to set up a first appointment and to have it broken or cancelled. It is common for the patient to be late or early. Some patients carry the therapist's number around for years before calling. All of these phenomena can be seen as transference manifestations (see Ms. B above). Everyone has fantasies about treatment, and some would rather keep those fantasies than check out the reality. Sometimes, the initial interview will quell the transference expectations, and sometimes the initial interview will be distorted to give credence to them. Things such as office furnishings, the people in the waiting room, the therapist's look, the lighting in the office, and the pictures on the wall are used—to fortify the patient's fantasies or to calm them.

"Well, at least she has taste."
"Ugh! I hate this office."
"So many books—at least she knows something."
"So many books—he ought to get a life!"
"Her bathroom is bigger than mine."
"He has more closet space than I do."
"What crummy hangers."

"The rug is worn—must be a lot of people coming in here."
"She can't afford a new rug—probably has no patients."
"He must be out of shape—so heavy."
"He looks so strong—I could cry on his shoulder."

CONSIDERATIONS

- Be aware of transference and the quality of object relatedness in the first call.
- Look into your thoughts after you hear from the patient. How did you feel?
- Was it difficult to set up a time to meet?
- Did the patient seem hostile on your message tape?
- Did the patient seem compliant?
- Was the patient behaving appropriately? Was she overly anxious, overly confident, overly familiar?
- Did the patient forget to leave her phone number?

SCENARIOS

"Hi, Jane. This is Lois. Fred told me to call you to talk. I might want therapy. How much do you charge? Call me back."
"This is Doris Gray. I'd like to consult about therapy. My home number is —— and I'm home after 7 P.M. or before 8 A.M."
"Hello. Jill Tobin gave me your number; I wondered if you were accepting new patients. Please call me at —— after 8."
"This is Mr. Brown. I am interested in therapy but I travel all the time. Do you do telephone therapy, and how much would it cost?"

The first potential roadblock is "Can we begin?"

CHAPTER 4

Inner Roadblocks

> One must never forget that, unconsciously if not consciously, [patients] are living in terror. They dread every kind of fantasized calamity, each of which is, in their psychical reality, as real as any objective danger and, owing to its infantile nature, far more terrifying.
>
> —Roy Schafer

No matter how troubled a person may be, the idea of change is frightening. This is largely due to internal pressures to repeat the familiar past, in order to retain feelings of safety. Every decision in therapy—including the decision to begin it—arouses resistance, and it may also arouse on both sides of the couch the particular kind of resistance that I call "roadblocks." By *roadblock,* I mean a resistance that has not been fruitfully incorporated into the analytic process, and so instead of facilitating that process tends to hamper it. Such resistances are difficult to recognize by patient and analyst. Giving up the status quo requires exploring unknown territory and altering habitual and comfortable defenses even when they are on the verge of wearing out or breaking down. This chapter will focus on theories of resistance, with an emphasis on how resistance itself looks in treatment in its recognized and unrecognized forms.

Early in his elaboration of psychoanalytic theory and technique, Freud thought that a patient's symptoms would remit, and that cure would result, if the repression covering infantile trauma were lifted. When this proved untrue, emphasis shifted away from the lifting of repression and toward interpreting the resistance to (that is, the defenses against) remembering. Free association was thought to be the way to overcome resistance. Ideally, in once- or twice-weekly therapy, as in four- or five-times-a-week psychoanalysis, the therapist follows the drift of associations and connects them like dots to show the patient the pictures that emerge. But even in those early days, willingness and ability to trust in this method did not come easily to patients. Because it was a rule—the *fundamental* rule—it was an occasion for resistance itself, as all rules can be. Even beyond such social inhibitions as shame and embarrassment, people are not used to saying everything that comes to mind. In fact, we are taught as children to censor our deepest thoughts; the capacity to free associate comes only over time, if at all, and nobody can do it perfectly.

However, the recommendation of free association looks less threatening as the patient begins to see that it makes sense. To interest the patient in deciphering his own unconscious is to make an ally of his ego. This in itself deepens the motivation for treatment. There is a vast difference between a therapist who demands compliance to a rule and one who offers a key to understanding.

A SHIFT IN TECHNIQUE

In the 1920s, Wilhelm Reich began a theoretical revision that resulted in a significant change in technique. His work was based on Abraham's "A particular form of neurotic resistance against the psychoanalytic method" (1919). There, Abraham spoke of patients who would not comply with the fundamental rule—or the other rules of the analytic setting—to the point where they seemed to forget that they had come to treatment to be helped. This very recalcitrance became the lever of access in these cases, where links were discovered between rebellion, envy, and omnipotence, which became character traits. Reich thought that these patients hid a permanent attitude of disobedience and provocation behind a facade of good will. Their sensitivity to narcissistic injury led them to identify with the analyst and to wish to surpass him.

Reich (1933–34, chapter 3) proposed the existence of a latent negative transference that often went unanalyzed. Such negative feelings were hidden behind compliance and idealization. Many analysts, whose own treatments had never touched this aspect of negative transference, went on to perpetuate the problem with their patients. The analyst, said Reich, is seen as a disturber of the neurotic equilibrium (the status quo), and this leads to the patient's mistrust. He proposed strict rules of interpretation that would not ignore the negative transference, as manifested, for example, in a patient's persistent or even occasional lateness. Attention to and analysis of such resistances *before* content became the rule. Reich advocated a view of resistance as a character armor that is relatively ego-syntonic and defends against anxiety. He himself was very confrontational, often badgering his patients into an openly negative attitude. His use of the words *attack, dissolution, liquidation,* and *armor* gave his style of analysis a militaristic tone, but he had a tremendous impact on analytic work. Character analysis is very difficult, and confrontation plays a large part in it. Confrontation is a supportive technique, as it is used in the patient's best interest.

Anna Freud, in *The Ego and the Mechanisms of Defense* (1936), continued the delineation of the resistances as an area to study and learn from. Today, such clinicians and theoreticians as Roy Schafer (1983) present a gentler and more empathic view than Reich's, yet an insightful and important one. These authors emphasize the importance of identifying resistances and getting patients interested in them as a basic approach. Schafer gives the example of a woman patient who stifles her tears. He points out that the tears are not the resistance—it is the stifling that must be explored.

When resistance is not "attacked," "dissolved," or "liquidated"; when the therapist neither badgers nor hostilely confronts a resistant patient; when she tries instead to learn from the resistance and to introduce the concept with benevolent curiosity, she calls on the patient to make sense of a potential roadblock. But sometimes, perhaps many times, nothing works. It may be extremely difficult for the therapist to maintain a benign attitude when the patient consistently ignores and denigrates the method of treatment. This attitude can be a manifestation of rage and anxiety, and when it occurs, stalemates in treatment are not uncommon. Kernberg (1975) advocates confrontation while Schafer (1983) details strategies of resistance that undermines the analyst's empathy, reminding us not to forget how anxious the patient is. When the therapist keeps this in mind, her empathy often returns.

Connecting the resistance to a manifestation of negative transference—"I think you are late again because there's something you feel you can't say in words; perhaps it has to do with me"—gives the patient something to think about. It also informs the patient that thoughts about the therapist are welcome. The focus is not on the lateness itself, but on the patient's feeling that he can't talk. Whether the lateness is due to anxiety or hostility, it can usually be analyzed by reflection on the patient's underlying feelings. In this example, the therapist combines Reich's rule—"analyze the resistance before the content"—with an empathic approach. When it cannot be analyzed, however, it becomes a roadblock.

TYPES OF RESISTANCE: THEN AND NOW

As he articulated the structural theory, Freud saw resistance coming from several sources. Reactivation of original complexes in the theater of the treatment was a threat to the patient's long-term defenses and adaptations. This threat was guarded against both by resistance to awareness of transference feelings and by irresolvable transference.

The *secondary gains* from illness are not easily relinquished. Masochistic needs are served, and revenge is taken on those who must witness the patient's pain. Many symptoms invoke extra attention from the patient's family and friends; in Freud's day, fainting was one of these. Today, delinquency, self-cutting, and psychosomatic illness all demand notice.

Id resistance takes the form of holding onto patterns of instinctual gratification. No libidinal position is easily given up, especially if it is combined with aggression. Id derivatives include the libidinal and aggressive behaviors involved in oral, anal, phallic, and oedipal pains and pleasures. When these behaviors are sublimated, and therefore socially acceptable and tolerated by the superego, their resistive aspects recede. An ego that can sublimate or tame the drives is necessary, and so strengthening the ego is a goal in treatment.

Mr. R wanted a divorce from his seriously depressed wife but was afraid to act on this wish. In his third month of analysis, he admitted to the analyst that he masturbated while speeding in his car. He acknowledged the dangers of this behavior, but said that he couldn't stop it. Complex work involving his need for a sexual outlet, his embarrassment and shame, his murderous rage at his wife, and his suicidal guilt all played a part in this action. His attempt to worry the analyst succeeded; his wish to be rescued, worried about, and loved by his analyst was interpreted. Gradually, action yielded to understanding and to a degree of sublimation. Mr. R stopped masturbating in a speeding car and began picking up prostitutes. Later in treatment he met a strong, competitive, sexual woman at his country club and began dating her. Transference was interpreted along the way: masturbating left the analyst/wife out of the picture, prostitutes demeaned them, meeting a safer, competent woman meant he could recognize and tolerate an appropriate woman.

Superego resistance has to do with conscious and unconscious guilt. Suffering or unhappy children tend to blame themselves to avoid the terrifying reality of their helplessness. Their guilt may stay with them, sometimes for life, contributing to a harsh superego. A harsh superego threatens severe loss of self-love and self-esteem and creates a need to punish oneself. The very goals of treatment (an improved, enriched, happier life) can be undermined by a punitive and guilt-evoking superego. The analyst's availability as a nonjudgmental, benign, new object (Loewald, 1960) with whom to identify can soften the superego demands and help understand why the harshness evolved. Identification with the therapist is a first step. Strachey (1934) advocated "mutative" (transference) interpretation meant to address the superego. Whether this is called transmuting internalization (Kohut, 1971), identification with a "new" object, or interpretation of conflict, superego work is necessary.

Every time Ms. O got a promotion at work, she got herself in trouble with her boyfriend. In treatment, she began to realize the connection. She had chosen a man who did not approve of women in the workplace, especially women executives, and it emerged that her father left home when her mother had resumed her teaching career. Ms. O blamed her mother for her father's leaving, and she blamed herself for alienating her boyfriend. Her guilt about hating her mother fed into her reliving the abandoning-man scenario. It took her a long time to be able to look at the way she repeated her past, punishing herself with the choice of a punitive man.

Superego resistances can be delineated through the analysis of symptoms such as Ms. O's; another approach is exploration of the patient's internalized objects. The image of a critical, competitive, unloving caretaker (an agglomeration of the child's memories mixed up with her own envy and rage) is not easily given up. This image becomes an imago—an internalized object—a part of the self. To modify such representations is a more realistic therapeutic goal than getting rid of them; the need to cling to familiar internalizations (Shengold, 2000) is too formidable a resistance. As we will see more fully in chapter 5, the more abusive the original object, the harder it may be for the patient to let it go; we have all seen cases of abused children clinging desperately to the very parent that is doing them harm. But critical, persecutory internal objects do become externalized enough to work with in the treatment. The closed internal world becomes an open one due to the power of transference (Fairbairn, 1958).

Resistance to letting go of the analyst (and the analyst's resistance to letting go of the patient) explains the regression that takes place once (or even before) a termination date is set. In the context of impending termination, the patient often reproduces old symptoms and anxieties. Both parties in the dyad wonder if it is truly time to stop (chapter 9). This is why a termination period of up to a year and no less than three months is helpful. That period of time can be used to rework conflict, review gains, anticipate problems, and mourn.

Threats to quit. Goodbyes are painful, and efforts to avoid them are not uncommon—patients sometimes cancel treatment over the phone to deny deep feelings. When a patient ends treatment abruptly, the therapist may suggest one more session to gain a better understanding of the situation. Sometimes a threat to quit therapy is a test to see if the therapist can tolerate the deeper feelings that are about to emerge. Roadblocks—unanalyzed resistances—in the therapist frequently account for clinical errors in situations such as holding onto a patient when the work has reached an appropriate conclusion, perhaps, or going along with a patient's wish to quit precipitously. Lateness, seduction, boundary violations, and cutting down on sessions inappropriately are other roadblocks that may threaten treatment from the therapist's side of the couch.

Social resistance. Although this attitude is changing, most Americans view being in psychotherapy as a stigma, proof that something is mentally wrong. Outside of such sophisticated cities as New York, Los Angeles, and Boston, there is a widespread cultural resistance to exploring one's inner life. Interestingly, this is not so in Argentina and Brazil, where everyone from CEOs to cab drivers seems to be in analysis—in fact, if you're not in therapy, something is wrong.

Fear of parental disapproval. Patients often don't want their parents to know about their therapy: "Mother will think she did something wrong" or "Dad will say it's frivolous." This concern may change as well-known people who have benefited from treatment speak up publicly. Such celebrities as Mike Wallace and William Styron have been open in discussing psychotherapy and medication and sharing their experiences, thus offering hope to the public. The mental health field is working toward informing the public that psychotherapy is a valid, proactive treatment. Movies and television abound with positive examples of psychotherapy: Gregory Peck in treatment with Ingrid Bergman in *Spellbound,* James Gandolfini in therapy with Lorraine Bracco in *The Sopranos,* and Robert DeNiro in therapy with Billy Crystal in *Analyze This* are just some of the images that stir public interest.

Acting out, that is, expressing feelings in actions rather than words, is a form of resistance, but like all others it can also be a valuable source of information. A patient who was upset by a last-minute cancellation did the same thing to her therapist. At the next session, the therapist asked about the incident, wondering if the cancellations were related. "Oh no," the patient protested, "my cancellation had to do with oversleeping." The resistance was not directly translated into annoyance or anger at the therapist's cancellation; rather, it was the patient's refusal to explore the action that prevented understanding. The refusal to reflect was the roadblock that needed addressing. Further analysis revealed that the patient's feelings of abandonment were so intense that she had had to cover them by sleeping through the session. This realization proved to be a point of access to the patient's defensive style. The anger that was part of it had to be disowned for fear of losing the love of the object and of the superego.

Tiptoeing into treatment—hesitation about trusting the process—and staying on tiptoes for long periods is necessary for some patients. If the therapist shares the tendency to tiptoe around the work, however, a roadblock can result (chapter 7). It is necessary to respect the patient's fear, but when the therapist is intimidated by it, she gives the patient even more reason to be fearful. The therapist's tact, timing, respect, intuition, and clinical judgment, along with her confidence in a psychoanalytically informed technique, are all necessary to walking softly without tiptoeing.

> Tania began treatment on tiptoes. She was mistrustful after a failure with a former therapist who had given her homework, advice, and extra time in sessions, but who had frequently been late herself and had sometimes forgotten appointments. A friend gave Tania the name of an analyst, and from the start Tania began testing. She missed sessions, withheld her fee, repeatedly requested changes in scheduling, and then threatened to quit when the therapist adhered to her policies.
>
> The therapist enlisted Tania's common sense and her sense of justice. She explained in a calm but firm way that she had to be paid in a timely manner because this was her job. She pointed out that rescheduling appointments, except in emergencies, would not work for either of them; they both had work schedules, and the steadiness of their work together was important. She also explained the importance of consistency and how missing sessions would make that impossible.

These explanations were offered calmly and earnestly. They set the tone for serious work, and they gave Tania a new picture of treatment. She commented that some of her friends had therapists who would let them cancel with twenty-four hours' notice. The therapist explained once again that without consistency they would not be able to make the necessary connections, and that her work as a therapist was her livelihood and that she could not accept a policy that was financially self-destructive. These conversations about policy and its basis allowed Tania to see that the therapist's requirements were not frivolous or arbitrary and that they made sense. They also allowed Tania to see that she was working with a serious person who would take Tania's treatment seriously and treat her with respect.

The roadblock in this situation was Tania's tiptoeing. This was understandable, given her past experience, but only when the therapist showed her that the ground was firm could she move along. In the transference, she expected the therapist to be weak, uninterested, and wishy-washy like her previous therapist and, originally, her mother. Explaining the structure of therapy is a commonsense approach to a conscious form of resistance based on former experience, although the resistance usually proves too complex to be dispelled by a simple explanation. In fact, in Tania's case it returned in different forms and permutations as treatment proceeded.

Another patient, Pam, could not understand why she was not entitled to take time off when she wanted to as the therapist could.

> Pam's inability to see that the therapist had a business, that if all her patients took time off without paying she would not be able to pay her office expenses, was due to her difficulty in seeing the therapist as a separate person. Beneath the anger lay tremendous separation anxiety and a need to be in control. Therapy is like other professional commitments. The professional requires a fee. Pam could not face that reality and left treatment. This particular therapeutic partnership did not get through the roadblock. Warning signs were Pam's hostile, brittle approach to life in general; the power struggle about paying for missed sessions was Pam's way of holding on to the status quo.

Another major roadblock is a patient's *inability (for whatever reason) to look beneath the surface*. When we walk along a road or sidewalk, we rarely wonder what lies beneath it. But if that question is brought to our attention, our responses can range from curiosity through interest, fascination, and dismissal (as in "who cares?"). This is equally true about what lies beneath actions, thoughts, inhibitions, or obsessions. It is the therapist's job to educate those patients who have never thought about the past's influence on the present, or the internal world's influence on the external. The therapist must explain and illustrate as her interventions show the patient connections between outside and inside, present and past. The therapist's stance of benevolent curiosity can do much to break up the resistance of this kind of concrete thinking.

It often takes time for a patient to accept the concept that ideas can be explored. Every time Miriam felt that she accomplished something, she punished herself. Arousing her curiosity about her masochism became the focus of treatment.

After several months in therapy, Miriam mentioned in an offhand way that there had been five children in her family, but that one had died as an infant. She went on to talk of other seemingly unrelated things. I asked what had happened to the fifth child, and as Miriam talked the theme of the treatment began to unfold. At first, Miriam didn't see any connection between the death of her baby sister and her present life, but as she explored her history, her family's reaction, the fact that hardly anyone remembered much about it, she became curious. Miriam's capacity to reflect on and explore an incident that had been pushed underground by the whole family made analytic work possible. It evolved that buried feelings of omnipotence and resulting guilt—Miriam thought that her hateful wishes had killed the baby—conflicted, causing a compromise in the form of a sadomasochistic character. A facade of cooperation and niceness hid the rage Miriam felt when things did not go her way. This became the focus of her analysis, over and above the content of the trauma.

Guilt and fear of loss camouflaged Miriam's sadistic transference reaction to the disappointment of not being in control. The fact that I could maintain a separate existence between sessions and over weekends, let alone during vacations, clashed with Miriam's omnipotent picture of herself. Her resistance nearly reached the stage of the negative therapeutic reaction, where the analyst loses all effectiveness. Putting her rage into words, however, and seeing that I could tolerate it, helped Miriam learn that her wishes for the baby's disappearance were coincidental with, not causative of, her death.

Miriam was not a murderer, even though she had wished for the baby's disappearance. But the resistance to and working through of her awareness of being an ordinary person without magical powers lasted for many years—when dangerous fantasies come true in childhood the effect can be serious (Greenacre, 1956). After years of work, Miriam and I decided to terminate. Miriam mourned the loss of the baby, of her mother's attention, and particularly of her fantasized omnipotence. The fear that her mother (the analyst in the transference) would let her die ebbed. Marriage and family were rewarding, and her growth was impressive to us both. Five years later, she resumed treatment to work on the depression that had followed her relinquished omnipotence and to achieve a new, realizable ambition. We considered that in her unconscious she was still wondering if I had survived her rage and if the remnants of her masochism would make her new goal unreachable.

OTHER COMMON ROADBLOCKS

Other roadblocks include consistent lateness, prolonged silence, and incessant chattering.

Lateness is a form of procrastination that can often be seen as acted-out fear or rage. It stands to reason that the shorter the session is, the less time there can be to look inside and to experience feelings. The therapist's reaction to being kept waiting is a clue to what the action means. If the therapist feels annoyed by persistent lateness, she can surmise that the patient is provoking her. If she feels relieved at the shorter sessions, she is usually picking up the patient's fear of expressing anger and her own fear of experiencing it. If she rejoices in the patient's lateness, she must face her own rage at the narcissistic injury that can come with feeling mistreated. In the following vignette, reported in the therapist's own words, interpretation of the lateness is done without exasperation and with patience and respect.

Emma is forty-eight, divorced ten years ago. She has a twenty-five-year-old daughter who functions well. She grew up in a self-made, wealthy family—her father was a dogged businessman, cruel, determined, compensating probably for an orphaned, poor background and deep ambivalence about being Jewish in a Wasp East Coast community. Mother is alcoholic. Emma's parents were excessively abusive to her (verbally mocking, taunting, shamelessly critical) and told her repetitively she was ugly, stupid, and fat, while actually Emma is quite attractive and definitely very bright. They pitted Emma and a younger sister against each other mercilessly. Not surprisingly, Emma married a verbally abusive and sadistic man. She lived with him for ten years. She had several years of active alcoholism (but has been sober several years now, and was so before beginning treatment with me).

She has a small travel agency and gets along with her customers, but has no close relationships.

Emma was referred to me after a series of therapists had either retired or moved away. Her high level of grandiosity and superiority and her chronic lateness probably put some of them off. Alcohol counseling and short-term work had not been productive in the past.

I have been seeing her for two years. We started (as her retiring therapist had) at once a week. Emma was always at least twenty minutes late. For that and other reasons, a year ago I suggested that she come twice a week. Still she was always late—arriving harried, self-effacing, with many somatic complaints, and very defensive about her "strengths" and accomplishments. It was hard to get a word in.

Over time, she has come to understand the distance she keeps as protective. As we pursued an understanding of the lateness, she began to talk (and be listened to) apparently for the first time—about the childhood abuse (including sexual abuse by her father) and about the psychological pain in her marriage. About four months ago, she began to arrive closer and closer to the appointed time. Emma is rarely late now.

Countertransference issues of course had to do with my being irritated and frustrated at the lateness and realizing how unimportant she feels to people. There were many times I would have gladly given up. Now I'm glad I did not. I find her to be a very impressive woman.

Generally, whenever she was late—which was literally for each of her once-weekly sessions—I would start by greeting her with something like "I'm glad to see you." This greeting was probably due to my annoyance, but in her case I think in retrospect that the consistency of the greeting was helpful. She would inevitably bombard the initial minutes of the (remaining) hour with comments about how unwell she was feeling—so depressed, stomach so upset, been awake all night, at times (saying) "I should just kill myself." Part of this, of course, was literally true, but there was also defensiveness about it—I always felt I had to interrupt to bring her to the topic of lateness (i.e., asking if the malady had contributed to the lateness, etc.). She'd brush the inquiry about lateness off—as if it were not important.

Eventually, and then repetitively, I told her that her lateness was important to me, that it had an impact on the effectiveness of our work together, and that it was frustrating not to have the full time we had allotted for our work. She went from disparaging that to frank surprise that I would want to spend "any more time with me than you have to." Over several sessions, she talked of various movie and TV "shrinks" who either joked or maligned their patients behind their backs, were driven crazy, or had inappropriate sex with them. Still, at weekly—late—appointments, we did get into more of her background. She hated her cruel, malicious, alcoholic mother, who eventually went "crazy" when the patient was thirteen or so and was hospitalized for a time. Emma was blamed. She told me that her father molested her in her bed at night. Ultimately, I interpreted that perhaps she worried that spending more time with me would cause harm to one of us. She agreed, essentially with a litany of failed relationships, hurts, self-blame, and anecdotes that she and others are better off with her alone—as lonely as she is—as she has been for most of her life.

Still she was always late. It was about here that I suggested that since she seemed to need to protect our relationship by shortening the hours—that is, by being late—we might be wise to schedule two appointments a week. Clearly, there was very important work to be done, but also considerable anxiety about using the full scheduled hour. It was a bit of a flier for me as I remember (realizing the paradox in the suggestion), but she was delighted. We added the second hour, and within a week or so she started coming earlier and earlier to both sessions. Now, for all intents and purposes, she comes on time. She verbalizes her continuing horrible low self-esteem issues as they play out in the transference, and she is gradually gaining insight. Overall, the quality of her life is moderately improving—she is gaining more autonomy in her contacts with her parental family, has actually had some dinners out with business acquaintances, has lost about thirty-five pounds, and is doing some nice things for herself.

She will probably be in psychotherapy for another three to five years—or forever to some extent. If I were an analyst, I think she might be a candidate to "cross the waters" to psychoanalysis, but I could argue on the other hand that the more interactive and overtly supportive style that psychotherapy allows may really be better for her.

Silence, usually seen as blocking forward movement in therapy, may be a clearer communication than words. Some possible meanings of silence are:

Thoughts about the therapist
Shyness (conflict about inhibition vs. exhibition)
A wish to be prodded
A wish for symbiotic merger

An angry response
A way of isolating the therapist (to show the therapist what it feels like)
Embarrassment
Depression
Secrecy

Nonstop *chattering* also has defensive and expressive aspects, such as:

Testing the therapist's stamina and patience
Fear of feelings
Expressing rage by not letting the therapist in
Exhibiting extreme anxiety
Isolating the therapist
Covering up painful or embarrassing feelings

As with lateness, in assessing the meanings of silence and chattering, the therapist uses her reaction. She may feel curious, assaulted, abandoned, mesmerized, angry, helpless, bored, sad, empathic, and so on. These reactions can tune her in to what the patient is communicating.

FROM RESISTANCE TO ROADBLOCK: INTRACTABLE SITUATIONS

Sometimes, a patient's resistance is insurmountable. Negative, perverse, and erotic transferences and the negative therapeutic reaction can all be covered or disguised by compliance or expressed overtly. All are frequently hard to overcome. The analyst stands for a hated object or part of the self. The patient's projective identification allows her to experience her hateful feelings as coming from the therapist, instead of from herself. Any positive feelings, wishes, or hope in the patient cause intense anxiety or fear of loss of the object, loss of love, punishment, fragmentation, or annihilation. Negative, perverse, and erotic transferences protect the patient from experiencing imagined devastation. The idea of depending on, relying on, or loving the therapist demands a kind of trust that may be unavailable to the patient or perhaps deeply buried. Clinging to an abusive object (chapter 5) often feels safer than letting go and replacing it. The best the therapist can do is to try to modify self- and object representations by offering herself as a new, consistent, benign object and by analyzing the patient's defensive feelings of omnipotence and helplessness. This is not an easy job. In fact, working with a patient who exhibits such fear of her unconscious fantasies—often murderous and sadistic—often proves impossible, as with Pam (above).

The therapist may lose her cool and express her own frustration—and sometimes this helps, if the patient can realize that the therapist is human and can get angry, and that they can both recover. However, patient and therapist cannot always last it out. Some patients have an unconscious sense of guilt that manifests itself in fear of success (Freud, 1916) so that every step forward is followed by several steps back. Therapists also have different levels of tolerance and patience. Cases that end prematurely are not uncommon in the field of psychoanalytic psychotherapy, but opportunities to read or hear about them are. This is unfortunate, because it creates a false standard. When two people do psychodynamic work, a certain amount of motivation on the patient's part is required. So is a large amount of humility and self-awareness on the therapist's part. The therapist who neglects to examine her own motivations and resistances risks failing both the patient and herself, as happened in the case of Alan.

> Alan wanted to take a job out of state. But his analyst needed to continue the analysis to complete required control work, and instead of analyzing why Alan felt he needed to leave his present job so suddenly, he offered phone treatment. He was afraid that a break in contact would jeopardize the hours he needed to fulfill his training requirements. Alan might have experienced the value of the work differently if he had had the opportunity to stop and resume when he could. The therapist, a neophyte in the field, with needs of his own, thought the solution lay in continued work. He did not consider that Alan was equally responsible for the analysis and could have chosen to stop for a time or to continue and look for another job.

Phone treatment does have a place in our work with certain patients for brief periods, but it cannot replace the person-to-person interaction that analytic work requires. The clues provided by vision (gait, manner of dress, bodily tension, facial expression) and smell (heavy perfume, body odor, flatulence) are just a few of the cues that are lost over the telephone. Questions of lateness, earliness, and waiting-room fantasies and actions are compromised. The symbolism of mouth-to-ear communication is not addressed in most instances that I have heard about. In this case, however, the main unresolved question was the motivation of both parties.

If Alan was unconsciously looking for a way out of treatment (resistance or irresolvable problems with his analyst), the therapist's offer undercut him. His fear of losing the case—his own resistance to analyzing Alan's decision—prevented him from analyzing the situation. Alan confided later to a friend that he just wanted to get out of the treatment, and that the offer of the phone sessions felt like an obligation. When he did return home, never having understood his departure, he found a different therapist. In this case, the therapist had a roadblock—his need to hang on to Alan instead of understanding with him what was really going on.

This brings up once more the matter of the therapist's policies.

Starting on time and not going overtime
Adhering to a regular appointment time
Giving notice well before vacations
Regular payment schedule
Establishing an agreement about how missed sessions will be handled

When patients balk at these policies, they are testing the therapist's ability to be firm, to establish boundaries, to take care of herself, and to tolerate anger. These policies are few, but they establish the basic working conditions for the therapist, and they must be sensible responses to her own personal and professional needs as well as the needs of her patients. We rarely talk about the therapist's personal needs, which may include the need to feel appreciated. Gabbard (2000) has discussed the analyst's need for gratitude and the roadblock encountered when a patient consistently denigrates and tortures the analyst. Being paid does not make up for such transference experiences, but it certainly helps. Granted, some patients will not consent to committing themselves to paying for missed appointments. They can usually find a therapist who will treat on an as-needed basis. I charge, however, or else offer make-ups, unless a patient knows she will be away for a period of time in such a way that I can plan my own time constructively. I try to schedule make-up sessions when there is illness or death in the patient's family because this can be a particularly stressful time for the patient. But colds, subway strikes, storms, and other short and unexpected outside situations are not my doing—my electric bill still needs to be paid. My experience has convinced me that while patients may gain something from less-structured treatment, they often outgrow it. The therapist's resistance to structuring the treatment is a major roadblock in many of these cases—if we return to the analogy of traveling, this type of treatment can be thought of as meandering. It may also be a way for the patient to test the therapist's strength. Can she stick to her policies? Is she afraid of the patient?

When therapist and patient meet, there are always subtexts having to do with how the parties resonate with each other preconsciously, subconsciously, or consciously. Who does the therapist represent from one second to the next? Who does the patient stand for? Is a projection of some part of the self or object occurring? Is there jealousy, hatred, lust, or merger going on?

THE THERAPIST'S ROADBLOCKS

One resistance for the therapist is *becoming sleepy* during a (superficially) interesting session, or when the patient speaks without affect (chapter 2). In struggling to stay awake, I have sometimes blurted out the words, "Something's going on right now. What are you feeling?" If the patient joins me in exploring, I become alert immediately. If not, I might get up to open or close the window. But nothing really breaks the spell except connecting with the patient. When this doesn't happen, resistance may become a roadblock. None of this happens intentionally or consciously; rather it is a powerful expression of unconscious, affect-laden material of the therapist or the patient.

Such subtexts are the essence of the work. The talk that goes on is like a net. If safe enough, it permits a plunge into heretofore suppressed, repressed, or acted-out material. Every therapist grapples with the resistances to subtexts when she is doing in-depth work.

Acting out is a resistance that often turns into enactment—that is, the therapist becomes involved in the action. If the therapist cannot eventually analyze her own role, an enactment, too, may become a roadblock. Acting out must sometimes be tolerated over a long period of time before trust grows. It must be put into words, interpreted, and explained, while the therapist's ability to remain constant, consistent, and steady is tested over and over again. This ability grows with experience, but the therapist who never loses her equilibrium or her cool is a myth. When two people meet on a regular basis to understand the unconscious, there will be intense moments of love and hate.

I will conclude this chapter with two extended vignettes illustrating several of the resistances and roadblocks discussed in this chapter:

- Primitive oral rage and neediness
- Reluctance to see the "other" as separate
- Resistance to giving up self-medication
- The therapist's countertransference anger
- The effect of the therapist's confrontation

Portia

Portia grew up with a controlling, critical, and cold mother and a father who worked at night and slept during the day. He died when Portia was a teenager. A sister, two years younger, was the favorite and much resented by Portia.

Portia had been in treatment for over three years. She was overweight nearly to the point of obesity and used marijuana and men to assuage her uncontrollable appetite and her hunger for love. She had sought treatment in order to end a sexless marriage, which she accomplished after a year of work. The therapist was experienced in the transference as weaning her from her various sucking activities, which included performing fellatio on her boss at work, overeating fast food, smoking pot, having sex with married men, and talking nonstop. Portia frustrated her therapist in subtle and overt ways, which helped the therapist to imagine how Portia must have felt as an infant and child.

Portia would overwhelm the therapist with examples of how nasty she was at work and then bemoan the fact that people stayed away from her. The therapist would reflect back how others were likely to feel when Portia unleashed her temper and disdain: "You seem to push people away and then wonder where they are." It became increasingly difficult for the therapist to be neutral, empathic, and patient as Portia became more and more sarcastic, demeaning, and bratty.

Portia: How dare you decide to work on the Thursday before the long weekend? I just won't pay you because I'm going away.

Therapist [calmly]: You are so angry about the idea that I have a separate life—your words about that will be more helpful than acting your anger out by threatening me.

Portia [coldly]: You don't have a life—you just sit here—in this office. [A long silence follows. Portia glares at the therapist.] Aren't you going to say something? Or don't you know what to say? Maybe you're stupid.

Therapist: I know that you're very angry and it would help to talk about it.

Portia: What's to talk about. You can't do anything about my anger. No one can. If you don't like it, fuck yourself.

Therapist: You're treating me like you treat others in your life—disdainfully. It pushes us away and makes us angry. It is important to express your anger, but when you do it this way it boomerangs and ends up hurting you.

The following session begins with silence and sulking.

Portia: I was so upset last time—didn't think I could face you again, or wanted to. I've never felt so misunderstood, frightened—I was gonna run. But I took Gail's [best friend's] advice to think twice—because I can always quit. I went from hurt, angry feelings to consciously feeling grateful to you for shaking me up. I went home. Lou [married lover] upset me, and I saw Gail and gave her all my grass. Today is my fourth day without it, and I said to myself I could do it with or without you. I'm still waiting for the other shoe to fall.

Therapist: How does that feel?

Portia: Funny. I never thought I would give up pot. Gail was glad because she knew I was smoking too much. From then on, I began to see things differently. A few years ago, I wouldn't have seen your point about how I don't take care of myself and would've blamed you. But now I don't blame you. I went from mad to worried about myself—promised myself to show up—and I didn't want to come. Afraid you'd still be angry and you had a right to be angry. That's why I'm scared. I mentioned it here as much as I could, but I know you didn't realize how bad it was. I was afraid you would take it away, and I didn't think I could stand it. Whatever happens here, I know I can do without marijuana. I called Mona [a friend] and asked her not to smoke. She agreed. Eating junk food is the next thing. For the first time, I made myself a regular meal.

Therapist: What did you make?

Portia: Hamburger and salad.

Therapist: How did it feel?

Portia: Strange. I gave myself permission to eat what I felt like and I haven't been overeating. I threw away ice cream. I have to try to help myself. This was spiraling in on me and I couldn't grab hold of it. I told you I wouldn't pay you the fee we agreed on without even saying why. You were right to lose your temper about my not valuing you—but I felt stunned. I know you're human, but it took days to get over my wish for revenge, by not coming back. Gail said what'll I do if don't go back. I don't demean therapy—I've said bad things and criticized a lot, but I show up.

Therapist: You've always had trouble understanding the effect you have on people. That's why you missed out on a promotion and why people stay away at work. You've said many times that you drive people away. You were trying to drive me away before I left on vacation.

Portia: Most of the time you don't respond to my insults—you let me run.

Therapist: It's important for you to express your anger at me, but sometimes it's not easy for me—I think you need to know that I'm not made of steel. Neither are others.

Next session:

Portia: I thought you'd be cold today. I had a dream: A sex dream, a variation on being late. Never got to the end of the dream where I could have sex with a man. In the dream, I couldn't find my diaphragm—couldn't catch up. The feeling was everything is ahead of me and I'm running along behind it. In real life, I've never been ready. Whatever I do, there's frustration and helplessness. I can't fit in. I remember in the dream—if I would do a few things that he wanted, he would have sex. He was mean and nasty but I wanted him in bed. There were a series of tasks like packing a suitcase—was trying to figure it out last night. Like in death dreams. I'm not ready for the end. In this dream, I came close but he withheld sex. In the dream there was someone with jagged teeth, scowling face, dark hair—a gargoyle—not human. A tormenting spirit. Is it me or you? I fear your anger but look at what my anger does. They're after me but I didn't deserve it.

Therapist: What about not wanting to be ready, like a kid not wanting to go to school.

Portia: At age five, I went to a playground/summer camp. The counselor was teaching us to dance, but I couldn't learn. She had no patience. At the performance, I wasn't ready. I was holding a girl's hand—I wouldn't go on stage. My parents asked me why and I said the girl wouldn't let go—but I knew I needed more practice and I knew I wouldn't be any good. My parents never wanted to know—they asked but they didn't understand. If only they'd encouraged me to speak up. I felt bad that I disappointed them. I didn't like camp. My sister was two and could stay home. If I got individual attention from the counselor—I could do well, but not in groups. One counselor gave me attention. She was black and my mother didn't like her. I asked the counselor when she'd be white, and my mother was embarrassed. My sister got all the attention and my father was working shifts. I had problems learning to read. So much pressure. I tested high—but from my perspective now, I can see a sensitive little girl needing more attention. They didn't understand that. I resented them a lot. Now at thirty-four, when will I be ready? I always felt gypped. My sister skipped second grade and got ahead. In ninth grade, she told me that I had a genius-range IQ and teachers had such high hopes for me. I got criticism and impatience. I spited them all by withdrawing into books.

Therapist: When you withdraw you don't feel ready—like in your dreams and with me.

Portia: In all the dreams, there's always an adult who has control. What am I late for? A question I'll never answer. It seems so much a part of me. The little girl who needed so much help. I'd like to go back and help her. She needs someone to help her.

Therapist: You and I can help her—together.

Portia: I need strict encouragement, not gentle. This girl is in a cave and would like to come out, but she's balking. Saying "please" and reasoning won't help her. She needs to be pulled. She's afraid and doesn't trust—she's in the dark waiting to feel good enough to come out.

Therapist: You've told us that you felt such pressure to perform that you refused in order to spite the grownups. I think that goes on here—you push me to pull you and then you get angry. Sometimes caves feel safe and it's hard to leave a safe cave. That's the struggle.

As treatment continued, the struggle eased. Portia became more trusting.

Richard

Richard, thirty-four, in treatment for three years, is homosexual. He has taken Valium, barbiturates, and amphetamines in varying amounts for many years. He works under great pressure in the fashion world and is quite successful, but he is always on the brink of losing clients. His beneath-the-surface rage is acted out in procrastination and subdued by drugs. His therapist sees him twice a week and feels that his sadomasochistic character structure requires more intense treatment. Richard assumes the role of masochist, feeling tortured by his clients, but at the same time he tortures them in turn by disappointing them constantly. His work is in demand, but his narcissistic and demanding clients (much like his parents) threaten him with abandonment. Procrastination hidden by his pleasing facade is his main weapon. His life is a repetition of his childhood, and although he has begun to make this connection and has stopped his drug abuse, he is losing his reputation in his field. The work is focusing on Richard's self-destructive pattern of disappointing others as a way of expressing anger.

Richard [begins by sitting in the chair instead of using the couch]: I think I'm not as nice as I thought I was. I've been angry several times this week—at Lisa [his associate] for being jealous of Ann [a client] and at the lady in the photo store for goofing. She was so nice I couldn't yell at her. Also angry at the delivery company and the hardware store clerk. It's uncomfortable. I used to be able to take the other person's side and avoid my anger. I see my anger as a little-boy thing to feel.

Therapist: It's not "little boy" to feel angry with someone you rely on when they don't fulfill their commitment. It reminds me of your mother, being so nice you couldn't feel angry. Last time, you said she'd have cardiac arrest if anyone spoke up to her—and today you're keeping your eyes on me to see if I'm OK.

Richard [walking to the couch]: I'm thinking of going skiing in Austria—but I know I can't afford it. You think I should come here three times a week, and I spend $40.00 a day on cab fare. My brother thinks I'm crazy about skiing—he knows I'm in debt.

Therapist: It's what you think that matters. And since you brought up three times a week, we should talk about it.

Richard: I have so many fears—subways scare me, being mugged, going out at night—like an old woman. My father is that way—always worried. What do you think?

Therapist: I think it has to do with your anger that you've been covering up and pushing down for so many years. The fear of being harmed may be related to your fear of harming someone else. Some of your dreams have told us this.

Richard: I dreamed my teeth were falling out. If that happened I couldn't call my dentist because I owe him $500. I really know he'd see me.

Therapist: And if you get angry here, at me, you know I'll see you. Not paying bills, by the way, can be an expression of anger.

Next session (Richard is ten minutes early, eating in the waiting room).

Richard: I have a headache, a callus on my foot. Sounds like I'm on the rag. Lisa thinks you have children because you're going away on Washington's birthday weekend. [Teasingly] How many? I'll go where you're going to embarrass you. I'm so curious about you.

Therapist: Specifically?

Richard: I want to look through your window and watch how you have sex. You have orange shoes and you're nude. What interests me is how women show passion. I could never imagine my sister-in-law in bed. She's cold and hysterical. I think women have teeth down there—just kidding . . . [silence]. . . . I guess I do really think that. I learned about women's periods when I was eleven. I played with my mother's tampax as if it were a gun or a syringe. Maybe I wanted to use it—if I wanted to be a girl why didn't I have my penis bitten off and use the tampax? Once, I knew a girl—Bunny—I got her all excited, hot. We were in bed. She grabbed for me and she was in a frenzy. I just stopped.

Therapist: What were your thoughts?

Richard: I hate women—I can't believe it. I like women. There's a mystique. You won't tell me things—and it's not for my good. I know everything about my friends and have always had my curiosity satisfied.

Therapist: I don't think so. I think there were secrets in your house that upset you. [Richard had talked previously about his father's secret safe, where he kept a gun and family jewels. His parents often went into the bathroom together, locking the door.]

Richard: I think you're right—sounds like you do your homework. I didn't think you thought about me when I'm not here.

Therapist: Do you think about me?

Richard: Yes—all the time [His mood changes. He is reflective for just a minute and then goes back to teasing.].

Therapist: I think that earlier when you said you wanted to go on vacation with me it was because you'll miss me. And then, rather than face those feelings, you switched to your sexual curiosity.

A major roadblock in this treatment was Richard's teasing. His need to avoid experiencing the object as separate resulted in efforts to get inside of the object, or to negate it by diminishing its importance. Teasing expressed both needs. The therapist often felt thrown off guard.

In his sixth year of treatment, Richard increased his Placidol (the sedative his mother took) use before the therapist's summer vacation and came to sessions staggering and falling asleep on the couch. The therapist was worried and knew that withdrawal would require hospitalization.

Therapist: Richard, we cannot continue our work unless you withdraw from drugs. I must ask you to check into a hospital so that the withdrawal period can be monitored. I can't sit here and watch the dangerous chances you're taking by using drugs.

Richard [sitting up, crying]: I never thought you cared about me except for my money. [Sobbing like a baby.] I never thought anyone really thought about me—about my life.

Therapist [very moved and concerned]: Will you call your doctor now?

Richard: Yes.

Here the therapist made a decision based on her patient's suicidal behavior. It was emotionally draining—like pulling someone out of dangerous waters. She didn't hear from Richard for several days; his phone machine was full, and she worried constantly. Finally, he called from the hospital to say that he was going through hell but was glad to be there. He resumed treatment the following fall and continued to work. Needless to say, suicide is the final roadblock, and an irrevocable one, so the therapist must take whatever steps necessary to avoid this drastic behavior.

Both Portia and Richard, in their own ways, upset the therapist, Portia with her rage and self-destructiveness and Richard with his teasing and suicidal behavior. In such situations, the emotional toll on both parties in the dyad is intense, and there may be roadblocks for both parties. The therapist may not be able to maintain her calm, neutral stance. However, it may be necessary for a patient to see that she has limits to her tolerance. The therapist's ability to draw a line for the patient is both important and welcome.

Inner roadblocks are ever present—during treatment and even after it ends. Wishes to merge and murder never die, but with treatment, they are hopefully joined by wishes to join and create and the ability to empathize.

❖ CHAPTER 5 ❖

Attachment to Abuse

Tommy is three and when he's bad
His mother dances with him.
She puts on the record,
Red Roses for a Blue Lady
And throws him across the room.
Mind you she never laid a hand on him
Only the wall laid a hand on him.
He gets red roses in different places,
The head that time he was sleepy as a river,
The back, that time he was a broken scarecrow
The arms, like a diamond had bitten them,
The leg, twisted like a licorice stick,
All the dance they did together,
Blue Lady and Tommy.

You fell, she said, just remember you fell.
I fell, is all he told the doctors
In the big hospital. A nice lady came
And asked him questions but because
He didn't want to be sent away, he said, I fell.
He never said anything else although he could talk fine.
He never told about the music
Or how she'd sing and shout
Holding him up and throwing him.
He pretends he is her ball.
He tried to fold up and bounce
But he squashed like fruit.
For he loves Blue Lady and the spots
Of red roses he gives her.

—Anne Sexton, "Red Roses"

Anne Sexton's poem horrifies us with images of child abuse at the same time that it shows us in heartbreaking detail how Tommy survived. His attempts to make the abuse into a dance are both pathetic and heroic. Even more tragic, however, is his attachment to it—one that he will never fully relinquish. Tommy needs his mother if he is to survive. In his helplessness, he must somehow tolerate her abuse to maintain his sense of her love. Perhaps, to him, love and abuse are the same. Tommy's mother is his lifeline. Without her he is alone, and as any child needs its mother, Tommy needs his. He takes the good where it is offered and when he can get it, and he endures the pain by removing himself from it (*dissociation*) and by making it feel like pleasure (*masochistic pleasure*).

He holds on to the pleasure/pain, developing a masochistic character, a paranoid personality, and perhaps a psychosis, living his life according to his fantasy dialogue:

Mother: I hate you. I never wanted you. Leave me alone.
Tommy: What can I do to make you happy? To make you love me?
Mother: If you're bad I'll let you play with me. I'll throw you against the wall and you bounce back. Then I'll throw you again. Now are you happy?
Tommy [sobbing]: Yes, I love it when you dance with me. Throw me again.
Mother: I will. When you're bad you're a good boy. Then we are one.
Tommy: I am bad. Punish me so that we can be one.

Wishes to retaliate, wishes to make mother (and, in the transference, the therapist) suffer, are repressed, split off, denied, projected. Tommy buries his rage and camouflages it with compliance until the day he can pass it on—to his wife, to his children, or to some stranger sitting in a diner.

Tommy may or may not have suffered the extreme abuse that he imagines. Although I am treating him as real, he is a fantasy, a figure of poetry, and his abuse may be metaphorical. For the real Tommys, the story is more complicated. Psychoanalytic theory once tended to hear stories like Tommy's as the projection of the child's own innate aggression, rather than a causal reality. Today, however, we are becoming ever more aware of how many children are maltreated, tortured, and even murdered by their caretakers—and that these external realities do not preclude aggressive fantasies. On the contrary, they enhance them.

Growing up always involves pain. But when there are especially painful circumstances in the growing up process—abandonment, illness, loss, neglect, violence, abuse—the chance to mature is severely diminished. Any sustained trauma scars the ego.

By *trauma* I mean any set of conditions that prevents a child from developing normally. Even sporadic abuse, because of its unpredictability, requires of the child an unnaturally vigilant state that he hopes against hope may protect him from a recurrence. Nonabusive trauma is perhaps not quite as damaging as abuse is, but it takes its toll as well. A child may deal with a loving parent's illness with fantasies of omnipotence and obsessional rituals; these defenses fill a void in the absence of an attachment that could better have supported a developing self, but they also deprive the child of a developing sense of reality. This chapter focuses on *real* abuse and real trauma, filtered as they always are through normal, innate love and aggression, and on the possible repercussions. It is horrible to think about sadistic treatment of children. It is a tribute to humanity that we are becoming more able to see abuse, take it seriously, and not push it under the rug. The sadism of humankind, and the masochistic surrender to it that is the response of so many, is overwhelming, but if we focus on individual evils suffered and committed, perhaps something can be learned that will eventually temper it. In *Psychoanalysis and the Maltreatment of Children*, Steele wrote:

> My own interest in maltreatment began in 1960, when Henry Kempe, a pediatrician, asked me to see some parents who had injured their

> children. He was distressed by the number of beaten babies admitted to the hospital and wanted me to find out why in the world parents attacked and sometimes even killed their own offspring. The idea of child abuse was new to me.
>
> The first few abusive parents I saw were seemingly ordinary middle-class or professional class families, but I was shocked and dismayed by their cruel behavior. I thought there was little or nothing in my psychiatric and psychoanalytic training that [had] prepared me for what I was seeing and hearing: parents who were bruising, burning, and fracturing their babies. Fortunately my curiosity kept me involved enough to take intensive histories; the first patients I saw were able to tell me about the experience of being abused and neglected in their own earliest years (Kempe et al., 1962). I could then relax and understand I was not listening just to bad, cruel, adults but was seeing grown-up abused children. The impact of trauma in childhood is intimately related to the adult behavior, a quite acceptable psychoanalytic concept. (Steele, 1994, p. 1002)

Steele interviewed abusive parents and found four commonly seen elements in physical abuse:

- A history of abuse and neglect in childhood
- A lack of empathy, or the inability to feel and respond to a baby's needs
- Unrealistic expectations that the child will fulfill the parent's needs
- Perceptions of the child's behavior that threaten the parents' sense of self

It is difficult to imagine Tommy as an adult, as a psychotherapy patient. What would he say to us? Something like this, perhaps:

> The moments when Blue Lady was loving and caring were heavenly moments. What did I know about life without mother? Mother was life to me, but she spent most of her time in another world—except when I was bad. Then she came to life, and I was allowed to be part of it. Pain became pleasure and pleasure was pain. They were intertwined as I grew up. They were the familiar texture of my world. Mother was my mind and soul. I put all my

> bad thoughts, all my murderous, vicious thoughts away somewhere—covered them up, buried them. To be her victim was all that I craved, because only as her victim could I survive.

Underneath such observations might lie others, less available to him:

"How dare you blame my mother? She is mine—through the ecstasy and torture we have shared. I will never give her up—she is me."

"She throws me because I'm bad—and I'm bad so that she'll throw me."

"If I stay with you will you be my mother? I'll give you reasons to mistreat me, too."

"If you say my mother was bad, then I am, too. I keep her alive by being her—so she will never leave me. It was all my fault, anyway."

"Sometimes I hear a voice that tells me to kill. Someday maybe I will."

A battered child grows up anticipating and expecting to be battered. This expectation becomes addictive—the child needs to be battered, because the battering is the expression of the batterer's love—and without it fragmentation of the self can occur. As Sandler and Sandler (1998) remind us, even a painful reality is familiar, and what is familiar feels safe. Abused children can seek out the battering they need in the form of blows, of words, or in other kinds of hurtful or neglectful action. It can be found in competition (some sports attract young athletes by their brutality), in abusive relationships, and in cutthroat business practices. Self-mutilation is also connected to early childhood maltreatment (Farber, 2000).

Childhood abuse (both verbal and physical) and neglect leave permanent scars. If and when the adult who suffered a traumatic childhood comes to treatment, the therapist must be prepared for a long and arduous trip, with plenty of roadblocks along the way. The transference drama in therapy will repeat the early relationship of abuser and abused, and as Anne Sexton and I have tried to show, this is a very complicated one. The patient may manipulate the therapist into acting like the abusive parent imago; she may be charming and lovable and good, hoping to be rescued; she may idealize the therapist to avoid seeing her as human, or she may frustrate the therapist with silence, intrude upon her with phone calls or odor (one patient of mine farted repeatedly), or frighten her with suicide threats.

The major roadblock on this journey may be a similar one for therapist and patient—the pain of bearing witness to tragic and unspeakable acts. It is terrible to hear of some of the things that parents do to their children, and the patient who has suffered childhood abuse, be it mild or as severe as Tommy's, has become by the time he grows up a master at perpetuating pain himself. He needs pain, so he invokes it by evoking the sadism of others or by torturing others directly. Patients who maltreat children or spouses or who abuse animals are so hard to listen to that the therapist's inner roadblocks may make treatment very difficult or prevent it altogether.

The patient has his own reasons for avoiding his memories, as we have discussed above and will elaborate shortly. The therapist, for her part, must recognize that she can neither change the patient's past nor fix it. This challenges her own narcissism, her own grandiosity, and the wishes to rescue by which she may contain her own fears. She must remain aware of countertransferential wishes to save and to harm the patient. Otherwise, provoked into anger, she may lose patience and decide to end the treatment, either directly or by provoking the patient to quit. Or, feeling frustrated and impotent, she may join the patient in castigating the original abuser. This is dangerous, however, and a real potential threat to a successful treatment. The abuser most often had good qualities, too, and it is important that the patient not be discouraged from remembering and keeping these. The very fact that the adult victim of childhood abuse comes to treatment means there is some hope—some memory of kindness. Because the relationship between an abused child and her abuser is so multilayered, the therapist must be careful to listen without joining in with the patient's hatred. Concern, empathy, sorrow, yes; but hatred must belong to the patient alone. That way, if good memories of the parent or empathy for the parent's situation emerge, the patient is free to modify perception of her early objects without feeling that she can please the therapist only by keeping her hatred alive. A therapist who joins a patient in her hatred for the patient's parent does not offer herself as a new object, an empathic but neutral listener. Instead, she becomes another hater—a type perhaps all too familiar to an abused child. The therapist's ability to remain calm in the face of the patient's rage gives the patient a new experience with which to identify. Furthermore, a patient's portrayal of the past may be consciously or unconsciously inaccurate, for any of a number of reasons—sometimes to shock the therapist—and it is important that the therapist not take too simplistically a very complicated situation.

> I once saw a patient who knowingly exaggerated her maltreatment. It took years for her to tell me this, but she finally acknowledged that she felt that no one would listen to her otherwise. She came from a large family where no one was treated tenderly or fairly, and her fantasy life included sadistic retaliation for feeling ignored. Beneath her preoccupying and defensive retaliatory fantasies, however, she uncovered some experiences of loving caretaking as therapy progressed, and memories of an adoring father (who died after a long illness when she was nineteen) and a consoling sister emerged in sessions.

A TRIPLE BURDEN

The patient who has suffered abuse carries a triple burden: she is victim, she is abuser by identification or even merger, and she is helpless witness. Even normal, momentary narcissistic injuries can feel abusive to children, converging as they do with the instinctual life that throughout development, and in all of us, includes wishes to devour, expel, and murder. To resolve the denials and dissociations that result from persistent maltreatment (such as Tommy displays in Anne Sexton's poem), to analyze the patient's own fantasized role in her perceived abuse, and to allow the good qualities of a "bad" object to surface so that reparation and forgiveness can occur become the work of treatment. The therapist must be able to bear the tragedy with her patient and to identify with her empathically, while always respecting the boundary between self and other. How the therapist handles stories of torture and abuse without resorting to her own capacity for denial is crucial to the patient's ability to mend the ego splits that are characteristic of these patients.

Adults with histories of maltreatment may—intentionally or unwittingly—not reveal them to their therapists for months or even years. Such memories may be suppressed, split off, and dissociated to such an extent that it is primarily through transference, countertransference, and enactment that abuse is discovered—by patient as well as by therapist.

> Diana, an artist, wife, and mother, described her childhood as one of constant turmoil. Her father was a professor whose position required that the family move every other year. Her mother was experienced as cold and critical; Diana recalled being tethered to a tree when she was two because her mother was too busy to respond to Diana's normal rapprochement needs. Diana remembered this as a humiliating and frustrating experience. When Diana herself became a mother, her mother reminded her of the tethering, saying that Diana was always running away. In treatment, she wondered why. She imagined that being at home was unbearable. A younger brother who was seriously ill required most of the mother's attention. At age eight, a car hit another brother, whom Diana was supposed to have been watching. She felt guilty.
>
> Diana came to therapy admitting to fears of harming her son with a knife. Her rage often took the form of delusional thinking ("there is someone evil behind the wall"). Occasional amphetamine and LSD use heightened her fears. She refused prescribed medication, however, saying that it dulled her talent. One day, after three years of twice-a-week treatment, Diana announced to her therapist that her husband had AIDS. He had admitted to his homosexuality, and he left the family to live with his preferred partner. Diana's drug use increased, and she blamed this on someone whom she called "the other person." She told the therapist that there were in fact two other people who took over at different times. The therapist, having no experience with such profound dissociation, didn't know what to make of this. Her inner roadblock was a skepticism and a disbelief that covered up her own feelings of incompetence. She thought that Diana's symptoms were delusional thinking caused by her drug use. Still, she felt that she had to work with her patient's own sense of reality, and this benevolent

curiosity saved the work. She tried including the "alters" in sessions, through Diana. For instance:

Therapist: Diana, you can tell her [the alter] that you understand her anger and that she doesn't have to act it out with dangerous drug use.

Diana: She likes drugs and her drug dealer won't let her go. [Diana hopes that the therapist won't let her go.]

Therapist: This drug user is the part of you who wants to hide from the memories and feelings you need to express in words. When you believe that this is safe, she will feel safe, too.

Diana: Maybe, but I don't know if I believe it's safe.

Therapist: Talk about that.

Diana: You go away in August and that's when I feel so vulnerable. She [the alter] wants to take the gun on our vacation.

Therapist: Diana, she cannot take the gun on vacation this summer. You must help her get rid of the gun.

Diana would not promise to do this, but she did write the therapist a postcard saying that she was fine. She later admitted to the therapist that she valued the therapist's concern.

Getting her therapist to worry was Diana's way of maintaining the connection. Her tremendous separation anxiety was the result (in part) of great rage, combined with grandiose fantasies that she could inflict harm. She feared that her rage could kill the therapist. Another summer, the therapist was going on a trip where she would not be accessible by telephone. Rather than accept the name of a substitute therapist, Diana asked to follow the therapist's route of travel on a map.

Healing the splits and taming the rage were the focus of Diana's treatment, and although she ended it before the therapist thought she was ready, much work had been accomplished. Her career was flourishing, her panic attacks had subsided, and the "stronger Diana" seemed to be in charge. In fact, toward the last months of work, Diana mentioned that there was a new person—an adult who could reason with the others. This figure appeared to be an internalization of the therapist.

In childhood, not to be rescued from trauma is a real tragedy. In times of crisis and danger, we always imagine someone coming to help. Superman and Spiderman are not only representatives of our grandiose fantasies, but they are also rescuers who can save the weak with their heroic, magical feats. They get the bad guys.

> Frank had dreams of flying and fantasies of being Superman. In treatment, these became connected to a helpless feeling throughout childhood due to the weakness and incompetence of his elderly father. He was constantly being overstimulated by his mother, who was young and attractive but also seductive and dependent, and Frank's wishes to be rescued by a strong, powerful father never came true. The "bad guys" of Frank's inner life were parts of himself, the parts that felt lust for his mother and hatred for his father. His wish to be Superman was based on his loneliness and his inability to live up to his mother's wish that he become her man.
>
> As treatment progressed, Frank realized that despite his father's failings and his mother's neediness, he could remember times when his father had been strong and decisive. He had arranged for the family to come to America when Frank was eight, and he and Frank's mother had maintained their relationship. Frank also verbalized his anger at having to be the grown-up before his childhood was over. His parents leaned on him—in the negotiations for an apartment and in learning the customs and language of their new country. Frank became a very competent man, but he always feared and resented his father. Castration anxiety made it difficult for him to achieve success in his field, but as this was interpreted he became more appropriately assertive and effective.

All children use magical thinking, and all retreat sometimes into fantasy life, especially when the outside world is threatening. Remnants of this fantasy life are present in adults, making adaptation to the realities of grown-up life possible. An identification with Arnold Schwarzenegger or Madonna in the movies gives us briefly a sense of control and power that we don't really have. However, wishes for rescue can inhibit the development of ego strengths that serve the establishment of the kind of reliable self-esteem that is based on accomplishment and survival.

> Leslie, thirty-two, identified with Snow White. Someday My Prince Will Come was her fantasy. As her treatment deepened, she learned that the prince stood for the father, who tried to rescue her from her cold, depressed mother. More than an oedipal wish, this was seen as a wish for the love her mother could not give. The situation was exacerbated by her mother's jealousy of the attention her father gave Leslie. Leslie's normal oedipal guilt, exacerbated by the lack of a loving mother with whom to identify, left her with poor self-esteem, an inability to make use of her talents, guilt, and depression. Falling asleep in sessions was her way of avoiding painful feelings of rage and loneliness, and the therapist found herself experiencing both wishes to rescue and boredom. The therapist's interpretations of Leslie's predicament led slowly to Leslie's ability to stay awake and feel.

In this case, sustained trauma of both pre-oedipal and oedipal kinds had occurred. Leslie's mother was punitive, demeaning, and remote; her father was a loving and seductive knight who nonetheless had failed to rescue her.

Events in an adult's life often resonate with childhood fears and anxieties. The World Trade Center attack brought forth many heroes, and these heroes fulfilled many dreams of rescue. Everyone shared the trauma and people helped each other in myriad ways. The abuse of the child, however, is a private affair and often ongoing. Family members are either perpetrators or too frightened to speak. Rescue rarely comes. Yet, the therapist as listener is rescuing her patient's ability to speak, to feel, and to mend.

CLUES TO THE HIDDEN PAST

An abusive past may be hidden by a variety of symptoms ranging from phobia to depression, obsessive-compulsive rituals, and even mania. Sometimes, an abused patient with remarkable resilience and survival capacity may seem very well put together. Many patients with difficult childhoods have forceful characters that bring them leadership roles, and their inability to depend on others makes them appear strong. Psychosomatic symptoms may mask the early trauma, especially when the trauma occurs in infancy, before words are available. In discussing what he called the *negative therapeutic reaction*, Freud wrote: "Every partial solution that ought to result, and in other people does result, in an improvement or a temporary suspension of symptoms produces in them for the time being an exacerbation of the illness; they get worse during the treatment instead of getting better. . . . We are accustomed to say that the need for illness has got the upper hand in them over the desire for recovery" (Freud, 1923, p. 49). Is this an attempt to hold on to the abusive object? Based on his own analytic work, Valenstein came to the conclusion that "a good deal impinges on the infant from within, viscerally and autonomically in terms of his own physiological functioning; and from without in direct or indirect consequences of the (mother) care giving surrounds" (Valenstein, 1973, p. 373).

Where in the child's development trauma occurs can sometimes be discovered in the patient's history. For instance, if in early childhood there was a separation from mother during the anal phase, stubbornness along with compensatory grandiosity can develop as a character trait. If neglect or traumatic separation occurs after a certain age, the child will obviously have a better array of defenses and ego strengths with which to cope. If there are other steady, loving figures in the child's life, potential trauma registers differently. If words are available, if the child has a chance to connect with an empathic other, the scars will not be as deep or as disfiguring. But trauma in the preverbal stage can lead to very serious difficulties with differentiation. Early childhood illness is traumatic, especially when it requires premature separation from the mother. If the trauma is what Kris (1956) referred to as "shock" trauma (a one-time occurrence), recovery is more likely than if it is an ongoing "strain" trauma.

How treatable the Tommys of this world are is an important question in itself. Some people who suffer the degree of abuse that we imagine Tommy did do try treatment, but some end up in prisons that they secretly hope will contain some of their rage. Is atrocious crime ever a call for help? What happens when an adult Tommy does comes to treatment? Shengold quotes a patient saying: "If you cannot trust mother and father, whom can you trust?" (Shengold, 1989, p. 312). This is where the therapist's constancy, consistency, and reliability are crucial. It takes years of treatment before such patients even notice that the therapist *is* reliable. In the above case of Frank, it was two years before he could count on the therapist, so normal are expectations of, and even wishes for, abuse in abused people. As mentioned above, the patient tests the therapist in numerous ways. Breaking appointments, not paying, not speaking, talking monotonously and without affect, provoking the therapist, and attempting to disgust her are just a few of the tools that a patient may use to assess the therapist's differentness from the original object. The most important thing a therapist can do is to be reliable. Being there, being on time, and being calm add up to consistency. Many beginning therapists whom I have supervised are surprised at how important consistency is to patients. They worry about what to say to their patients, not realizing that their attention and benign curiosity are their most valuable techniques.

HOLDING ON TO THE BAD OBJECT

The biggest roadblock in work with abused people, however, is the way that such patients hold on to the internal bad object. It is a real challenge for the therapist to stay calm, steady, and empathic when her patient is pushing her to behave as the original object did. Patients who respond to treatment with negativity and a refusal to improve are extremely frustrating to the therapist (chapter 8). Irene was a case in point.

> Irene had a brother whose teasing kept her in a constant state of hyperarousal. (The persistence of this relentless abuse makes one wonder why her parents didn't protect her, and in fact it came to light later in therapy that Irene's mother had been abused by a brother.) When Irene's parents went out, her brother, five years older, chased her, tickled her, locked her in the

closet, left her in the dark—overstimulating her and scaring her, and leaving her with the experience of never being able to contain or control her own feelings. As she grew up, this perceived incapacity for self-control took the form of overeating, promiscuous sex, and occasional delusional thinking.

In treatment, Irene constantly expressed her rage, blaming the therapist for her failed relationships and her inability to hold a job. This both tortured the therapist as Irene herself had been tortured and evoked the therapist's anger. In a session during the fifth year of treatment, Irene told her therapist that she was convinced that she had head lice. The therapist immediately became distracted, wondering how he could protect his next patient, who also used the couch. It turned out that Irene did not in fact have head lice, but that she had been concerned that the therapist would not be able to bear her dangerous, biting, inner fantasies and dirtiness, and would be contaminated. Her biting rage had long been a focus of treatment, but at this point a regression occurred that took the form of a delusion. In this case, the therapist remained quiet because such a dilemma had never come up before; he did not know what to say, except that Irene should make an appointment with the doctor to verify her self-diagnosis. Her delusional behavior, along with the hatred Irene displayed toward him, caused the therapist to reevaluate the treatment; Irene was getting worse and he felt enraged and impotent. After another tirade of which the two of them could understand nothing, Irene decided that she would prefer to work with a woman—and the therapist felt relieved. Treatment ended. Upon reviewing the case with a colleague, the therapist realized that he had been involved in a sadomasochistic enactment that he could not stop. Irene's provocative, frustrating behavior was a repeat of her relationship with her brother in the transference: "Go away, but chase me."

To some people forced into therapy by the courts or by drug rehab programs, therapy is just serving more time. They see the therapist as part of "the system," and thoughts about her trustworthiness are not even considered. Yet if the therapist can create a setting of consistency, constancy, and empathic concern, she has an opportunity to engage such people in important work. Most people who enter treatment involuntarily have never before been treated with respect and benevolent curiosity. The idea of trying to understand what caused the drug addiction or the criminal behavior is deeply unfamiliar. In these cases, the therapist's courtesy and respect go a long way. For instance, the desired effect of drug use—the "high"—is often a haven from the intolerable emotional pain of abuse and neglect. Drugs permit the patient to relax her guard against the expectation of further attack or abandonment. So can self-mutilation, which is another attempt to externalize internal pain. When internal pain can be expressed in words, however, the symptoms become less necessary. Revisiting trauma within the safety of the therapeutic environment eases the terror of the memory.

Giving up the familiar pain of physical or emotional abuse, whether it has taken the form of neglect, abandonment, or denial of separateness, is sometimes more than the victim can manage, and at those times the therapist becomes an impotent observer. Abused patients do not easily experience the therapist as separate. They use the therapist to relive and repeat past abuse in the hopes of mastering the trauma, and also in an attempt to hold on to the abusing object. Tommy's mother was his only mother. She was his lifeline. For that reason alone, he cannot easily relinquish his internal representation of her, however painful it may be. Modification of the badness of the bad object and internalization of a new object relationship with the therapist are two important goals in work of this kind. The therapist's respect and empathy are a brand-new experience and may register with the patient very quietly. Years into treatment—sometimes not until the end—the patient may tell the therapist how much it meant to be listened to and wonder how the therapist did it. Carla, in analysis for eleven years, said to her therapist in her last session: *"I will always be amazed at your ability to listen to and remember all the stuff I brought in here—and you were always on time, here waiting for me."*

The child with an unpredictable parent lives in constant fear, tiptoeing through life. She develops rituals, she dissociates, she dies to be good, and she lives by being bad, by being noticed, or by staying in the shadows. She develops a false self or "another" self (as in imposture or by developing "alters") to hide her pain, her rage, and her yearning for love. Closeness is frightening. Hiding is safer. No one is to be trusted. Sometimes she brings on abuse by being "bad," and sadomasochistic patterns develop. This way she is in control. A Blue Lady is a depressed lady, and a mother's withdrawal is traumatic. If Tommy sees his "red roses" as emblems—as proof that his mother loves him—he will fight to keep them. A new object must not take away what the roses symbolize.

According to Sandler and Sandler, "Affirmation from the object can be gained even when the object is experienced as a harsh and punitive one, because feelings of safety are gained through the perception of the familiar, even though that familiar perception is unpleasant" (1998, p. 61).

RAGE AND SADOMASOCHISM

Berliner (1958), Smirnoff (1969), Shengold (1999), Valenstein (1973), Asch (1988), and others writing on masochism have called to our attention how early childhood unhappiness caused by abuse and neglect sets the stage for a child's attachment to a punishing object. Because the early abuse or neglect is suffered at the hands of a caretaker, and because it occurs in a helpless phase of life, the child has to tolerate, accommodate, and adjust to a frightening reality. If this reality becomes familiar (as Sandler and Sandler imply above), it feels safe. This is why such a child will arrange to repeat the abuse and neglect with contemporary figures. Defenses such as denial, splitting, identification with the aggressor, appeasement of the aggressor, dissociation, projection, and turning passive into active are necessary for survival, and they put tremendous strain on the ego, weakening its functioning. Thus these necessary defenses and the distortion they cause become the lens through which life is seen. Pain and rejection are the life quest of the maltreated child, for pain is familiar, and what is familiar is safe.

The sadomasochistic person searches for bullies and unfair situations; where there are none, she creates them. He provokes his spouse to nag. She alienates her friends by making dates and breaking them. She loses her car keys all the time and misses vital appointments. His procrastination undermines his business endeavors until he feels that he fails at everything he attempts. She works late night after night for a boss who never promotes her. He sets himself up to be caught for trivial and not so trivial crimes (the white-collar crimes committed by accountants and CEOs often contain a very visible element of sadomasochism). She is raped repeatedly. He seeks out humiliation in sex. To sum it up—sadomasochistic people are losers. But to them, losing is winning. They need their punishment; they cannot live without it.

Masochism of this kind not only assuages a patient's guilt, but it also protects her from feeling her own murderous rage at the way she has been treated and experiencing her intense yearnings for love. Better to have the world mad at her; better to go without love than to feel such fury and such longing.

This leads us to the causes of rage beneath sadomasochism:

- An abusive early caretaker
- Lack of soothing
- Uncontrollable physical pain
- Lack of parental boundaries
- Lack of protection
- Neglect
- Abandonment
- Inconsistency
- Sexual overstimulation
- Lack of emotional connection with a caretaker
- Repetitive primal scene exposure
- Misattunement in general
- Intrusiveness
- Painful separation individuation

Psychoanalytic work with these people takes a long time, and it is constantly threatened by the powerful roadblocks that serve to protect the desperate patient's inner fantasy world. The therapist's counterreactions threaten the work, too. Being verbally attacked by a patient is not pleasant, but having the work itself attacked silently can feel even more devastating, and the therapist may react with hostile silence or abusive words. When the patient makes a connection, it is often the sadomasochistic kind that frustrates, repels, bores, deadens, or enrages the therapist (Bird, 1972; Gabbard, 2000). To tolerate the patient's rage (Hall, 1998) is not possible for many therapists; reciprocally, it is impossible for many patients to trust the therapist enough to express rage.

Countertransference is powerful and can be an important instrument. If the therapist anticipates her countertransference and girds her loins against it, she has a chance to contain and interpret the rage and pity stirred up in her. What she is trying to do is help the patient to see—gradually, lest he be overwhelmed and shut his eyes again—how huge his rage and sorrow are, that she is not afraid of his feelings, and that he will eventually be able to tolerate them, too. The abused adult has held on to his childhood omnipotence, and so he thinks his rage can kill. Every child goes through an omnipotent stage before he realizes that he is not at the center of the world. Letting go of the omnipotent fantasy happens slowly, as the child has experiences that balance the frustrations of his limits with the relief that he can't in fact kill with his thoughts. When the caretaker perpetuates the myth of omnipotent merger by not respecting the child's boundaries, enhancing the child's capacities for autonomy, mastery, and the toleration of frustration, or containing his rage, the child has no reason, no inclination, and no way to see the object as separate. Furthermore, success and individuation in any area incur the wrath of the masochist's inner object—an object that he can't afford to lose. Tommy in Anne Sexton's poem thinks that *he* has the power to make Blue Lady dance—and his only security is to go on thinking so.

A patient's fantasies and fears of disintegration and violence must be faced persistently in the reality of a relatively safe treatment situation (see chapter 9). A benign reality is not readily accepted—it may never be fully accepted—because of the attachment to abuse, but a softer reality emerges as the patient owns his projections and internalizes the loving, caring aspects of a new object.

> The therapist of the victim of soul murder (and of others not significantly traumatized or deprived as children but similarly psychologically burdened) requires the utmost in empathic tact and patience to guide the patient toward becoming able to tolerate the need for love (caring, *caritas*). (Loving and caring have been avoided since they have made the former victims so vulnerable.) Love must be felt in order to acknowledge and attenuate the terrible legacy of murderous hatred that has become too much to bear without destructive or self-destructive action accompanied by crippling inhibitions and defenses. Restoring the capacity to care about oneself and others is the therapeutic challenge. (Shengold, 1999 p. 286)

INTERPRETATION, EXPLANATION, CONFRONTATION, AND WONDERING

When things get difficult in therapy, should the therapist interpret, explain, or confront? Should she call a patient who does not return after vacation, or one who quits in a fury? The answers to questions such as these are matters of clinical judgment, and they depend on how the patient and therapist experience each other in the transference/countertransference.

Patients who have suffered childhood abuse employ defenses that protect their perceived fragility: denial, projective identification, and dissociation or splitting. But these defenses take a heavy toll on the patient's ability to negotiate life. With these patients, I often explain rather than confront, because confrontation carries with it a suggestion of blame in its connotation that "you are doing such and such." Confrontation can also lead to more narcissistic injury. Explanation, however, can include both halves of the dyad: "We seem to be spinning our wheels," or "We seem stuck in a battle," or "I find myself feeling anger—perhaps it is easier to see me be angry than to feel it yourself." Such comments are followed by an invitation to the patient to explore what's going on. This technique does not sweep away the difficulty, but instead attempts to engage the frightened, belligerent, silent, or overly loquacious patient to join in an exploration. The patient in such a quandary will often say, "I know you're right, I know what you mean—but I can't feel it." At this point, the therapist can explain how frightened the patient is of his feelings because they are imagined as extremely dangerous or powerful. The whole purpose of splitting and dissociation is to keep the murderous rage under control.

This technique sounds intellectual, but to interest a patient in her fantasies is a very important step. The fantasy of grandeur, of omnipotence, was once age appropriate. The abused child holds on to it because he feels so powerless underneath. Grandiosity, however, does not serve adults well. It makes relationships impossible, because it prohibits empathic connection (see Mr. M in chapter 8), and it makes ordinary experiences of rage and hatred much too frightening. Each time the patient lives through a separation and sees that the therapist did, too, both breathe a silent sigh of relief. They have both survived. A break in therapy does have some positive aspects—more time to oneself and less money to pay out—but the patients who insist that they will be merely relieved at a break are denying their truest and most fearsome feelings.

Some abused or maltreated patients live in such terror that their rage is inaccessible. Defenses against it—such as splitting and denial—are built in so deeply that they become an intrinsic part of the patient's character. Awareness of violent outbursts or ongoing furies are suppressed to such an extent that these people may commit crimes of which they feel completely innocent. The provocative patient begs for retaliation. Whatever the manifestation of hidden rage, the therapist must point it out over and over.

Confrontation of a patient's disavowed anger, however, can sometimes help to make it reachable, to "put back" into the patient that which he projects. If the therapist says something like "You can express your rage with words" or "You can own your rage," she implies both that "You really are very angry" and that "Both of us can tolerate it." But she must decide, based on her assessment of the patient's strength or the fragility of the patient's ego, whether the patient can tolerate the confrontation. If not, she might try *explanation*, a milder technique: "I think your fear of feeling angry at me has to do with your mother's inability to tolerate it." A milder approach still is to *wonder* with the patient about what is going on. Such wondering shows the patient that the therapist is not a mind reader, and that when she doesn't understand something, she tries to reflect on it. It is an invitation to the patient to reflect with her: "Let's try to explore why you told me your dream at the end of the session."

Confrontation may be inevitable, however, when a period of negative transference is threatening the treatment, or in the context of the *negative therapeutic reaction*, as described by Freud above. The therapist may have responded to the patient and his material in the most appropriate way possible, but the patient gets worse. "Rarely have these very serious, very difficult, and very puzzling reactions been regarded as an attack upon the analyst" (Bird 1972, p. 292). Bird goes on to say that, when the resistances are used to attack the analyst, the analyst must confront instead of interpreting: "Resolving this destructive situation depends on speaking of it directly, even assertively in terms of action. . . . Whatever the [patient's] response, it will no doubt be a welcome relief, for the patient as well as for the analyst, from what has probably been a monotonous, many-month-long stalemate."

However she addresses it, perhaps the most important thing the therapist can do is demonstrate to the patient that she is not afraid of rage. Sometimes, she may not be able to keep from showing her own anger; an abused person's power to evoke sadism is remarkable, and the sadomasochistic game needs to be played. But after the game is over, it can be interpreted—and it must be, time after time after time.

Vacations and other separations underline the fact that the therapist has a separate, outside existence, and thus, as we have seen, they are powerful provokers of terrifying feelings of rage and longing. The periods before she leaves and after she returns are potentially treatment-threatening times. Threats to end therapy abound then, and some patients do not in fact return after a break. In psychoanalytic psychotherapy with fragile patients, the therapist can contact the patient if the patient does not return; such a call will assure the patient that the therapist is alive and ready to talk about what happened. It is a matter of clinical judgment and gut feeling whether to call a patient who quits angrily. An opportunity to review what has happened can save the treatment, or at least offer closure with a comment such as "I think it would be helpful if we could talk more about your decision, and I will be here for your next appointment." Sometimes, the therapist herself has had enough of the treatment and feels relieved that it is over; a therapist is neither a savior nor a sacrificial victim. If the patient does return, however, it is important that she be able to express her anger, and the therapist must tolerate it. She must also explain what is happening. The patient who has been sufficiently damaged by early abuse has learned to deny the pain of loss or of missing someone. Intellectual understanding is often a first step, before emotion can be felt.

These patients have many anxieties—about annihilation, separation, castration, loss of love, loss of the object—and may need help to face these fears sufficiently that they do not get acted out self-destructively. When a planned absence is looming, pointing out references (or a lack of references) to it may help the patient prepare for it: "Our separation might be evoking feelings. What comes to mind?" "Where do you picture me?" "Our break in therapy hasn't come up" (Hall, 1998).

CLINGING TO MISERY

Some patients hold on to the abusing object through the pain of repeated injury, ongoing stress and tension, mental anguish, and anxiety about needing yet fearing closeness. They may court physical pain, visiting doctors frequently, complaining, yet never letting them succeed in alleviating the pain. This kind of interaction expresses both the wish for closeness and the fear of it. Pain is addictive, a fetish, a perverse attachment to an internalized abusive object. It has magical powers: it can assuage guilt about being separate, it can contain rage and its attendant anxiety, it can protect against unbearable loneliness, and it is always available. The internalized abusive object representation is threatened by treatment. Wishes for something better cause anxiety, and medication may be necessary. As the patient begins to realize her accomplishments, she may leave treatment abruptly, perhaps by setting up a situation that requires a move, by running out of money to pay the therapist, or by slowly provoking the therapist into ending the work.

One psychotherapist described how this almost happened with her patient Barbara:

> Barbara is seventy, was married for forty-eight years. She has significant physical ailments: hepatitis C, glaucoma, high blood pressure, tinnitus, migraines, arthritis, gastritis, urinary track infections, hypoglycemia/diabetes, dermatitis, and a year ago she had breast cancer that required a double mastectomy. She has a thirty-six-year-old son with Asperger's syndrome and a thirty-two-year-old son who lives with her and suffers from crippling arthritis. Barbara was born with deformities of the spine and of one arm. She was raised in a large city by a lower-income family. Her childhood was bleak.
>
> Barbara's mother, who also had physical problems, died unexpectedly in surgery when Barbara was ten. Her father, whom she describes as verbally abusive, died when she was eighteen. After her mother's death, Barbara was cared for by a grandmother and aunts who denigrated her, and by a mildly retarded sister ten years her senior.
>
> At age twenty, she underwent a series of spinal surgeries requiring a one-year hospitalization. At twenty-two, she married a man who was unable to perform sexually except for the few times that led to her pregnancies. The marriage was conflict ridden throughout.
>
> Barbara has been in psychotherapeutic treatment for depression since she was twenty: psychoanalysis for ten years after which the analyst ended the treatment, cognitive/behavior psychotherapy, and now weekly psychotherapy—all with little relief. She remains depressed, needy, morbid, rageful, isolated, and somatically preoccupied. She has poor interpersonal relationships. She states that the only people she can talk to are those people she pays.
>
> After years of work, she continues to resist any moves toward improvement, stating that she has given up trying to feel better and comes to treatment only to keep herself out of a mental hospital. Her belief is that by "spewing out her feelings" she can survive from week to week. Although she comes to sessions seeking advice, she refutes all interventions and interpretations. She lists all the terrible events of her life: her deformity, her health issues, her bad marriage, her sick children, her financial difficulties, her husband's poor health. She believes she should never have been born

or had children of her own. She believes there is a curse on her family. The therapist finds herself working to maintain empathy. She is frustrated, dreads sessions, watches the clock, and feels as helpless and hopeless as the client.

In the second year of treatment, Barbara arrives with her weekly complaints of severe migraines and tinnitus. She describes in detail how she sits daily in pain with a wet rag on her head—just as her mother had done before her death. This is a strong identification with her dead mother, which she easily endorses; however, she then states that these are real headaches, physically derived. As she has done for the past two years, she becomes angry at all references to possible psychological causes of her physical distress. She talks about her pain doctor, with whom she was very angry and who recently gave up on her. Her need for empathy is palpable. The therapist, sorely tried, gives a sketchy interpretation, pointing out that the patient's lifelong depression might be contributing to her headaches. This is not an acceptable response in Barbara's view, and she becomes annoyed. The therapist interprets that Barbara is angry that the therapist seems not to understand the depth of her pain. Barbara then negates this interpretation with a litany of the physical problems people blame her for inflicting on herself. In the meantime, the therapist, who rarely has headaches, begins to develop a headache so painful that she has trouble focusing on Barbara. With trepidation, she decides to share this information: "I must tell you, Barbara, I can count the number of headaches I have had on one hand. I came into this room fine, but now I have an awful headache. I'm telling you this because it tells me that your mind has incredible powers." Barbara asks, "You think I gave it to you?" "It would seem that way," responds the therapist in a surprised and curious tone. Barbara appears happy—some sort of victory for her that frees her. Although she never mentions this again, in the years to follow she will state that the headaches are much less intense and less frequent.

This vignette exemplifies how tenaciously people can cling to misery. Barbara has no idea that anything different is possible. Her symptoms are her crutches and her friends. They will never leave her. They serve as a fetish, physically making her alive. They bind her rage. To expect anything different—to upset her delicate balance—would be terrifying. The therapist, who has become another constant in her life by not demanding or even trying to make her change, tolerates Barbara as she is (albeit with difficulty and frustration). This is therapeutic in itself. A new balance is created, as long as the therapist can last it out. Barbara's therapist feels that her own frustration and rage were bound by the headache and that sharing the information with Barbara is saying: "I can feel how angry you are—you affect me, you can reach me."

Barbara's ability to frustrate her therapist is the connecting link between them. It lets the therapist know how she (the patient) feels; the patient experiences sadistic pleasure in torturing the therapist; the sadomasochistic enactment serves as an object connection; the patient is depositing her bad feelings (headache) with the therapist in the transference. Reciprocally, the therapist is letting the patient know that she is still there and in this case can feel the quality of Barbara's pain (through projective identification).

The therapist must realize that an adult survivor of childhood abuse will never fully trust another. Even to realize that there *is* an "other" is a major achievement. The act of differentiating causes great pain, but this pain can lead to growth. Barbara's therapist, by interpreting the enactment, gives Barbara a glimpse of herself as a separate object, and at the same time a glimpse of Barbara as a separate (and influential) object herself.

> To accept the analyst as a separate person and then as predominantly a benevolent one takes years of seemingly endless repetition and testing. One must never assume that the analyst will be felt by the patient as working for the patient's welfare; even with the "average expectable" patient, these anticipations of benevolence are at best intermittent. The analyst and the patient must be able to last it out. (Shengold, 1989, p. 313)

Sometimes a person imagines or evokes negative attention because positive attention cannot be trusted to last. This is why a patient may guard against feelings of closeness. Closeness means danger and thus is to be avoided. A collaborative atmosphere or working alliance can take years of steady, patient work—and it may never happen. Overly ambitious goals may blind the therapist to real gains. The work may feel like a war zone at times, but if the patient is talking and the analyst is listening, a collaboration exists.

Still, therapy is a hard and painful undertaking for Tommy and his siblings, and sometimes no collaboration is achieved—or even the beginning of one is too frightening for the patient to bear. When a treatment ends prematurely, no matter how experienced the therapist is, her self-esteem suffers, her interest wanes, and she feels guilty and defensive, and to varying degrees narcissistically injured. She reviews the case, wonders if it was ever workable, looks for what she may have missed or done differently, reads intensely, and finally writes about it. Is this to vindicate herself, to share her vulnerability, to help others in similar situations? Probably all three. The lost opportunity to understand with the patient is like the inability of the child to reconcile with his past and his abuser, and the therapist mourns this lost opportunity.

SAVING SOULS

Masochism serves many functions:

- It provides suffering intended to avoid retaliation, loss, and abandonment due to forbidden erotic and aggressive wishes.
- It maintains the tie to mother, buying the mother's love with suffering.
- It turns passive into active; hurting oneself diminishes the hurt from outside oneself.
- It holds on to the abusive internalized object.
- It defends against success by perpetuating victimhood.

At the same time, the patient who has voluntarily crossed a therapist's threshold has a hope—a wish for something better—based on some positive past relationship, some ray of sunshine. It is this hope that must be nourished by the therapist's concern, patience, tolerance, and love. Listening to a patient is a loving act. Being there consistently is a loving act.

Shengold (1989) calls the abused patient the "soul murdered." Many therapists are drawn to the work of soul healing by their own rescue fantasies. Only when the therapist's fantasies have been to some extent identified and worked through is she prepared for the difficult, sometimes lifelong, work with damaged patients. Boundary setting must be done with empathy and explanation, but it must be done, because the violation of boundaries is dangerous and can lead to regression or flight. The patient will eventually be gratified by the therapist's ability to contain and explain what is happening in the patient's relationships—both inside and outside of treatment.

Enactments are recognized today as normal occurrences in analytic work, but with abused patients they can be deadly. Although it may feel safer to the patient to reenact than to revisit the pain of childhood terror and guilt, the danger of feeling retraumatized in therapy is an important issue. The need to repeat the sadistic treatment of the past is pressing, and some patients have an uncanny ability to elicit hurtful interventions from even well-meaning and well-trained therapists. This is why the most important things the therapist has to offer are a safe environment, empathy, respect, patience, and benign curiosity. The patient will not let go of her abusive self- and object representations until she can imagine other ways of keeping herself safe from further pain. At first, respect and curiosity themselves appear threatening and dangerous to the patient, and this is why the sadomasochistic transference is enacted in treatment. It is as if the patient says: "I need my past to survive. I know what it's like, it's familiar, and I can handle it. Don't even think about shining light on it. It is safer in the dark." Whether acknowledged or not, however, the patient who comes willingly to a therapist is looking for a light, and the light is the therapist, who can use the transference to explain this wish to stay in the dark. "It's so hard for you to trust me—it's not logical for you to trust based on your past relationships."

It is often difficult for the therapist to respect a patient who does not come to his sessions or is consistently late to them, who doesn't pay in a timely manner, or who, in short, refuses to improve in any way. This is where the therapist can work with the patient to separate the patient's actions from the patient: "You are acting as if you hate yourself. It seems that part of you wants to hurt me and yourself. You are acting out your rage instead of verbalizing it."

Mr. M in chapter 8 angered his therapist by missing many appointments and being late for the rest. Each time the therapist confronted, explored, or interpreted his actions, he agreed with her, and for a while he would attend his sessions promptly. These periods lasted for two weeks at best, and then the lateness and absences began again. One day, the therapist issued an ultimatum. Either he change his pattern, or therapy would end. Therapy ended.

When the therapist loses her cool, several things happen:

- The patient feels a sense of victory.
- The patient feels cared about.
- The patient is relieved that the therapist is human.
- The patient reacts to the confrontation with anger—a step toward connection.
- The patient becomes outraged and frightened.
- The therapist feels better and/or guilty.

Provocation cannot be ignored.

Sara was cold, arrogant, and uncooperative. Her sessions left her therapist enraged. He tried mirroring her empathically, engaging her, ignoring her, and understanding her. But after a long period of sadomasochistic enactment, he got mad.

Therapist: Your silence and refusal to cooperate are getting us nowhere. Nothing will change in here unless you speak up and express your feelings. Acting them out with silence is irritating and useless.

Sara: How can I talk to you? You are stiff, uncaring, and demanding. I can't stand you.

A connection was made. Therapy came alive.

Projective identification (an unconscious communication by which the therapist comes to feel the patient's rage and hatred) can cause the therapist to retaliate as the patient would like to do to her abusers—and to herself for abhorring and enjoying the abuse. The therapist may start coming late, cancelling or even forgetting sessions, or interpreting in a sarcastic way. She may feel angry, then guilty, impatient, or depressed. At such times, it is helpful for the therapist to talk with a colleague or supervisor—not necessarily for answers, but just to verbalize her feelings of rage and impotence. There really are no answers to these dilemmas, and the therapist should understand this. Secret fantasies of grandeur and omnipotence give an abused person (therapist or patient) unrealistic fears and hopes. The therapist wants the patient to change and the patient wants to change the therapist.

But change, as we have seen, is hard to come by. The patient with an abusive parent feels not only pain but also guilt for enjoying the pain and for having (in his fantasy) caused it. This fantasy gives the victim of abuse some feeling of control. As we have seen, too many patients who have been "soul murdered" injure themselves by self-mutilations of one kind or another or medicate their anxiety and depression with drugs or food. They are often accident prone and may be suicidal. Furthermore, when change does come, it may come very quietly indeed.

Mr. M's abominable behavior toward his children, friends, business associates, and wife (who turned out to be as involved in their sadomasochistic relationship as he was)—and therapist—was hidden by a kindly exterior. He thought he could get away with anything. He thought he could gain something from therapy without putting in the time required, that his business would continue despite his absence, and that his marriage would last. These thoughts were products of an unconscious fantasy system developed in childhood to ward off the pain of neglect and loneliness. Perhaps the lack of consistently empathic parents kept him from developing the ability to imagine how another person felt. Instead, he provoked others, feeling that by doing so he was in charge of any pain that came his way. Mr. M was caught between the wish to hold on to an unpredictable object (an internalized mother representation) and the fear of trust and closeness. Every time he achieved some trust, his fear of loss caused him to ruin it. (Mr. M is discussed further in chapter 8.) Treatment with a person attached to pain is slow, torturous, and depressing. Many treatments end prematurely because murderous attachments are often the only attachments. Mr. M's rage combined with his fear of closeness prevented him from using the therapist as a new object. Every time the possibility arose of trusting the process of therapy, he ruined it by running away, either emotionally or literally. Mr. M was a serial killer of relationships, and serial killing may be a way of holding on to abuse and abusive internal objects. The killing can never stop, because acted-out rage cannot satisfy; it must be repeated over and over.

Like Mr. M, every masochistic character has a sadistic side and is therefore an inflicter of pain, and so the outcome of the treatment depends on the therapist's capacity to confront in a productive way and on the patient's eventual ability to let herself feel. Intellectual understanding cannot take the place of feeling. The defensive isolation of affect is extremely difficult for the abused patient to give up. When intense affect begins to surface, it is like a game of hot potato: neither player can hold on to it for very long. There are times when neither therapist nor patient can take the heat of such intense rage and despair. As in the game, once the hot potato begins to cool—when words are used to express affect—it becomes easier to handle. The connection between patient and therapist strengthens, and an alliance develops. This is when the therapist can begin to interpret the material. But sometimes the alliance is made by a false self (Winnicott, 1971) whose wish is less to grow than to appease (as with Mr. M). The therapist is lulled momentarily into a false sense of security, only to realize that the roadblock is impassable (chapter 8). This is what happens to abused children who are lulled or seduced periodically into feeling secure and are then suddenly attacked or abandoned yet again. Mr. M. repeated this experience in treatment as he did to the therapist what had been done to him.

PERMANENT ROADBLOCKS

The real crux of psychoanalytically based treatment is the work in and with the transference, for this is where the patient has a chance to examine her deepest feelings in relative safety.

If the transference is so important and useful, however, how is it also the most powerful resistance, as it very often is with abused patients? The cases mentioned so far have illustrated transferences of mistrust, rage, and clinging. When the therapist is at last recognized as separate, she becomes the bad object, finally externalized. Her consistency, resilience, and benign curiosity give her a staying power and an influence that modify the negative transference to some degree, making the therapeutic work tolerable. And sometimes the very roadblocks that complicate life within the treatment make life outside of it smoother—in some ways, at least. When the therapist has "become" the bad object, having her to focus his fear, anger, and desire on may take pressure off of the patient's other relationships, making his life more comfortable and less tense. But these are self-perpetuating compromises that may take on a life of their own without ever leading to substantive change and real growth. Sometimes, even after years of therapy, the wheels keep spinning in the same old ruts. The patient comes to his hours, sleeps, complains, bores the therapist, enrages the therapist, and pays the therapist—but no more than that. His pathology seems to be contained in the transference, and he never becomes able to see the therapist in a different light. And if this is his way of holding on to the original disappointing and sometimes abusive object, it may be as good as it gets.

The original object would otherwise have to be let go of and mourned, and for abused patients this is not an option. In his book *Is There Life without Mother?* Shengold addresses repeatedly how difficult it is for the adult who has been maltreated to let go of the abuser:

> The most destructive psychological effect of child abuse is the need to hold on to the abuser by identification (an unconscious becoming like him or her); this is part of the compulsion to repeat the abuse—as tormentor (enhancing sadism) and as victim (enhancing masochism). (Shengold, 2000, p. 25)

> The hardest legacy of childhood abuse is the need to hold on to the tormentor (body and soul) by some personal mixture of identifica-

> tion, hatred and rebellion, and longing and submission, a mixture that leads to psychic conflict and pain. (p. 58)

> The continuing chief terrifying expectation for those people whose liberation in analysis was predominantly successfully resisted seemed to be that of losing the parent. (p. 192)

A childhood that involves being tortured or witnessing torture exacts a hefty toll. Even if one does not grow up like Tommy or Barbara, events such as losing a parent to illness or death weigh heavily on future development. Inner conflict is difficult to resolve in the best of circumstances. When circumstances aren't good, the child's normal oedipal wishes may lead to vengeful, envious, competitive rivalries that become the motivating forces of life (Loewald, 1979). With a good-enough therapist, some of the damage may be softened. But it is important for the therapist to have humility, and having humility means taming her own grandiose rescue fantasies.

Accomplishments and success are not well tolerated by masochistic patients whose guilt has become their safe haven. It takes conscious work to allow happy moments to add up to happiness. "Mother always said I was a piece of shit and deserved to be flushed down the toilet," said one patient. The therapist must work to encourage and support the gains the patient has made and to help her face the anxiety she feels about giving up mother's message.

No therapist with a long professional life will escape without encountering some Tommys. They are artists, cops, surgeons, serial killers, pederasts, analysts, politicos, models, movie moguls, CEOs; they are envied, hated, pitied, loved, admired, idolized; they live on the street and in mansions; they are poor, rich, weak, strong. Tommys are us.

❖ CHAPTER 6 ❖

The Many Faces of Rage

> In this work we encounter paradox, for rage combines the urge for life with the impulse to destroy. Fire is a metaphor for rage, as flame is a metaphor for hope. Confronted with our patient's rage we try not to be burned ourselves and not to fuel the conflagration. Despite our fears, we cannot douse the fire; we must let it burn and can only hope that in the relatively safe and nonflammable container of therapy it will burn itself out. Our task is to help our patient find within his rage the feeble sparks of self acceptance and of disowned feeling and experience that might, if tended, grow into the gentler flame of hope.
>
> —Jeffrey D. Nason

Rage has a place in growing up, whatever one's experience has been. In a relatively smooth childhood, rage takes its place among the many affects that make up the fabric of life. But when conditions of development have been consistently or severely negative, rage, hate, envy, and spite stand out in harsh colors. This is a most powerful quartet of affects, especially when it remains in the darkness of the unconscious or in split-off parts of the self. How often do we hear a murderer described as a "nice, quiet person"—a person whose crime shocked those who knew him? How often do we read about a respected, hardworking father who, seemingly out of the blue, murders his wife or his entire family? How many mothers hear voices telling them to kill their children? We tell ourselves that such things happen because of chemical imbalances, but does an explanation like that really account for murder? Something must have snapped, we think to ourselves. She could not do such a thing otherwise.

The only weapon against destructive, sometimes crippling, often murderous feelings is recognition and understanding through verbalization. Medication is an important adjunct in many cases, but medication without psychotherapy is often not enough and may be dangerous. In psychoanalytic psychotherapy, shying away from these aggression-fueled affects is not uncommon on either side of the couch. A therapist may fail to recognize a patient's rage and instead be courted and won over by the patient's idealization, cooperation, and improvement; the patient basks in the analyst's approval and feels calmed by soothing techniques and the fantasy that patient and therapist are one. But cracks in this mutual idealization eventually occur, and it is through these cracks that the rage, hatred, envy, and spite emerge.

Rage is universal. It can be found across the entire diagnostic spectrum, although theoretical controversies sometimes obscure this universality. The different influences of Kohut and Kernberg over the past several decades dictate treatment techniques that are at variance with each other. These theorists/clinicians have assigned rage to the so-called narcissistic and borderline categories, with different treatment strategies for each. Kohut (1971) describes a patient whose narcissistic line of development has been derailed. He stresses empathy and mirroring, which in his view lead to transmuting internalization and more mature forms of narcissism. Kernberg (1975) recommends confrontation as a major technique when splitting and projective identification fragment the personality. "Neurotic" people also suffer from the effects of rage, however, and this rage, combined with anxiety, often shapes their lives. Obsession, phobia, inhibition, paranoid ideation, self-destructive behavior, destructive behavior, and drug abuse can all be seen as behaviors or styles of thought that to some extent bind deep-seated rage. Rage and its attendant shame and guilt lie at the core of the sadomasochistic character. Punishing, or being punished by others both contains and displays the rage in an ongoing manner. In treatment, the patient often succeeds in making the therapist feel impatient and angry, even sadistic, while the patient feels excitedly punished. Such sadomasochistic enactments can go on for long periods of time and can lead to stalemates and guilt in both patient and therapist unless recognized and interpreted (see Mr. M in chapter 8).

Throughout this book, I refer to the rage engendered by abuse and neglect, distinguishing it from the universal anger we all experience. Klein (1932) thought that the roots of envy and rage were constitutional, appearing with the infant's greedy, envious relationship to the breast. But in my view, such factors as early trauma, sustained trauma, failure in attachment, neglect, physical pain, and illness all contribute to rage—an uncontrollable affect that may consume the patient. I see a continuum between the sort of anger that can be used effectively, to anger that is experienced but not constructively dealt with, to the severe frustrations and powerlessness of a not-good-enough childhood, to rage. The abused child's ability to recognize and relate to the object empathically is often permanently damaged, and when she becomes a parent, her children will be exposed to unempathic parenting. Abused people enlist fantasies of grandiosity and omnipotence as protection from the devastating feelings of impotence that are at the center of their worlds, but both children and adults experience rage when the protective power of these fantasies fail.

The psychotherapist, with her patient, respectful, consistent, empathic stance, has a chance to do real repair work. Work in the transference/countertransference is the vehicle for improvement. The therapist's ability to permit and to tolerate the patient's feelings without retaliation allows for a new experience that becomes internalized (Carpy, 1989). The therapist's endurance illustrates that the patient's rage alone cannot kill. This kind of work is a long, often exhausting process that demands flexibility, creativity, and careful attention to the therapist's countertransference. Much of the work with the traumatized adult takes place between patient and therapist, in the here and now. As much as the patient tries to recreate the past in the present, the therapist must try valiantly not to reenact the old script. The enactment that occurs in the therapeutic dyad is a pivotal point, and when analyzed it leads to growth through understanding.

Severe narcissistic injuries along any of the developmental paths guarantee a group of defenses that take years to modify. Denial, dissociation, splitting, projection, projective identification—these are protective techniques that may be necessary to survival even while they pose formidable obstacles to growth. A traumatic environment, and the reactions to it, cause character structures that are highly resistant to change. Patient, long-term psychoanalytic work provides an opportunity for the patient to modify defenses by softening self and object representations and recognizing the analyst as a new object. The key to such work is the therapist's ability to introduce the concept of benevolent curiosity and show her patient that she, the therapist, is trustworthy. Some of the cases in this chapter illustrate this process. The therapeutic dyad will face many roadblocks, for the road to change and growth in rageful patients is not a smooth one.

TAMING RAGE

How rage spreads, strengthens, and grows, and whether it takes over the landscape or shares it with the roots of love, kindness, and safety, depends on many things, among them the quality of the attachment to the mothering figure. Attunement, soothing, and "good-enough" mothering offset the minor traumas and narcissistic injuries of the child's everyday life. The taming of the child's normal grandiosity takes place naturally. Experiences of normal separations, falling down, teething, illnesses, arguments—all the calamities of growing up—give the child gradual glimpses of frustration. When caretakers ease these disappointments, these falls from grace are tolerable. Soothing, appropriate stimulation, constancy, love, kindness, consistency, boundary setting, and positive attention are the things that good-enough parents provide to make the journey through toddlerhood as comfortable as possible. When good-enough conditions do not prevail, however, rage is not tamed. The individual may hide the rage as best she can, but it erupts at times of frustration. From road rage to serial killing, untamed rage has serious consequences.

Sadomasochism, perversion, anxiety, and depression all share a large component of rage and its three cousins: hate, envy, and spite. When people suffering from such conditions become patients, the therapist has to be ready.

The therapist's goals include:

- Being benevolently curious, constant, consistent, and reliable.
- Permitting the patient to experience and to recognize the fact that her rage will not kill unless it is acted upon, and that words diminish the need for action.
- Understanding how hard it is for the patient to see that a once-adaptive feeling of grandiosity is no longer necessary and in fact impedes development.
- Allowing the patient to modify gradually the internalized abusive object and to substitute for it (or at least superimpose on it) a more benign object who respects the patient as separate.
- Tolerating and explaining the rage the patient expresses in the transference.
- Encouraging the patient to recognize and to express her rage with words.
- Translating, and helping the patient translate, actions into words.
- Helping the patient realize that she projects her own rage onto the object, thus contributing to her perception of the object as bad.
- Understanding and interpreting the sadomasochistic enactments that are bound to occur.
- Explaining the patient's provocative role in present maltreatment.
- Containing the patient's projected rage.
- Empathizing with the patient's stories of horror and neglect.

The methods used by the therapist will vary with individual patients. A well-structured patient will do better experiencing her rage if the therapist stays out of the way, letting the transference build, showing the patient that she's not afraid. This is the classical analytic approach, used when the patient is motivated to do deep work, and appointments are frequent enough for a sense of security. If the patient's anxiety level is high and her defenses are not able to contain it, the therapist will be more active, often explaining what is happening. With a very fragmented patient or a severely depressed one, the goal of understanding remains, but medication becomes an option—not as a replacement for therapy, but as an adjunct to it. The therapist is obliged to interpret—make sense of—the patient's inability or disinclination to experience feelings or to connect them to symptoms (Carpy, 1989).

WHEN THE THERAPIST FEELS TRAPPED AND ANGRY

These are all ideals, however, and not necessarily easy to live up to in the face of an enraged patient. However, the therapist's struggle to maintain a therapeutic stance, even when she sometimes fails temporarily, in itself offers a healing message to the patient.

> Mrs. E frightened her therapist from the beginning. She was loud, demanding, and bossy. She told her therapist that under no conditions would she pay for missed sessions, and she proceeded to miss many. Mrs. E's therapist began to feel relieved when Mrs. E did not come. She felt trapped and frightened by this angry, hostile person. She had to choose between going along with Mrs. E's demands until she and her patient could understand what was going on and telling Mrs. E that she could not effectively work without the framework she proposed: regular appointments, with Mrs. E financially responsible for her time. The therapist told Mrs. E that when they understood her objections to the therapist's policy, they could decide better if working together was possible. The therapist used her benevolent curiosity to contain her own fear and anger.

She might also have said:

- Can we look into your angry, adamant reaction? Why is missing sessions coming up right now—at the beginning of our work?
- Perhaps we will not be able to work together, but we might learn something useful to you if we explore your feelings.
- If all my patients said that, I would be out of business. This policy is based on my need to pay my bills—it is not meant to hurt you.
- You sound very adamant. Can you tell me about that?
- My policy really upsets you. It would be helpful to understand what it means to you.
- Your tone of outrage is clear; can you talk about it?

In this case, it turned out that Mrs. E's former therapist had recently retired. Mrs. E felt abandoned, frightened, and angry. She felt she needed to control the situation to protect herself.

Mrs. E: Dr. S really jilted me. One day, he announced his retirement. He said we would talk about my feelings for the next two weeks. I never went back.

Therapist: Feeling jilted is really painful.

Mrs. E: You're damned right. We had worked together for two years, and it was helpful. And suddenly, out of the blue—he left me. What was there to talk about? I was so mad I couldn't see straight. He had a hell of a nerve! What's two sessions to talk after two years!

Therapist: Sounds like there is a lot to say—a lot of feelings never expressed.

Mrs. E: I guess so—but how do I know you won't do the same thing? So, I'm going to do this my way, not yours. I'm sick of being passive. My mother did the same thing. One day without warning she died. I was a kid—sent to my grandmother's—no one told me. "Your mother went to heaven" they said. Where was heaven? Why did she go? Why didn't she take me? Or tell me?

This material came out over months of work—and as Mrs. E talked, patient and therapist, both emotionally moved, came to respect each other. The journey continued despite the initial roadblock. As the work deepened, the therapist reiterated her policy when Mrs. E was contemplating vacation.

Mrs. E: Why do I have to coordinate my vacation with yours?

Therapist: You don't have to, but our work depends on consistency—like in school. We set up a structure in the beginning—something you weren't ready to do initially—and we do our best to stick to it. It's your choice to go away when I'm working, but when I take my regular vacation, we'll have an extra break. It makes sense to coordinate. I need to be paid when I'm here to work.

Mrs. E: It still makes me angry, even though you're being logical. I feel like a kid when my mother had bedtime rules. I had tantrums. My mother told me later that I used to bang my head as a baby. My friends got to stay up later. But it turned out that my friend's mother just didn't care about her kids—and they got into a lot of trouble. But at the time I carried on—and then she died. I thought I caused it by being bad. And with my last therapist—he retired abruptly and I wondered if I made him sick.

Therapist: Your rage did not kill or even harm anyone. But by blaming yourself it seems less out of your hands. You feel less impotent. Here, when you began therapy, you were adamant about my policy because you were feeling so impotent. But now, you can tolerate expressing your anger in words and you don't have to act it out.

Had the therapist not mentioned her policy again before Mrs. E's contemplated vacation, she would have lost an opportunity to let the patient see that she was not afraid of the patient's rage.

Similarly, a therapist who does not adhere to other necessary clinical stances or policies runs the risk of leaving rage unexplored. Sharing personal information on a steady basis, socializing with the patient outside of the office, letting the patient overstay her hour, and having sex with the patient are all enactments that cover over the patient's rage or hunger and the therapist's fear of that rage or hunger. They enable patient and therapist to diminish or ignore the patient's expression of oral deprivations, anal struggles, and oedipal disappointments in the transference. Rapprochement and separation crises may be seduced into quiescence. Patients often feel better once treatment begins and decide to end before their rage surfaces.

After the initial relief of feeling listened to in a nonjudgmental way, the honeymoon phase of treatment—which corresponds with what Modell (1976) has called the "cocoon phase"—the patient begins to notice that the analyst is a separate person with needs of her own. Vacations, weekends, changes in appointments alert the patient to the fact that the therapist has another life and is not attending exclusively to her. One patient used to get furious if I sneezed. Many therapists find it easier, more humane, and more empathic to gratify the patient by giving extra time, by answering questions, and by not charging for missed sessions. This falls under the heading of tiptoeing to avoid the patient's anger, as described in the inner roadblocks chapter.

Explaining professional policies to a patient is much more useful and ego strengthening than tiptoeing. The therapist conveys, in words and in posture, that she can tolerate the patient's reactions. The patient's rage, once hidden by denial and avoidance, can surface. "This rage in some patients takes on murderous proportion and may lead to a defensive indifference" (Modell, 1976). "In contrast to the rage that accompanies the Oedipus complex, the wish to destroy the parent of the opposite sex, this rage is not aimed at the analyst as a parental imago. It is less definite and more diffuse. [The therapist] becomes the target of rage directed against external reality. This rage may also be fuelled by envy" (p. 297). As therapy continues, the patient no longer feels falsely self-sufficient and her needs to depend are no longer denied. "With this, comes the beginning of individuation, a sense of separateness, and the development of the therapeutic alliance" (p. 298).

TREATING RAGE

As treatment progresses, the therapeutic dyad builds bridges that allow the patient to explore. Feelings long buried by the weight of life begin to emerge. Anxiety, despair, hatred, and panic are felt and tolerated as the work deepens. The only thing that makes these feelings bearable is the patient's growing awareness of the consistent, reliable therapist (Loewald, 1960; Hall, 1998; Shengold, 1999). The patient, sometimes for the first time, is treated with respect and concern, and as a person with thoughts and feelings separate from anyone else's. The awareness of separateness, although gratifying, is also frightening. If the patient has her own feelings that no one else can control, so must the therapist. This is an alarming possibility for people whose survival has been based on the need to control. The therapist may feel the patient's devastation, hatred, and even panic as she struggles with the complex issues of separateness.

Roadblocks occur when the patient succeeds in pushing the therapist away—making her feel useless, even dead. Sleepiness in session may be a therapist's response to this attempted murder, and her feeling of deadness may be a defense against the deep rage and deprivation of the patient. To survive and explain the enactment is the therapist's job; if she cannot do this, the roadblock may prove insurmountable.

Case analyses show the variety of ways that individuals defend against rage. One of the defenses against feeling rage is depression; another is addiction. Once the depression is understood, the sadness and mourning for missed opportunities and losses can be faced.

> Lois began to experience both intellectually and affectively that she controlled and criticized her staff at work as her mother had controlled and criticized her. Her mother had been dead for twenty years, but Lois had avoided the recognition of this loss by behaving like her mother and by overeating, which stuffed down her feelings. As she began to talk about her mother's illness and death (for the first time in treatment) she started to mourn the loss.
>
> Lois's ambivalent feelings toward her mother made the mourning very difficult. Sometimes she expressed her rage at the therapist: "How do you know I didn't mourn my mother? You have no right to even talk about her. You didn't know her. You don't even know me. I'm nasty and mean at work. I get furious when the secretary slips up. I yell and scream. And I feel like you're the same—slipping up. You take a month's vacation! How dare you leave—and where do you go? What difference does it make anyway? You're useless. I hate you. (Silence) No, I missed you—but it's easier to hate you."
>
> Her rage and guilt were painful emotions to uncover, but after a long period of mourning, she felt things shift inside. Lois was seventeen when her mother died in a car accident. She felt that if she had been a good girl, this would not have happened. By internalizing the tragedy, she kept her mother alive in fantasy. She became her mother. After some years in treatment, she began to selectively identify with the therapist and to soften the mother representation. Lois's treatment deepened as she became able to examine her rage from all angles: "Mother's screaming was not as terrible as I think—it seemed worse because of my own rage at her. Our rages got confused—I have to separate out my jealousy of her and her jealousy of me. My father probably contributed in some way.

The survival of the therapeutic dyad is what makes the treatment work. The patient's frightening feeling of omnipotence is slowly chipped away as the therapist tolerates and interprets each assault. During the last session before a vacation, a patient expressed worry about how he (the patient) would get along. The therapist replied, "I'll be fine." This tongue-in-cheek statement addressed the patient's murderous fantasy. (This interpretation could be made because of the many years of work that had gone on about anger and separation.) Later on in this treatment, the patient's anxiety about others' safety was acknowledged as his own anger. Wishes for someone's failure, injury, even death are often hidden by overconcern. Richard (above) reported that, as a child, he would wait by the window until his parents came home from an evening out. He worried that they had been killed in a terrible car accident. In treatment, he realized that this worry was based on his own rage and his own wish that harm would befall them for excluding and abandoning him.

Years are spent erecting the walls that contain the rage of the abused or injured child, and they are not easily taken down. It is important that the therapist respect the defenses that cover rage; she must treat them with patience. Intellectual understanding can take pressure off the superego. A therapist might say to Lois, for instance, "It sounds as though you didn't have very much attention when your mother died. It would be only natural for you to feel angry and deprived about that."

It often takes years of testing before a patient trusts the therapist enough to risk facing angry feelings. In many cases, the therapist must become aware of the rage first—or at least think to suspect it—by hearing the patient's history. That was true in the following case vignette, which was presented in a class. The participants had varying reactions, and some of these are given here at the end of the presentation. This early session in a long treatment gives clues about underlying rage and despair.

Laura, a twenty-four-year-old black woman from the South, is attending college on a writing scholarship. Sexually abused between the ages of four and seven by a cousin and beaten by both of her fundamentalist parents throughout her childhood, she presents herself as an articulate, pleasant, depressed little girl. She was referred for counseling by her school because of her visible depression—crying, insomnia, listlessness, and staying in her room. She eagerly accepted the referral and began talking about her mother's recent death. She felt homesick, although there was no one at home who she wished to see, and she connected easily to her therapist.

Session #8 [three minutes late]:

Laura: That is some hill! I'm not used to these hills. They gotta do something with this campus [chuckles]. Let's see. I had this nightmare this morning. Gosh, I just woke up at 11. Didn't get to sleep 'til 3 in the morning. This was a crazy dream. I died but I didn't really die. My family was looking for my body. . . .

Therapist: Tell me more.

Laura: Well, it was so strange. I was laid out in the coffin, but I never got to see my face. Every time I got close enough, the coffin would be shut . . . and I knew I didn't really die. Then I went to my friend's house because the coffin was there. She was a friend I used to take dance lessons with. But she wouldn't let me in. It was like she knew I was in the coffin but could see I was not in there. Then, we went to my grandmother's house and there was a great flood. I don't know—this dream is crazy.

Therapist: It's very interesting. Keep going.

Laura: OK. My whole family was there. They could see my face and I was so mad because the funeral director had a brochure about my death.

Therapist: Brochure?

Laura: Yeah. It was a picture book of all the steps it took to make me up. What makes me up is my perception of my childhood. Everybody was looking at it. I don't know—what do you make of this?

Therapist: Well, with dreams, what matters is what the dream means to the dreamer. So, what does this dream mean to you?

Laura: I've been thinking of that. [She pauses.] When I'm chasing the coffin from place to place, it was like the day when no one would tell me where my momma was. First, I went to Florence [a neighboring town]. She wasn't there. Then to Columbia—she wasn't there. [Pause] But my grandmother and the flood—I don't know about that. And I'm dead but everyone sees I'm not really dead.

Therapist: Last time, you were talking about going home and everyone seeing your mother's face when they looked at you.

Laura: Oh yeah. They never see me. When I was little, I remember being at school and I couldn't wait to get home and tell momma about my good grades. She wouldn't even look. She would say: "I gotta look at your brothers' grades because they get all Ds." And I was such a good kid—I'd say "OK, Momma." My momma always said: "Your little brother is special. He was born for your father." What about me and my older brother?

Therapist: Yes.

Laura: What does that mean and why would she say such a thing?

Therapist: What does that mean?

Laura: When my older brother was born, our father was in prison, so he didn't get to see us grow up. I was four when he came home from prison. Momma said he wanted to raise a toddler. What is that! They gave my little brother all the attention.

Therapist: How about you?

Laura: Not when I was younger—but when I was older. [She pauses, thinking.] I hate to say this—it seems so childish to want to be noticed. I noticed this pattern all my life—of having one friend. I still do it, even today. It's like I know on one level that my friend has friends other than me, but on another level I think I have her all to myself. Then, sure enough, something happens and I get hurt and I end the friendship. I don't have a lot of friends—even now. You know, I think I exhaust my friends.

Therapist: I think it's important that you shared this information after talking about how your mother paid little attention to you—and so much to your younger brother.

Laura: Oh, that is interesting. . . . I feel so clingy at times. I don't know—let me ask you—how can I just keep my emotions in the one situation?

Therapist: Do you mean dealing only with the emotions that are a direct result of a current situation?

Laura: Yes. Once something happens it sets off a lot of other thoughts and feelings from the past.

Therapist: Well, part of our work together will require that you talk about your past and visit these memories and emotions—but you will do it as an adult looking back on the past.

Laura: Oh. OK.

Therapist: Understanding these emotions will help you with the current situation.

Laura: I see—there's a lot there. When I think about my father and the way he treated me . . . he never gave me a reason why he disliked me. [Laura's eyes fill with tears—one rolls down her face.]

Therapist: I see you're upset. Why don't we start here next time and continue to talk about your father.

Laura: That would be good.

After discussing this vignette in class, we came up with the following questions and ideas. In this eighth session, Laura is telling the therapist how depressed she really is (the flood), why she is so depressed (the loss of mother, past and present), and her own fear of deadness. Does she dare to feel alive? Will her therapist be able to tolerate her clinginess? What about her rage and envy about losing her mother's attention to father and brothers? Will Laura end the relationship when she feels disappointed or when she sees that there are others in the therapist's life? These faces that she can't see in the dream are her own faces—faces of rage and longing hidden by sadness and tears. The feelings about the beatings and rape she endured may or may not surface except in the creative writing she will do. This beginning therapist shows how gentle she will be. She is alert to the message of Laura's reference to the hills that must be climbed. The journey will be tiring but hopefully rewarding for both parties.

Laura's history of rejection, punishment, and sexual abuse all point to hidden rage beneath her depression. Her fear is that she is responsible for the way she was treated. She must act like a good girl, never revealing that her rage is alive underneath the depression that makes her feel and look dead.

RAGE IN DISGUISE

Unmodified rage has some uses, such as maintaining distance by denying otherness, making a connection to another without risking engulfment or merger, or abreacting and taking revenge against internal objects or external situations. Rage often takes the form of psychosomatic symptoms. Physical pain (headache, back pain, stomach pain, jaw pain, intestinal spasm), often a result of tension and stress, can also be understood as hatred toward an internal object or as a compromise between ego achievement and superego punishment. As with most symptoms, secondary gain is part of the package. Physical pain and illness bind rage and usually guarantee attention.

Self-injury and accident proneness can be an expression of rage as well.

> Joan reported her fury at her husband, who was in the process of leaving her. He had not acknowledged hurting her feelings, and this enraged her. Ten minutes after an argument, she tripped and fell. She bruised herself badly, but strangely, she felt better. It was as though she was punishing someone—her inner self and object representations. As a child, she had been ridiculed and physically abused by her mother. As Joan grew up, she silently hated her mother, envied her, and adored her. Hurting herself was Joan's way of expressing rage—at herself, her mother, and her husband.

And:

> Hannah grew up with an alcoholic mother and became a drug addict when she was sixteen. Her pregnancy at age eighteen forced her to remain abstinent until the baby son was born, but the stresses of motherhood and her rage at her mother contributed to her going back to heroin. After six months of dangerous drug use, she was accepted by a residential drug treatment center. She finished the program and began analysis shortly after that. In the initial stage of treatment, Hannah talked about her past and present, pretty

much ignoring the analyst. In the second year, however, the analyst had to cancel several sessions. Hannah never asked why but began coming late to sessions. When the analyst wondered to Hannah whether her canceling and Hannah's lateness were related, Hannah scoffed at the question: "You have nothing to do with my lateness. I've been getting diarrhea, headaches, and stomach cramps before my appointments." But as this pattern intensified, both therapist and Hannah realized that Hannah was ignoring and distancing herself from her son as her mother had ignored her. "The doctor says there's nothing wrong with me and asked if I was tense. Of course I'm tense; when I used heroin I could relax. I can't tolerate the demands you and Tom put on me. They make me sick. My mother got sick when she cut down on drinking. But then she'd disappear again—like you did a few weeks ago." The analyst, still feeling distanced and at times bored, told Hannah that he thought her physical symptoms were her way of avoiding painful feelings.

One day, Hannah said, "Stop nagging at me. You sound just like my mother. First you're silent and ignoring, then you nag." Hannah's expression of anger was a relief both to Hannah and to her analyst. As the transference intensified, both the analyst's boredom and the patient's physical symptoms stopped. Verbalization allows the body to rest.

Along the same lines:

Lila married a widower with three sons. The boys were difficult, and it took a long time for them to accept her into the family. A passive, soft-spoken, and basically depressed person, Lila took the situation stoically. In therapy, she began to realize how angry she was—complaining that her husband didn't seem to understand how difficult her life had become. During this time, an ovarian cyst was discovered. The week before Lila was scheduled for surgery, she allowed herself to "let go" in her session. She yelled and cried and called her husband and the boys names. Suddenly, she felt a tiny pain, which went away immediately. When she went in for her pre-op sonogram, there was no sign of the cyst. It had vanished, and both Lila and her therapist wondered if the expression of anger had had something to do with it.

Another illustration of somatic compliance:

Barbara, who appears in chapter 5, was plagued by physical symptoms. The basis of many of these symptoms was physical, but the psychological component was clear. Barbara's therapist felt that her pains were a way of holding on to past objects, bad as they were—the mother who had died when Barbara was ten and the father who had died when she was eighteen. Her family life had been filled with misery, and only in sickness did she find caring doctors and nurses. When Barbara's therapist, after years of treatment, let Barbara know that she could feel her pain in the form of a headache, Barbara stopped having headaches. The therapist did not fully understand this, but the class speculated that Barbara felt a connection to the therapist that allowed her to let go of one of her symptom friends. The rage encapsulated by the headache symptom was tamed by Barbara's internalization of the therapist as a good object—thus softening her internal object world. Of course, the therapist had been the only one to listen nonjudgmentally to Barbara over the years, and this is what had allowed her to feel free to address the headache the way she did.

In treatment, the patient's underlying and tenacious conscious and unconscious rage can lead to a cluster of defenses that may make the therapist feel impotent—useless—and a failure. Projective identification of this kind can cause a roadblock by making the therapist feel as though she is losing her way.

Susan projected her rage on to the therapist. She would sit calmly while the therapist clenched her fists, held her breath, and silently cursed at her patient. The therapist had to interpret what was happening lest it become further enacted in treatment.

Susan decided to visit a friend the day before a national holiday. The therapist would be working that day, and this interfered with Susan's plan. She knew she would be charged for the missed session, but resented the therapist's decision to work. The fee was less important to her than her envy of other patients who would have their sessions. Susan behaved as though everything was fine, but she came fifteen minutes late to her sessions on Monday and Tuesday before the holiday. In her Wednesday session before the Thursday she planned to take off, she chatted away about an office mate who had recently been given notice.

Susan: What a shame—Marla was a nice person, but the boss hated her. She got fired. You could tell by the look on his face when he talked to her. I wonder what she'll do, now.

Therapist: You would like to fire me today.
Susan: No, I don't know why you say that.
Therapist: I can see the anger on your face and I can hear a tone of indifference.
Susan: I feel fine. Maybe you feel upset. I'll pay you and that will be that.
Therapist: I think your lateness Monday and Tuesday was your way of expressing your anger. [The therapist feels something shift. She has invited Susan to share her anger and no longer feels the intensity of Susan's projected anger.]
Susan: I hate you for not taking my plans into consideration. Everyone is taking Thursday off to make a longer weekend. But not you. You and your schedule are all that matter.

This vignette is meant to show that Susan is beginning to acknowledge the therapist as a separate object with her own needs. The rage she expresses has roots in the past that can be reworked with the therapist in the transference.

Ann's roadblock was repression and dissociation.

Ann's mother had been afraid of setting boundaries because of her own inability to separate. Ann became her extension. By never providing boundaries, the mother prevented Ann from true individuation. Ann's was a case of neglect. Her narcissistic mother was an alcoholic and let Ann do and have what she wanted. A maid did household chores, but did not seem to like children. Ann skipped school frequently and played with her toys and read books (Cinderella was her favorite). Her mother was there but not there—shopping and drinking and sleeping. Notes and phone calls from the school were ignored. Once, a truant officer came to the house, and Ann's mother assured him that Ann would be in school. Both mother and daughter lived in fantasy worlds. Ann eventually married a man who gave her everything and expected nothing. Ann was his beautiful doll. When he left her, she fell apart.

Ann's treatment gradually enabled her to see that the rage she had repressed, split off, dissociated over the years of emotional neglect was safe to express. At first, she took it out on herself. Suicidal ideation, depression, and drug use preceded her acknowledgment of rage. Her wish to make her mother sorry or to make her mother (the therapist in the transference) suffer by threats of self-injury did not work. She became angry when her mother continued to ignore her in times of crisis. "Where is she—doesn't she care? She must hate me—no, I hate her. I always hated her, but I wanted her love so badly—her acceptance meant so much to me." When Ann verbalized her hatred in the here and now of treatment, the therapist did not retaliate. He listened empathically. Over the years at different times in the therapy, he was experienced as a transference object, a transitional object, and a new object.

As with Ann, Miriam's therapy was colored by negative transference.

Miriam, discussed in chapter 4, grew up with the grandiose fantasy that she had power. Her baby sister had died when Miriam was almost three—her wish that the baby would disappear had come true. But when her "power" didn't work, Miriam became enraged. She threw silent tantrums at indications that the therapist had a separate life and that Miriam could not control her. She lay rigidly on the couch, feet crossed, arms folded, and silent. Before the therapist's vacation, she skipped sessions, came late, and withheld payment, to the therapist's annoyance. When the therapist returned, Miriam said that she did not really need therapy and wished to end treatment.

When a fantasy such as the death of a sibling comes true, it may take years of analysis to work through the implications (Greenacre, 1956). Miriam's belief that she had the power to kill her sister made it terrifying to her to be so angry at her therapist, whom she needed and feared she could kill. The therapist felt Miriam's rage and her own, and her interpretations seemed to fall on deaf ears. There were repeated conversations such as this:

Therapist: I feel frustrated and at the end of my rope. I know that you feel anger, too, but you express it in your actions instead of in words.

Miriam: All you care about is your work and making money—you don't care about me.

Therapist: Why are they mutually exclusive? I think you would rather I not be human and vulnerable like Ella [the baby sister who died] was.

Miriam: You couldn't stand seeing me angry.

Therapist: You're afraid I won't survive like Ella didn't. But you didn't kill Ella, and you can't kill me.

Miriam [cries silently and finally says]: No one knows how evil I am. Everyone thinks I'm good and reasonable and kind.

Therapist: You can be angry and good and kind. One feeling doesn't mean the others go away. We all have mixed feelings.

Exchanges like this were not unusual. There had been many like it and there would be more to come, for Miriam needed to be sure that her rage could be tolerated. When children are left with an overload of unmanageable rage, the superego may take over the ego's capacity to develop, much as the early object thwarts the child's ability to individuate. Going through life as a "soul murdered" person (Shengold, 1999) is a tragedy that can be modified only with dedicated work by the dyad. To witness and tolerate the intolerable is terrifying work, but rage is necessary to some children's survival. It has a real life and a legitimate place that cannot be ignored, and so the therapist must hear both the patient's rage and the circumstances that called it forth. This is not easy. Both patient and therapist may often be tempted to give up the work, but not giving up may save a soul. This is where a rescue fantasy on the therapist's part, however "theoretically incorrect" it may be, is useful, even necessary, as sometimes the patient gets a sense of it and internalizes it. I am not advocating an evangelistic approach, but I believe that a wish to rescue is one reason why one goes into a healing profession.

Lack of feeling is another disguise under which rage can hide. Mr. M, who is described at greater length in chapter 8, organized his rage in repeated scenarios of control and frustration.

Mr. M chose to marry a compulsively neat, controlling woman. His procrastination enraged her. He could experience his rage only vicariously. This passivity evoked her sadism, and he responded to it passively, enraging her once more. This choreography ruled the couple to the point where spontaneity and change became impossible, and it threatened Mr. M's treatment as well. Lateness, silence, and whining were offset by brief periods of hard and impressive work that titillated the therapist into wanting more. Teasing the therapist was eventually seen as a reliving of a childhood seduction. Mr. M was saying, "Yes, I can do the work but I won't." Each time the therapist despaired, feeling that the patient was hopeless, Mr. M bounced back. Impasse after impasse added up to stalemate, but neither party declared checkmate. As long as Mr. M could bury his rage, hatred, spite, and envy by enacting them in the treatment and in life, he could avoid experiencing these feelings.

After years of playing with the time, coming late, and skipping sessions, Mr. M came to a session early, and when the therapist came to the door she was startled to see him reading a magazine.

Mr. M: I have to change my life. I don't do my work and hate doing things at home . . . would like to get away with doing nothing. I felt spite when you opened the door. You didn't expect me to come on time, and I'm here partially out of spite—to show you I can. I grew up with spite. It's as deep as I am old. I don't like who I am—a shell. My older sister called to say Mom is in Europe visiting my uncle. Fear and paranoia—they know about my business problems and the investigation. Want to kill them off. The investigation is very scary.

Therapist: The investigation in here is scary.

Mr. M: I see a small boy—me—mother and sister bathing me, humiliated.

Therapist: What do you see?

Mr. M: Genitals—small penis. Sister stimulating me—teasing. It's humiliating—a seed of hatred and anger and powerlessness. I'm standing with a girl—apple cut in half with two seeds. I'm mixed with feelings of meanness and playfulness. You, she doesn't have a penis—castrated. Playfulness and spite. There was a whole houseful of spite and not enough love to offset it. Image of subsisting off a rock like a mummified monster . . . cold, mean, and ruthless. I thought a serial killer would have a profile like me. Gregarious, white, nice.

Therapist: It's how angry you are.

Next session:

Mr. M: I got here for spite.

Therapist: Other reasons?

Mr. M: (1) Wanted to get here (2) to be with you—a chance to be with you. Just felt fear—hesitancy to say that—embarrassed like I'm denying myself feelings and desires. I have an image of a boy in the living room, next to father—thinking I'm wanting something but with a neutral face. I'm a bad boy if I let on. I'm the baby—until my sister came along. I was laughed at but it was some kind of attention. I was a jokester—never taken seriously. Then my sister was the baby and I lost my place.

Therapist: I think this is all connected to wanting to be here—wanting something from me and fear of that.

Mr. M: It's safer to make this into a spiteful game than to really feel sad . . . don't want to admit I need you.

The patient can't let on to his parent/therapist that he wants something. He would rather come late to sessions than face his desires for soothing and sexual closeness. He rejected interpretations of this material for the same reasons. His theme song was "I see what you mean and I realize you are right, but I don't feel it." Isolation of affect, the "not feeling," served him in many ways:

- He avoided pain (along with joy, excitement, desire, and love).
- He disappointed and devastated others without feeling guilt.
- He appeared helpless while maintaining his imagined superiority and power.
- He protected his grandiose position by avoiding vulnerability.
- He managed to appear masochistic and pitiful while torturing others.
- He made the therapist feel as he felt as a child—helpless and furious but hopeful.

INJURIES FROM WITHIN AND WITHOUT

Inner turmoil, anxieties, inhibitions, and compulsive character traits are present in everyone. The real outer circumstances of childhood are part of the story, but only part of it. Even with good-enough parenting, a secure upbringing, and a "normal" childhood free of traumatic events, narcissistic and neurotic difficulties are ever present. The envies and jealousies of everyday life affect us in different ways. The childhood athlete or star is often weighed down by expectations of the envy of others. The child whose mother is a beauty may feel she can never measure up, let alone compete, and so takes no care of her appearance. Childhood fears blossom on their own, in the absence of outside factors. Where complicating outside factors *are* present, however, the ordinary fears and fantasies of childhood, like the ordinary angers, can become much more intense and threatening. Envy and jealousy are cousins of rage—they are universal and are often numbed by alcohol, perversion, comedy, and helplessness.

Mrs. N came to treatment after a face-lift and other plastic surgery did not help her depression. She lived in luxury, traveled first class, and had successful children. "Why do I feel so empty?" she asked. "I go to parties, I go shopping, I go to the theatre, I have servants." In therapy, she was listened to for the first time in her life. No matter what she said or who she blamed (including the therapist at times), she felt heard. As she told her life story, she began to understand her loneliness.

Mrs. N and her mother were war refugees. They left their homeland when Mrs. N was seven. Mrs. N was shuttled from place to place and left for long periods of time to fend for herself. During the times that they were together, roles were reversed, and Mrs. N had to take care of her dependent mother. She always felt like an outsider, and indeed she was one. Mrs. N went to school by herself, learned to speak a new language, and behaved stoically every time she and her mother had to run once again for shelter. Her mother slept with men in front of Mrs. N, and sometimes the men made advances toward her. As frightening as this life was, Mrs. N adapted. She even felt a sense of competence and self-esteem in her role.

When she and her mother moved to America and were taken in by relatives, life suddenly changed. Her mother remarried. A teenager by this time, Mrs. N felt excluded by the other kids in school, not needed by her mother, and generally lost. She missed her past adventurous life and the intense closeness with her mother. She missed the sense of accomplishment of surviving.

Mrs. N eventually married a wealthy man and had children. She found herself feeling distanced and aloof—even envious. Having grown up in poverty and danger herself, she could not adjust to her new life. In therapy, she began to understand her resentment and envy toward the children who had grown up safe and with every imaginable luxury, and who excelled in business and the arts. Rather than let herself be overcome by her embarrassing emotions, or to express them, she tried taking advantage of her opportunities. But she felt wooden and disinterested, and eventually became depressed.

In therapy, she revisited the past. Only then did she begin once again to feel animated and enthusiastic. Her childhood had made her feel special, and she had every right to protect her memories. Her experience had left her self-sufficient and strong. Her tie to her mother was strong, too—they were like sisters in some ways—but real mothering (or good-enough mothering) had been out of the question due to her mother's preexisting inadequacies and the realities of war.

In treatment, Mrs. N. idealized the therapist, at first, partly because she needed a good object who provided steadiness and interest, and partly because she was holding back negative feelings that she feared would be alienating. But as she began to focus on transference fantasies about the therapist's clothes, imagined lifestyle, and other such things, a heretofore hidden side of her emerged. Sarcastic remarks, demeaning opinions, and general nastiness took the place of idealization. "How can you wear the same shoes so often?" "Why do you work at all, why can't your husband support you?" "This office is gloomy; you have no taste." "How could you charge me when I went to Hawaii last month?" "How can you decide when I go away?"

These comments and questions came after a period of work that permitted Mrs. N to realize how angry she was at her mother for having another life, a life without her. She learned that her problems with her children were influenced by her own mother's inability to cherish her as a separate person. Rage entered the treatment, and Mrs. N gradually saw that it harmed no one. As the idealizing transference shifted and the therapist was allowed to step down from the pedestal, Mrs. N became angry at the therapist about vacations and other breaks in treatment, evidence that the therapist too had another life, separate from Mrs. N. The illusion of exclusivity was shattered, as it had been when Mrs. N and her mother came to America.

Mrs. N [bitterly]: How can you ever know what it was like? I was alone—scared to death. But could I tell her? She would have cried. She was an idiot—but I needed her—where could I go? The neighbors thought she was so brave. I knew she was a self-centered bitch. Just like you. All you care about is my paying—not what I go through.

The therapist listened and saw that when Mrs. N confronted these feelings toward her mother in treatment, she opened a door to communication on a new level. Rage at the mother and the therapist was also about Mrs. N's own helplessness, her feelings of rejection, and her pervasive sense of guilt that had been covered by the false self-esteem of her precocious wartime years. Expressing the rage was cathartic, but it also helped her realize that she wanted and needed closeness. Connecting with rage is often a first step toward loving feelings. The buried rage surfaced, freeing her to connect and to individuate (Winnicott, 1969).

Her new life in America had distanced her from her wartime sense of herself as strong and self-sufficient. Many years of treatment helped her put the past in perspective and reconnect with and develop her sense of her own vitality and competence.

Mrs. N. began to tell her children about her past; this enabled her to let them share her memories. Pride in her strength replaced the "outsider" feelings. She became engrossed in art history–a way of finding beauty in the past. She allowed her past deprivations to recede so that she could take pleasure in the present. Mrs. N had never experienced appropriate mothering, and this had prevented her from emotionally nurturing her children. Luckily, and intuitively, she had married a giving, steady man who helped make her survival possible. Treatment helped make her survival happier. She was a wonderful grandmother–showing her grandchildren the love she had not been able to feel with her own children.

Mrs. N was fortunate. For her, the expression of rage was a turning point in her treatment and her life. But sometimes rage is the final roadblock—the patient needs to hold on to it, and the therapist can't do a thing about it (Gabbard, 2000). The patient may provoke the therapist into ending treatment; sometimes the patient abruptly quits. Other times the treatment is terminated mutually.

Rageful feelings are like the PCBs in the Hudson River—they stay mostly buried until they are stirred up. Both leak poison slowly, chronically, and imperceptibly. When they have to be dredged up, things often get worse for a time on the way to getting better. They must be dug up, exposed, and transformed. If not, future generations will inherit them and pass them on.

❖ CHAPTER 7 ❖

Professional Dilemmas

> They hang on, they persist, and eventually many of them prevail. Living out their years in a climate of hatred and dependence and torment, they nevertheless maintain that the life of man has meaning, can be understood, and that his suffering is in part remediable. . . . They stand by. Hatred they endure and do not turn away. Love comes their way, and they are not seduced. They are listeners, but they listen with unwavering intent, and their silence is not cold.
>
> —Allen Wheelis

"What's it like to be a therapist?" "Isn't it depressing listening to people all day?" "Do you take it home?" "What happens when you go away?" "What drives a person to do this?" These questions are familiar to every therapist. People are fascinated by the field of psychotherapy and the lives of the people who practice it. The fantasy of rescuing and being rescued is one shared, I think, by most therapists. The wish to understand is another motivation. Curiosity, shyness, voyeurism, identification with one's own therapist, and a wish to repair, relive, relieve, and forgive are often involved. There are also drives to be successful, to make a living, and to make a difference. But it is important to keep in mind that however fascinating the work may be, to become a psychotherapist is to make a commitment to professional responsibility.

What is unique to the work of the psychoanalytic psychotherapist is the amount of self-reflection and awareness of countertransference it requires. Access to the unconscious is hard to come by, and without awareness of her own inner life no therapist can understand how difficult, dangerous, and exciting it feels for the patient to explore her own. The joys of enlightenment and understanding make the difficulty and danger tolerable. When a patient starts to see life through different lenses and to feel emotions that have been buried, psychoanalytic work is rewarding for both parties. But it's hard work.

Gertrude Blanck (personal communication) always taught her students that in the consulting room, the therapist is the professional, no matter how inexperienced she is. The therapist has been consulted because of the patient's stress, and whatever else she does, the therapist must put her own stresses and insecurities aside for the meeting. "You are the professional in the consulting room," she would say, "and remembering that is important." Patients, especially those who begin treatment in a state of high anxiety, require a calm and professional demeanor in the therapist.

> The first aim of treatment must be . . . to penetrate the panic and relieve some of the anxiety. . . . The composed, firm, assured attitude of the analyst is of the greatest importance. . . . A word about reassurance: most patients tend to react badly to direct reassurance. A quiet attitude of knowing one's business usually suffices. . . . The same thing is true of advice. Although emergencies occur at appalling frequency, . . . the analyst is in a better position if he does not permit himself to be drawn into the role of advisor. (Greenacre, 1969, p. 58)

Expertise usually comes with experience, and so it is at the end of her career that a therapist is wisest. But it is at the beginning of her work life that a therapist has the most energy and eagerness. It always seems that new therapists have the most difficult—and the most interesting—cases, and so assuming a professional role is necessary from the beginning. This includes establishing a consistent and reliable schedule, keeping rules and boundaries clear, tolerating the patient's feelings, keeping track of the therapist's own feelings, and maintaining an atmosphere, both physical and emotional, in which the necessary work can be done.

The therapist is always susceptible to the pull of countertransference, especially in times of stress, and this may seduce her into offering concrete help. Of course, there are times when action must be taken (where there are suicide risks, illness that requires hospitalization, homicidal threats, battered or battering spouses), but most of the time, even when faced with outside crises, the therapist can do most for her patient by listening and supporting autonomous functioning.

> Dr. J's patient is a twenty-one-year-old college student who reported that she had been abused between the ages of seven and ten by an uncle. She told her parents, but no one believed her. While she was in treatment, she got into a number of troubling and dangerous situations, and Dr. J found herself making phone calls—once to the security department at her school and on another occasion to the patient's doctor. As Dr. J observed her own actions, she realized that she was trying to undo the patient's early experience by taking care of her. She saw that her behavior was infantilizing her patient and taking away age-appropriate autonomy.

The temptation to try to be a better parent is common, especially with abused patients. But patients are rarely strengthened by, or satisfied with, a therapist's outside involvement. When the therapist involves herself by making phone calls or seeing the patient's family or friends, she is enacting with the patient instead of interpreting. (Many senior analysts do not seem to understand the value in ego building and give advice and direction to their psychotherapy patients.) Instead of taking over for the patient, the therapist might say something like, "Let's try to understand what gets in the way of your calling or going over to the security department at school." This conveys the idea that the patient is not helpless and that the therapist is in fact confident in her ability to take care of herself. If the intensity of treatment and the patient's ego strength allow it, the therapist can interpret the enactment. "You would like me to be a better parent to you than yours were and to protect you, and I can understand that wish, but it is more important that I help you help yourself." When the patient is clearly unable to function or poses a danger to herself or someone else, an exception may be in order, but it can still be analyzed.

The demands of abstinence and neutrality pose dilemmas for therapists all the time. It is difficult to be benignly curious when a patient is demanding, threatening, or acting out. Ms. C got a new job after a year in treatment. She informed her therapist that she needed an hour after 6 P.M. The therapist did not have an hour after six, and Ms. C threatened to quit. A dilemma: should the therapist add an hour to her day? The treatment was going well, and she felt obliged to continue it. After discussing the realities of the situation, Ms. C shared a fantasy that she wanted proof of her specialness. The therapist explored with Ms. C why she should need a proof that might deprive her of treatment. A compromise seemed in order. Ms. C would begin her job, and after settling in she would ask her boss if she could work late and take a longer lunch hour. This plan satisfied both parties. During the transition, the therapist added an hour to her schedule, and after a month Ms. C felt comfortable and secure enough at work to arrange a daytime hour. Another therapist might have let Ms. C wait to continue treatment.

THE USE OF THEORY

Responsibility, responsiveness, attentiveness, empathy, curiosity, and seriousness are attitudes that add up to professionalism. The wielding of theoretical knowledge may assuage a therapist's anxiety, but theory must be used wisely. I heard one therapist present her graduation case using every psychoanalytic concept and term I have ever heard. But when she was finished, I knew nothing about what had happened in treatment or even who the patient was. Her need to feel expert got the upper hand over her ability to listen to her patient.

The simultaneous needs to be expert and to be open sometimes conflict, but the paradox can be tempered by benevolent curiosity. Because psychoanalytic theories shift every ten years or so, the therapist who realizes that all patients are unique and cannot be pigeonholed by diagnostic labels will never feel out of date. Structural diagnoses based on ego strength and assessments of where a patient may have faltered developmentally are helpful to a point, but overdiagnosing or dwelling exclusively on pathology sets a tone in treatment that can hamper progress. To greet a patient with regard, courtesy, respect, and of course, benign curiosity is a gift that in itself quells fear, sparks the patient's interest, and helps to create a safe space.

Psychoanalytic theory has fashions: classic, modern, avant-garde, traditional, Freudian, Mahlerian, Kohutian, Kleinian, modern Kleinian, relational, interpersonal, attachment—the list grows ever longer and then seems to double back. Strachey (1934), Sterba (1934), and Loewald (1960) made contributions many years ago that should still be read by students today, and *The Evolution of Psychoanalytic Theory* (Bergmann and Hartman, 1976) is filled with historical papers whose ideas are being reflected, but not credited frequently, in present-day discoveries.

Doing psychoanalytically based work is very much like being an explorer (Hall, 1998). Which theory of technique does the therapist choose to aid her on her travels? Each patient presents the therapist with a unique terrain. It is advisable, therefore, to survey all kinds of geography and weather, keeping an open mind. Reading the literature acquaints the therapist with theoreticians and clinicians of different points of view. The list of authors is very long, but if the major theoreticians and clinicians become the therapist's friends, the trip will not be quite so arduous and frightening. Each vantage point offers an assortment of ideas that can enhance a therapist's capacity to listen and understand. I am not recommending eclecticism, but the development of a well-rounded therapist requires openness to new ideas. Fred Pine's article "The Four Psychologies" (1988) makes this point. The complexity of the patient requires the therapist to be knowledgeable, intuitive, and open-minded. "Each patient writes her own theory" (Martin Nass, personal communication). Therapeutic dilemmas cannot be solved exclusively by theory, however, because each case is complex and unique. Intuition must be valued as well. Most mistakes are rectifiable, and when one is made, often the patient can become a partner in resolving it.

A user of *Kohutian theory* may lose sight of the passion and power of the Oedipus complex at the same time that she gains techniques suited to problems of extreme narcissism. A classical Freudian's consideration of pre-oedipal pathology may be limited, but her awareness of conflict may be especially acute. Relationalists make fruitful use of the dynamics of the dyad, but may run the risk of not letting the patient explore the roots of her behavior. Is narcissism pathological, a line of development, or a defense? Are eating disorders based on oral fantasy, oedipal defense, compulsive adaptation, addiction, fixation, or regression? Are procrastination and stubbornness anal fixations, defenses against success due to guilt, expressions of rage, or character traits? These symptoms are always compromise formations. Theoretical concepts provide a shorthand for therapist-to-therapist communication, but they can also be limiting. Labeling people may ease the therapist's anxiety, but it may also take her away from her real feelings about a patient. The broader the therapist's life experience, the more comfortable a traveler she will be. The therapist who understands that people are truly unclassifiable will understand more about the patients she treats than will one who believes that complexities can be wrapped up in a diagnosis.

This understanding informs technique. Decisions about when to interpret, when to reflect, when to connect to the past, and when to stay in the present are made according to the moment, the terrain, and the strength of the dyad. There are times when every therapist finds herself worrying about her demeanor—how warm and giving to be, how quiet and empathic, how confrontational and directive. But just as each patient is unique, so is each therapist. Indeed, personal style may dictate the kind of theory one gets training in. A cognitive therapist may not be comfortable with, or interested in waiting for, unconscious derivatives of a patient's maladaptive ideas. A family therapist prefers groups to one-on-one work. It is not unusual for a person to study the theory and technique her own therapist practiced. Yet flexibility and common sense, along with consistent availability and a therapeutic frame, are threads common to all clinical approaches. The current debate among therapists about how revealing to be, how much to disclose, whether or not to answer personal questions must be resolved by each therapist using her own clinical judgment and experience and taking into account each patient's ego strength and capacity to reflect. The capacity to reflect and to wonder is enlisted by the therapist's examples. Such phrases as "I wonder"; "Let's figure out"; "Have you ever thought about it this way?" "What comes to mind about it?" and "Have you ever felt this way before?" are helpful in encouraging the patient to reflect.

Travel does require equipment. Some tools I have found to be helpful are:

- A genuine benevolent curiosity (Hall, 1998; Sharpe, 1947)
- A comfortable place to sit
- A passion to learn
- A good sense of who you are and the capacity to be flexible
- A professional attitude (which does not mean coldness, rigidity, or lack of caring)
- A good ear
- An appreciation of how others get through life
- A tolerance of rage and hatred on both sides of the couch

THE OFFICE

Setting up the office is a very personal process, but it is also an important presentation of the therapist's professionalism and so requires attention. Many therapists believe that the office should be sparse, with little to distract the patient. Freud, however, had his collection of antiquities in sight. It is true that the therapist is reflected in her office decor, but each patient reacts to that decor based on her own fantasies, needs, fears, and transference requirements. A therapist with a clinic or hospital office may have little choice, but the choices she does make—to do something or to do nothing—are meaningful. My first placement in social work school was in a clinic where I rarely had the same office twice in a row. The dilemma was what to tell the patients. I chose to tell the truth—that I was a student and was given an office that was available. The main dilemma, however, involved the fact that I would be leaving in June. Some patients used that knowledge to resist involvement. Others resented the arrangement. All of the patients had to face separation anxiety and so did I.

Every scenario has its pluses and minuses. Patients' reactions to office surroundings are interesting and informative. A patient of mine after two years of work suddenly commented on a new painting. The painting had been there all along; her noticing it indicated a growing awareness of me as separate. Another patient could talk about nothing but the office, avoiding for a long time any (direct) notice of me. A friend was referred to a therapist who did not have a waiting room; he found this so upsetting that the treatment never took off. Perhaps that was resistance, but a waiting room was an important requirement for him. Another friend was so put off by a waiting room that she never returned. Criticisms—too ostentatious, too sparse, no magazines, boring magazines, shared waiting rooms—can all be seen as symbolic of the patient's fears and needs.

Related matters, such as answering the telephone while in session or whether or not to take notes, must also be considered in the context of the needs of both parties, and it may be helpful to explore the patient's reaction to the decision. I find that note taking distracts me during a session. Many patients feel important when notes are taken; others find that it impedes needed eye contact. Many therapists jot down a few notes after a session or at the end of the day. Again, such issues may sound like beginner issues, but in fact they come up repeatedly, even for therapists of many years' experience.

TO TELL OR NOT TO TELL

Here a professional approach requires that the decision be made in the context of what will facilitate the therapy.

Questions are natural. A patient's curiosity provides a good opening in which the therapist can explain the idea of fantasy and support the patient's capacity for self-reflection. Every therapist has heard different versions of the following words:

> How can I have thoughts or feelings about you? I know nothing about you. If only I knew if you had children or were married or were ever divorced or used drugs or liked to cook or went to movies—then maybe I could trust that you'd understand me.

Therapists often have difficulty not answering personal questions; they fear that this is a deprivation that might damage the alliance. My experience has taught me that once the therapeutic attitude of not answering questions is explained logically, the patient feels safer and the treatment deepens. There may be exceptions to any guideline because each patient is unique and because different clinical situations require different responses. The stance of benevolent curiosity, however, usually saves the therapist from making uninformed decisions.

Mrs. T asked her therapist where a new lamp had been purchased. "I must have a lamp like that; where did you find it?" Therapist: "It would be so easy to answer—but your feelings and fantasies about it will tell us much more than any information I could give you." Mrs. T went on to describe in detail her own living room. This led to taking about her husband's criticisms of her taste. As she expressed her feelings about this, she began to see her wish to have a lamp like her therapist's as a way to counter her husband's criticism. Mrs. T had joined with the therapist's benevolent curiosity approach and realized that her original question had more to offer her than just a source of electrical fixtures. Helping a patient wonder about her curiosity is a far more giving act in the long run than diminishing that curiosity with information.

When a patient asks me a personal question, I explain as tactfully as I can that questions are very important to the work of understanding, but that answering personal questions or giving personal opinions would cut short an important learning opportunity. The opportunity is the patient's fantasy about the answer. I say something like: "Your questions are very important to me, and in a different setting it would be polite for me to answer them. Here, we want to learn about your thoughts and feelings. Your questions about me are valuable ways to explore them. It would be easy for me to answer, but in doing so I would be depriving you of a chance to wonder about me and picture me any way you want to." Such an explanation is basically reassuring to a patient. It says to her that there are boundaries, that this is not a social situation where politeness is required, and that her therapist is interested in helping her reflect. Offered early in treatment, it helps educate the patient about how the work is done.

A therapist's vacation may be particularly distressing when patients need to deny the separateness of the therapist—as their caretakers may have denied their separateness. The patient is faced with the irrefutable fact that she does not and cannot control the therapist and that the therapist has a separate life. But here, too, the fantasies that come up in the absence of "knowledge" may be very helpful in the work.

> In the first year of treatment, Nancy pictured me on an island with my children as my only company. (She would be visiting her parents.) The next summer, she sent me to London, specifically the Tate Gallery, where I would be studying the Turner seascapes. (Nancy was a painter and longed to visit the Tate Gallery herself. That summer she was going to the shore.) During the last summer of our work, Nancy let me plan my own vacation, and all she required was that I have fun. Taking away Nancy's opportunity for fantasy by giving her facts would have deprived her of the chance to work at her own pace and to understand her fantasies. As inner self and object representations soften, the patient's ability to see the therapist as separate increases. As envy, often hidden by inhibition, receded in Nancy's life, she became less controlling. She learned to value what she had, and her own talents blossomed.

There are some patients who cannot seem to tolerate a therapist's nondisclosing stance. At these times and with these patients, clinical judgment, common sense, and experience must guide us. Mrs. L suffered from separation anxiety so severe that it seriously disrupted her functioning. She was able to maintain stability by arranging weekly phone contacts.

It may seem a minor point, but if the therapist starts sharing personal information, how, when, and where does she draw the line? Telling a patient a little can be tantalizing, like saying "Take a peek, but only a peek." My preference is to give the patient the space to explore in fantasy where I go. When it appears that a patient really cannot tolerate not knowing, the therapist might say something like: "I will answer your question but can you work with it first? This way we will learn more than if I answer you quickly. Then, if you still feel that my answering will be helpful, I will."

A different kind of challenge occurred when I came down with a debilitating virus during one August break. I needed to regain my strength and did not return to work until a month after I had been due back. I told my patients over the phone that I would be taking another month, and I told them why. Each patient had a different reaction (besides hoping I would feel better soon). One M.D. I was treating was highly skeptical and threatened to leave unless I "told him the truth." It took him six months to realize that I was not lying; even then, he remained angry at being left out of my medical life. He wanted to make sure I was having the proper treatment—that is, he wanted to know if *he* would get the proper treatment. Another patient thought I was sicker than I had said—and he reviewed a time when he was six and his mother had stayed away longer than she planned to. He had felt betrayed and anxious and had become school phobic for a time. His fantasy that I was sicker than I said was an expression of anger at his feeling of betrayal. Some patients were so relieved when I returned that my being away seemed to be quickly forgotten. The following summer, however, one patient teased me, "Are you going to pull that virus excuse this year?" Beneath the question were serious concerns that she had kept to herself about my health.

Some therapists might not have mentioned the virus and just said that something had come up that required taking an extra month off. My self-disclosure in this case had roots in my own unconscious. My need to explain overshadowed their right to imagine. When a therapist makes a decision to disclose personal information, it is most helpful if she can analyze her decision to do so. I decided to tell the truth probably to make it easier on myself and on my patients. I wonder, if I had just said that something had come up, if I would have felt that I was depriving my patients. I know that they would have been angrier at me. The point is that there is no absolutely correct way for the therapist to "be" in the myriad situations that come up when working analytically—except to understand as best she can what motivates her and to preserve the frame whenever possible.

She must also take into account the fragility of the patient. With a patient who suffers from severe separation anxiety, the therapist might offer phone contact.

How many of us have never answered a personal question? Therapists who do psychoanalytic work understand the idea of abstinence, but most of us have answered a personal question or been tempted to offer advice. Experience is the best teacher, and what we learn from these experiences is that rather than helping the patient trust, these answers often do the opposite. If the therapist answers one question, why would the patient not expect all questions, or at least most, to be answered? If the therapist offers advice and the patient chooses not to take it, guilt, embarrassment, and shame may result. Answering questions, however well intended, diminishes the patient's room to wonder and to explore her own fantasies. I have heard patients ask questions and then reassure me that they really don't want me to answer.

Despite the current debate on "self-disclosure," in which some therapists advocate the sharing of personal information and others prefer a more traditional approach, it seems to me that if the therapist understands and respects the patient's right to imagine, she will look for the best ways of protecting that right.

BOUNDARIES

There may be exceptions to every policy, but there are no exceptions to the therapist's responsibility to pay attention to boundary issues. This does not mean that the therapist cannot reveal something about herself or her thinking at appropriate times in therapy: "I would be nervous walking home alone after midnight." "I would probably be angry if such and such happened." These comments can be used when the therapist senses that her patient is denying feelings or feeling alone.

Boundary violations have been the subject of many discussions in the psychoanalytic literature and at many meetings over the years. Recently, Gabbard et al. (2000) have written on the subject, and interest and consternation have grown as evidence accumulates that some very highly esteemed analysts have taken sexual advantage of their patients. Dr. R reports in her own words the following vignette of a patient who managed to provoke several analysts to overstep the bounds:

> In trying to think through what touching meant in psychoanalysis, I recalled a seminar from my student days. The senior analyst conducting that seminar responded to a question from a fellow student by saying that the student should respond to a patient who tried to hug him as she left a session by saying: "Ms. S?" His shocked manner and stepping back from the patient would convey all that was necessary. The senior analyst also counseled discussing the matter with the patient when she came in for her session the next day. None of us analysts-in-training dared to voice our doubts that she would come back the next day, or ever, if we shoved her out in that peremptory way. The senior analyst, I thought then, had plenty of patients. He could be cavalier about losing one. He had a great deal of experience. He could be sure that the transgression was the patient's fault. But I would not be so sure. And hugs between two women were different, weren't they? I wish that I could say that I had been brave enough to voice all that. Like my fellow students, I pitied the man who had had to ask the question, and felt grateful that I wasn't in his quandary. I never found out how it turned out.

Dr. R went on to say:

> I had ended my own analysis with a handshake after considering all sorts of alternatives—from a fantasy of hugging my analyst, to thanking him for the wonderful result I felt I had gotten, to crying so bitterly that he would not let me end. In the years that followed, few patients had even talked about touching me or having me touch them. Being a professional woman implied to me staying in my role as a professional, keeping the boundaries firm, and being compassionate toward patient's wishes for intimate physical contact while conveying the impossibility of it by the gestures of formality and politeness that would keep it from ever coming up. I made sure that I held the door open for patients as they came in and went out. I always stood up when a patient did. I sat only after indicating the chair or the couch for the other person. I believed that this conveyed the idea that I wanted to be the caretaker and that the patient could count on my setting the limits and taking responsibility.

Ms. V proved to be a challenge. A very troubled person since she was nineteen years old, she began treatment with a propensity to cling, to act babyish, and to demand attention. She had seen a male analyst for five years. During that time, she married, had a child, divorced, and completed college. Settled into a profession and busy caring for her baby as a single mother, she terminated analysis with a sense that she had gained a great deal out of the treatment. Several years later, not having found another husband, and feeling quite desperate about her chances for marriage and more children, she saw another male analyst for several years. That treatment ended badly when she accused the analyst of boundary violations and threatened to bring charges against him for those violations. The case was settled when he "voluntarily" agreed to retire and not to renew his license to practice.

The patient came to me for treatment when she was thirty-four. Her son was a late latency child at that time. Ms. V had begun to question her treatment of him. Because she was a single mother, she had enrolled him in an all boys' religious school where she thought he would have male role models and mentors. She still hoped to be able to remarry and have at least one more child, the little girl she had always wanted. Her goal was to find out what made this so difficult for her. In the course of our treatment, she related horrific tales of what had happened between her and her second analyst. He had pushed her out of the office when she refused to leave at the end of her sessions. He had pushed her to the floor when she attempted to sit on his lap. He had spoken to her on the telephone late at night when she was calling him from her bed. She would sometimes masturbate during these calls. She claimed that this was the only way she could fall asleep. She understood that all of these actions were boundary violations. I understood that she had provoked the man constantly and mercilessly. While I initially felt only horror and repulsion at these tales, I gradually came to understand what had happened. As she provoked me, I also came to feel sorry for myself having this tiger by the tail.

She was unable to tolerate the deprivation involved in our treatment when I would not touch her to push her out of the office when she refused to leave at the end of one of our sessions. After having to ask the patient who had the hour after hers to come back another time, I explained firmly that if she would not leave at the end of each session, I could not continue to treat her. She refused to leave (the next) session as well. I referred her to a colleague who had a more flexible attitude toward touch in the treatment situation. He believed that nonsexual touch would be healing for such a severely deprived person. They worked together for some months. She believed that she was not getting any better with his treatment, so she called me for another referral. The person I suggested turned out to be the same person (her current therapist) had suggested. That treatment lasted for another few years. Eventually she felt that it was not helping her enough either.

At that point she began to consult experts in all different forms of psychotherapy. She "recovered" memories of sexual abuse in an intensive treatment program for survivors of sexual abuse. She tried interpersonal therapists, intersubjectivists, and a self-psychologist. Each consultation ended with the same disappointment. She called and asked to come back into treatment with me. I told her that I would agree to see her in consultation with a possibility of treating her in analysis, on the couch, four times per week, with the intent of putting her feelings and thoughts into words. I also told her that I could provide no more than that. If she needed more, she was to go to someone else. If we could accomplish something working in that modality, I would be willing to work with her. I was not going to undertake to rescue her from her troubles if she needed anything more than (what I was offering) or anything different from that.

Ms. V agreed to those terms, came back into treatment, and immediately began provoking me by sitting up, turning around, reaching her hand out to touch me, bringing me presents, asking to take home bits of things from my office: a pencil, a ball-point pen, some Kleenex, a plastic cup from the bathroom. I told her each time that she could put her wishes into words and that I would think about their meanings with her, but that I could not provide anything more than words. She wept, said that I hated her, that she was valueless, that she had no right to live, that I despised her, that she was hopeless, that all I felt for her was hate, and that I wanted her to go away and leave me alone. I began to think that the last accusation had some truth to it.

Meanwhile, she told the tales of her intervening treatments. The first person she had seen after she saw me was a follower of Winnicott. He told her that she wanted infantile comfort. He assured her that it was nonsexual. He therefore allowed her to sit on the floor next to him with her head in his lap during her sessions. He told her that he was not allowed to touch her, but that she could touch him. She said that she had enjoyed their sessions, but grew tired of them when (it) became clear that he would not help her attain her goal of getting a husband. She believed that her work life was deteriorating as a result of her increasingly infantile behavior. According to her, (her therapist) acknowledged that they seemed to have reached a stalemate and (he) referred her to his mentor.

His mentor had more experience with severely regressed patients and had developed a technique that involved talking to her, but also accepting gifts of food and other things from her. He introduced her to his wife and children. He held her hand when she was frightened. After a few years, she believed that she had been integrated into that therapist's family as an extra child. Eventually she decided that he was exploiting her, and left him. Like all of her therapists, he had told her that she was extraordinarily gifted intellectually. In addition, he encouraged her to believe that all of her symptoms were the result of her very deprived and abusive early childhood. I told her that I could not understand why she would want treatment from me when I was so much more withholding and so discouraging to her. She insisted that I had helped her in the first treatment, and that it was only that I had gotten tired of her and her provocations that had led me to throw her out.

She continued to provoke me by putting her hand in my face, by begging me to touch her, by telephoning at all hours. In every way she could, she invited rejection.

During much of the treatment I thought about the feelings evoked by my having broken off the treatment the first time. I constantly brought our conversation back to the last day of the treatment, to how she had felt and what she had thought. Sometimes I wondered whether I was just being sadistic in doing that, but it did make some space in the room so that we could talk to each other about what was happening between us as well as how that connected with her other treatment experiences. She was the one to bring in experiences of her early life, and we both tried to connect those to that fateful day. Whenever things got too hot for her she would reach back over the pillow and I would see her hand coming toward me. (Once,) I told her that her only chance to mature was to put her wish to touch me into words rather than into action. She cried and threw the pillows from the couch, but she managed to settle down on it the next time.

Dr. R continued:

Of particular interest to me were the feelings she had when she was allowed to touch the other therapists. Just as she complained about everything and everyone, she also complained about the therapists who allowed her to do that. They, according to her, were not as smart as she was. They did not know that she was manipulating them. I recognized that this was just a variation of her theme of seducing the therapist into feeling superior to the other therapists and to her parents, a fairly common and often successful countertransference enactment. I could see how the therapists who wanted to be better parents than her parents got pulled into this kind of thing, and that I was getting pulled into it also. I told her that all of her carrying on was in the service of not talking about what she was worrying about. She insisted that she could not talk about it. I insisted that if she could not talk, I had nothing to offer her. Having read the literature on perversions and the literature on boundary violations, I believed that the greatest danger to the treatment was her insistence on provoking rescue fantasies in me. I thought that as long as I saw her as an extraordinarily bright and talented person, I was playing into her grandiosity and allowing my own grandiose fantasies to overrule my judgment. I decided that I had to think of her as one of many patients, probably someone who could be helped, but neither appreciably smarter nor appreciably worse off than the others.

This attitude on my part enraged her. She insisted that I was not believing what she told me. All of her previous therapists had thought she was extraordinarily smart. She mischievously said as she was leaving a session: "I almost got you to hold my hand that time. I am the smartest patient you have." I was shocked to hear myself saying: "What makes you think you are the smartest among my patients?" When I interpreted her rage about my not playing her game, she became even more enraged. "Oh, you think I am dumb. You think I am not as educated or as professionally advanced as your other patients. But that's because I am an animal to you. I am subhuman in your eyes. I don't deserve to live." The alternation between grandiosity and catastrophic loss of self-esteem was amazingly rapid and extreme.

Again and again she attempted to get me to prove that I did not want her dead or that I did not feel disgusted by her touching her. Again and again I pointed out how she left no middle ground for either herself or me. After I said that, she would send herself flowers, signing the card as if it came from me. She grew more insistent that we should be lovers as I interpreted to her that she both wanted and did not want such a thing to happen. I felt her behavior was a constant challenge requiring me to steer between the regression-inducing gratification of her wishes and the communication of fear or loathing that I believed would be wounding.

Dr. R's material explains clearly how difficult and frustrating this work can be. With some patients, no matter what a therapist does, she is doomed to fail in the patient's eyes. This vignette could easily have a place in the chapter on resistance, but the focus here is on the therapist's dilemma—she wants to make a difference, to help the patient change her pattern, but she must do it as a professional and not be seduced into boundary violations by an exaggerated sense of her own power. Some patients cause therapists to lose perspective and get caught up in a never-ending battle over boundaries. It is helpful to keep in mind that a patient who has compiled a list of therapists over the years will probably keep adding to it. "But," said Dr. R, "the efforts made by the many therapists involved with this woman were in fact useful and important to her. Therapy had kept her alive. Her son went to college, where he excelled." Perhaps no one can be sure precisely what helped, but the efforts made paid off. Dr. R's ability to set limits made her unique to this patient and gave her a measure of impulse control she had never had before.

GIFTS

Gifts from a patient pose another dilemma. I never want to insult a patient and I usually (not that I get many gifts!) say thank you. I then ask the patient to talk about the feelings behind the gift, because ours is not a social relationship and understanding is our goal. Expensive gifts are not acceptable ethically and must be analyzed and returned. Among other things, gifts can be:

- An expression of gratitude and love
- A cover for rage, envy, and spite
- A distraction
- A wish for reciprocal kindness
- A transitional object to be held by the therapist

The details of gift giving (Is it frequent? Are the gifts obviously inappropriate? Do they make the therapist uncomfortable?) along with the structure of the patient's ego must be taken into consideration and each case much be treated uniquely. One patient had been depressed for months over a breakup with her boyfriend. She cut herself off from her friends, withdrew from her usual activities, got poor reviews at work, and overate. But someone at her office got involved with origami, and the patient became fascinated. One day she brought me a paper bird she had made. I accepted it with a sincere thank you and kept it on my desk. It seemed to me that this gift did not need to be analyzed. We both knew that it meant many things, and that they would come out in time. This was an intuitive decision, but intuition is an important therapeutic tool, too.

THE THERAPIST'S ILLNESS

Illness is a most difficult dilemma. Whether in the therapist's family or in the therapist herself, it is always distracting. When the illness is something other than a flu, a cold, or the like (things usually obvious to the patient), the question of what to tell the patient is a serious one. There is no one rule because each potential problem is different and each dyad is unique. In *Deepening the Treatment* (1998), I discuss coming back from vacation with a broken ankle and a black eye. I told the patients who asked that I had had a bicycle accident. Each patient put her own spin on the information, and I learned that telling a patient the reality makes no difference. Fantasy takes center stage no matter what.

Illness in the therapist's life requires her to evaluate as best she can what her choices are.

- Does she need time off?
- Is the time off for a relative or for herself?
- Is she disabled? (Disability can mean anything from a broken leg to chemotherapy.)
- Is her appearance changing?
- Is the illness (family or self) incurable, temporary, in remission?
- Is she dealing with a death or the possibility of one?

There are many ways to think about such situations. Peer groups, personal therapy, supervision, and consultation can all be enormously helpful to the therapist. While such peer support is crucial, however, a therapist may hesitate to tell anyone about a personal illness if she fears that this will cost her necessary new referrals—another dilemma.

One danger to consider is that a patient's knowledge about the therapist's illness, or even illness in her family, can cause a role reversal. The patient's concern and empathy distract her from the work, and in some instances she might think of herself as the therapist's caretaker. It is a challenge to make certain that this doesn't happen. The other extreme can occur as well: the patient panics, gets angry, and leaves treatment abruptly. Ideally, a dialogue about the reality of the situation leads to a decision as to what is best for the patient. Whether it is the therapist or the therapist's loved one who is ill, there are so many variables (prognosis, time in recovery, degree of pain) that it is impossible to make rules and difficult to make suggestions.

It is the therapist's duty to be a professional, but how she can best accomplish that is up to her. Being a professional, in my mind, means keeping what's best for the patient in mind at all times. If the therapist decides that she cannot concentrate well enough to be of service to her patients, she must consider taking a break in treatment or referring them to someone else. If possible, this can be done over a period of time so as to gain some closure. Many patients harbor death wishes about their therapists, and learning of a serious illness may be traumatic for them. Work on magical thinking, guilt, and grandiosity must be done.

When a therapist is ill, her patients often sense it. But some therapists try to keep this personal issue to themselves, and I hear sometimes about a sick colleague who is keeping her patients in the dark, with no preparation for what might happen. In the case of serious illness, the patient has a right to know. That way, the dyad can—we hope—take an honest look at possible outcomes. It is imperative that the therapist be in supervision, treatment, or consultation at such times. A seriously ill therapist has too much on her mind to go it alone. Her family and friends already have much to contend with emotionally, and ethically the therapist cannot share her professional dilemmas with them in any case. Some institutes and societies have private committees for support and guidance. I would like to see more of these support groups in our profession.

When a therapist's loved one is ill or has died, personal time usually becomes necessary, and the therapist can tell the patient that a personal situation requires her to take time off. When this is a limited amount of time, the patient can usually wait to resume treatment.

The therapist has a private life and a professional life. We have been taught to keep these lives separate. But this is often impossible. Many therapists have offices in or attached to their homes. Other therapists play roles in the community or in the schools or in the training institute. It is rare today to maintain an isolated, private existence. So complete anonymity of the therapist is not, and never was, a realistic position. However, the less the patient knows about the therapist's real life, the more she can fantasize and imagine. These fantasies and imaginings are precious opportunities for learning.

JOYS

But psychotherapy is not only dilemmas. One of its joys is the opportunity to work with people on enriching their lives. Needless to say, the process also enriches the therapist's life. Hearing and deciphering the unconscious is learning a new language, and it is enormously gratifying to both parties in the dyad. Both parties are involved in an ongoing learning process.

Teaching and supervising are another kind of learning experience, and they, too, play an important and exciting part in the therapist's life. Connecting with students is enormously fulfilling—each class or seminar teaches the teacher that there is more to learn. The greatest joy is to be in a field where learning never stops.

❖ CHAPTER 8 ❖

Stalemates and Beyond

What we see is a mechanism that entices others to give a particular sort of response, a response that must be wish-fulfilling in the sense that all object relations involve wishes, not only for instinctual gratification, but also for particular sorts of affirmation. The sadomasochistic patient needs the sadomasochistic dialogue, not only to gratify his sadistic and masochistic wishes, but also to secure the good feelings and safety that accompany the actualization of a wishful fantasy based on an internalized childhood relationship.

—Joseph Sandler and Ann-Marie Sandler

The most difficult roadblock of all, as discussed in chapter 5, is the need to hold on to internalized sadomasochistic object relationships. Only when more benign relationships temper the negative or bad objects, gradually taking their place and putting them to rest, can the patient begin to relinquish the need for pain. Realistically, this need is probably never completely eradicated, but with hard work the masochism can abate. The struggle requires patience and empathy on both sides of the couch. Shengold (2000) asks "Is there life without mother?" and explains how, when the internalized parent has been abusive or neglectful, the child's attachment to pain is incredibly strong. But for those people who find their way to a therapist's office, there is also a wish for something better. The therapist must understand and tolerate the competition, using all her strength not to throw in the towel. The patients discussed in this chapter, Mr. M, Ms. S, and Ms. L, were all headed for stalemates. When the terrain becomes rugged, the journey becomes arduous for both the patient and the therapist. The therapist's ability to work with the transference/countertransference and to endure, coupled with the patient's own endurance and willingness to do the work, can often break through the roadblocks that are intrinsic to the psychoanalytic journey. Sometimes, however, when there are insurmountable roadblocks on either side of the couch, treatment fails. The point I want to make is that as difficult, and at times impossible, as psychoanalytic work is, as antagonistic and negative as the transference/countertransference may become, the patient internalizes the therapist's effort even when treatment ends prematurely.

THE CASE OF MR. M

> Mr. M is tall, dark, and nice looking. He was referred for individual psychotherapy by his marriage counselor, and he accepted the referral to appease his wife. His wish for "something better" had to remain hidden because of his pride. To admit that something was wrong was just not done, at least not by men in his country of birth. Skeptical and unmotivated, he began treatment once a week, often cancelling and frequently coming late. After several months, the therapist began to lose interest in what seemed to be a hopeless case—this was partially a countertransference reaction alerting her to her own narcissistic injury and also a projective identification of Mr. M's deep anxiety, as well as experience—and told Mr. M that unless he increased his sessions and came regularly, he would continue to come late and cancel sessions, until he eventually quit. This candidness caught his attention and piqued his interest, and for a while he began to work.

What happened? Why the change? Looking at the situation from a transference point of view, Mr. M had felt pushed into treatment by two women (his wife and marriage counselor). He experienced the referral to yet another woman (the therapist) as a narcissistic blow. By pretending to acquiesce, he could express his anger at all three women. He was actually saying to the therapist: "I don't want or need to come here, because therapy implies I have something to learn. Since I am perfect, and since you don't seem to understand that, I will come here when it's convenient in order to appease my wife." Yet it seemed to the therapist that he was also saying: "Maybe I'm *not* perfect. Maybe the pain and anxiety I keep so hidden from myself could go away. I do need help. I do need to feel someone cares. But how frightening such thoughts are!" The therapist suspended judgment and remained curious.

> Six months went by. Interpreting this ambivalence acted out by being late or absent went nowhere. Mr. M always had a reason that made sense to him. The therapist's patience was tested, and though she was in her chair waiting for her patient at the time appointed for every session, she felt provoked and thought about giving up. Her wish to do the work she was qualified and prepared to do was being ignored. It was at these times that Mr. M, sensing his therapist's interest waning, would come on time, bringing important material and looking at it with a psychological eye. He was in effect saying, "Look, I can do this work, but don't count on me."
>
> Time and again, he would seduce the therapist into thinking she had a patient, and time and again he would run away. This seduction was interpreted over the years by both patient and therapist. After a particularly moving or interesting session, Mr. M would say, "What if I'm fooling us again?" or "Here I go again" or "We've been here before."

The therapist understood this behavior on several levels: as characterological anal stubbornness, fear of regression, narcissistic defense, anxiety on all levels, sadomasochistic excitement, and revenge. Explaining again that analytic work required frequency and regularity, the therapist gently, and finally firmly, interpreted the enactment and invited the patient to continue treatment on a regular basis so that it would be of benefit to him. She recommended psychoanalysis at this point because she felt that twice-a-week sitting-up treatment was not going to reach Mr. M. Character work requires intensive treatment, and Mr. M agreed to a four-times-a-week schedule and to using the couch.

> Mr. M accepted the invitation to begin psychoanalysis. He was able to hear the therapist's empathy and to sense her confidence in the clinical judgment on which she based her recommendation. But he also sensed unconsciously an opportunity to continue his sadomasochistic style. Beneath his wish to comply with a rational recommendation by the therapist and his

tentative, superficial interest in learning about himself, there was a private grandiose world filled with vengeful motives. (His country of birth had a strict code of revenge.) He protected himself from anxiety (about separation, loss of love, loss of object) by connecting superficially or with a charm that covered up hatred. He projected his hatred so that he became the victim, while his partner (his wife, therapist, or business associate) expressed the anger. These sadomasochistic interactions kept him feeling alive, attached, and secure in the status quo.

Mr. M had four older brothers and one older and one younger sister. He spent his first five years on a desolate farm. The family slept in one room with various siblings sharing beds. Mr. M reported that the custom was to bind the infants at bedtime for the first year of life. Beneath the house was the stable for livestock. The family used an outhouse. His early memories consist of playing in the dirt with a stick while the others were off working in the fields. His older sister, twelve years his senior, was his primary caretaker. Bathing, toilet training, and feeding him were her chores, and Mr. M remembered his humiliation when she taunted him about his penis being so small. In general, Mr. M felt that he was regarded as one more mouth to feed. As a toddler, he managed to amuse the family and developed a clown-like facade. Pleasing others to get attention was a survival skill, but it came at the cost of resentment, rage, and stubbornness. Several of his older brothers had a charm he described as a veneer, but one brother he described as being like an animal. This brother kept to himself and was famous for his raging temper and his brutality. Everyone thought of the oldest sister as crazy. Grabbing people's crotches was her way of showing affection. The youngest sister later mistreated her children by letting them grow up without attention or consistency. She was oblivious to their needs, and they became troubled and uncontrollable.

Over the years of treatment, Mr. M's descriptions of his childhood and his siblings painted a portrait of neglect and sadistic teasing. He regularly witnessed the slaughter of livestock, and one day when a neighbor complained that he had been bitten by the family dog, Mr. M's father killed the dog with an ax in front of the children to appease the neighbor.

Mr. M was masquerading as a docile, unpretentious, likable man, but underneath this image lay murderous rage. He was driven by an unconscious wish for revenge, and spite was the way he accomplished it. In treatment, Mr. M's expectations were based on his history with preoccupied and disinterested people who often treated him cruelly; always in trouble, he nevertheless managed to hang on to his innocent facade (see chapter 6).

> He and his family came to this country when he was five. He learned to speak English in school and generally fended for himself. He did not realize until after many years of work in treatment how angry he was about the torment and neglect he had suffered as a child. His repressed, rage-filled fantasies were projected onto his object world and affected those around him. Although he was apparently successful in hiding the rage from the world and from himself, in his masochistic lifestyle it was possible to discern the character formation of a silent destroyer. From team sports to career to marriage to fatherhood, he set people up to be disappointed in and devastated by him. As his marriage deteriorated, he was forced to look inside himself.

Unsurprisingly, he treated the analyst as he had been treated—seductively and destructively. He projected his inner self and object representations onto the therapist, who found herself beginning to experience his rage for him. In this way, he maintained his innocent bystander pose. This angry countertransference made it difficult for her to empathize with this patient. He could not tolerate any success. He carelessly lost work, then blamed it on his secretary before finally taking responsibility by saying, "I know I messed up, but I can't seem to do anything about it." Situations such as this frustrated both him and his therapist, whose benign curiosity became difficult to sustain. Her interpretations were greeted with "I know you're right, I can feel you're right, but I can't help it." Beneath these admissions was another message to the therapist: "You're useless, a failure, impotent to help me." As interpretations failed, confrontation became the main type of intervention. Years passed before he caught on to his own game, and more years passed while he recognized and fought his wishes for revenge. To wreak his vengeance he had to sacrifice his own emotional life and risk whatever good was in it. But finally as he began to see that he was repeating with his children and wife what he remembered experiencing himself, he seemed ready to turn a corner in his life.

Mr. M's vengeance, rage, and despair now became the focus in treatment. At times, the analyst was the object of his hatred and mistrust, and the transference became a battleground. Mr. M felt that he and the therapist were involved in a game. He would appear reflective and insightful, providing interesting material and making connections; then he would go on strike. The therapist would become disappointed and angry at this man who showed so much potential and then destroyed his chances—and hers—to do the work. Coen says about sadomasochistic excitement:

> The patient disclaims responsibility for his behavior. He plays the sadomasochistic game with the analyst, who is to try to stop him—or become so frustrated, angry, hopeless, and defeated that she is unable to help the patient. What is dissociated here is the patient's difficulty with autonomy and self-regulation and acknowledgement of the serious destructiveness imbedded within such sadomasochistic game playing. The excitement of the game denies the seriousness of the intended destructiveness. (Coen, 1988, pp. 51–52)

Two weeks before both therapist's and patient's planned vacations, Mr. M brought on a marital crisis by staying out late one too many times and not calling his wife. This was not new behavior, and this time his wife withdrew and began staying out late herself, seeing her old boyfriend. This state of affairs threw Mr. M into a panic. He expressed his love to his wife, who rejected it and him. His desperation led to a change in his behavior at home; he did chores that he had neglected and gladly took care of his children. He told the therapist that he was cured, that his character was transformed. He tried getting his wife into pastoral counseling at the church. She would have none of it. The tables had turned, and Mr. M began expressing his anger at the analyst. At first, he was horrified at himself, but when he saw the therapist's tolerance and ability to stay alive, he let loose. The therapist became a witch, a taskmaster, an unfeeling bitch: "You have no answers, you can't fix my life, you're worthless." During this period, Mr. M had images of himself as a young boy and of the revenge he wished to take. These pictures were devoid of feeling—like a movie with no soundtrack. The defensive isolation of affect was prevalent in the work.

Mr. M: I left in time—I had the car, there was traffic, but I still had time to get here. I was on the car phone and hit another car. I wondered if this was because I was avoiding being here on time. . . . I planned the whole day to get here and I looked forward to it. [Silence.] That's really frightening. I'm feeling paranoid—terror, not being in control, about to lose control.

Therapist: You're afraid to lose control with me—to hurt me—because of the vacation.

Mr. M: It sucks—I'm scared . . . feel alone, not really abandoned because logic kicks in. As a kid I felt it. I can feel my mom going to work—we needed the money—I understood she had to leave.

Therapist: You understood in one way but you felt abandoned as you do now.

Mr. M: Intense pain, kicking the dirt, kicking myself—like today. Wanted to be here but no. I let you wait. Have an image of you stepping away—hugely angry at you. How can you choose something over me? I need help and you're walking away. You don't see I need help—she didn't see I needed her. I feel blind rage, tantrum. I'm just getting to something and you leave. . . . I'm going to start swearing. I'll be here (his wife cancelled the vacation), toiling in my own mess. As a child with a grass skirt—steeped in my mess. Fuck you all! Anger across the board. It scares me when you say I destroy this work by not being here. How do you expect me to be on time? You're supposed to be here when I need you. It's like a parallel conversation: one with me and one with a child. Afraid of the bigness of things—the sky, the house, I see myself as small—there are wolves, bulls, and snakes. Scared to be alone. So happy when she comes back. I picture myself coming here and the door is closed 'cause you're away. Turning away so sad . . . alone. [Silence.] I have an urge to leave now. My thoughts went to the office and work. . . . Fine, you go away. I don't need you, I hate you. Would kick you if I could—throw rocks at you as you leave. I'll be fine—can't let you know. Where the hell are you going? See what a monster I am? It's better to be the mummy—all wrapped up and safe.

This is an example of how emotions set off by a planned vacation resonate with a childhood filled with loneliness. The regression frightened Mr. M, but he finally experienced a glimpse of rage with the therapist and connected it to his mother.

This session enabled the patient to begin understanding his rage. The "mummy," on the one hand, was wrapped securely and felt no pain; the mummy could not fragment; the mummy was safe; the mummy was him, wrapped as a baby, and the mummy was his mum. By being like her (unpredictable in his eyes), he could be with her. The "monster," on the other hand, was obscene. "He devoured raw meat, chewed up anything in sight like an alligator. He dismembered corpses. He smelled rotten from rolling in feces. He was a killer." The monster came forth in dreams and for brief moments on the couch. But mostly the mummy was in charge. Mr. M was frightened of his monster side, and the bulk of the therapy consisted of interpreting the grandiosity that hid the loneliness, rage, and impotence of his childhood. Mr. M recognized the importance of sessions during which he let himself have feelings—but then he began withdrawing again. This happened repeatedly. Whenever there seemed to be a glimmer of hope or forward movement, the conscious resistance of lateness and many missed sessions would begin. Procrastination was Mr. M's favored expression of anger. This was a character trait that enraged those around him, and so let Mr. M experience his anger vicariously instead of expressing it directly. He was always promising and always disappointing.

After more than five years, Mr. M and the therapist began assessing his ability to continue in treatment. Although the therapist was able to tolerate and interpret the situation for periods of time, soon enough she began to feel her own anger again, along with the anger projected by the patient. She informed him of her frustration, telling him once more that analysis was useless unless he came to his sessions (he would cancel weeks at a time). Mr. M agreed and began another cycle of seduction. "I know you're right. I can't give this up. I know I can do this. I know I am capable." He arrived promptly for a week. Thoughts and fantasies about the therapist were expressed in a monotone voice: "I can't feel. I see these images, but there is no emotion. I picture choking you, breaking your bookcases, smashing the wall, fucking you." These pictures had no emotional sound track. They were like frozen cartoons. Were the pictures meant to please the therapist—to supply what he thought she expected—or were they progress, even a beginning attempt to feel? Memories of childhood were revisited—himself as a young boy, alone, despondent, abandoned.

The work became once again engrossing and moving, and it was impressive in content (although devoid of affect)—but once again the lateness and absence began. The patient was well aware of his provocative style and of his fear. He realized, intellectually, that he repeated in treatment what had been done to him as a child. He repeated the seductions and abandonments, letting the therapist know how helpless and discouraged he was. Mr. M saw that he was taunting the therapist and destroying himself. He provoked his wife repeatedly and confused his children by adoring them and then abandoning them. This pattern was repeated time after time and year after year. His wife continued to see another man, and Mr. M was shocked into reforming, but it was too late. The marriage ended.

Mr. M's emotionless spree of teasing, anxiety, hatred, fear of closeness, and rage threatened every aspect of his life. The therapist continued to invite her patient to explore his actions—to put them into words—but he hung on to his monster/mummy image, unable to really feel or trust anyone. The therapist, indeed angry and saddened after years of seduction and withdrawal, interpreted the sexual implications of this behavior as a deep hatred of women, reviewing his sister's castrating behavior and his mother's absences, connecting this to the analyst. His foreplay ended with impotence. The therapist attempted to remove herself from the enactment time after time, interpreting instead: "You are trying to torture me as you felt tortured, by not participating in therapy." "You are in a lifelong tantrum that protects you from feeling deep sadness." However, interpretations fell flat because Mr. M understood only on an intellectual level and, as he said himself: "I agree. I can't believe I can't do this analysis. But each time we get to this point I show up for a few days and lift our hopes."

The therapist, feeling useless, punished, abused, and angry, finally issued an ultimatum. She explained yet again that therapy could not continue without his presence and that she would discontinue treatment at the end of the month (three weeks hence) unless the patient came to his sessions regularly and on time. But Mr. M dealt with the threat of loss by beginning an affair with an adoring woman in another city, and the treatment ended.

Mr. M's narcissistic defenses protected his status quo. He said to the therapist, through his actions, that if she could not accept him unconditionally, he would find someone who could.

The therapist, for her part, was responding both masochistically and sadistically. Putting up with this patient was painful and frustrating. However, her refusal to give up can be seen as a test of wills. Her unwillingness to believe she could lose the battle was part grandiosity, part stubbornness, part caring, and part not being sure what to do. In summary, one can hope that both parties learned something about perseverance, empathy, and constancy and acted-out rage.

Negative therapeutic reaction, perverse transference, and an *unanalyzable patient* are some of the terms that could be used to explain what was going on in this analysis. But such clinical phrases do not make clear that what was happening was an attempted murder/suicide (Bird, 1972). A potentially life-enhancing process became the opposite. The closer Mr. M came to recognizing his rage, the more he ran from this recognition, acting his anger out instead. His grandiosity, his omnipotence, and his power to defeat were the only lifelines he could see. Intellectually, he understood (to some degree) that he was afraid to give up his grandiosity. It had protected him from suicide. Altering his character defenses meant the death of all he was and all he knew. Analysis meant modifying his internalized self and object representations as he explored the unconscious fantasies of power he used to regulate his anxieties. The absence in his childhood of a caring, steady, loving person made it impossible to hope for more. And, as Sandler and Sandler (above) pointed out, the very same neglectful early objects are clung to.

One year after Mr. M's analysis ended, he called his therapist. Phone tag went on for a week, until the therapist finally reached Mr. M in his office. An appointment was made for the following week and unsurprisingly cancelled a few days later. It turned out that Mr. M was angry about having to wait so long for the first appointment; this was a cover for his anger about the ending of the analysis. Another appointment was scheduled, but already the therapist was consciously wondering whether to reengage with Mr. M. The game had already begun. Mr. M came to his appointment on time, complaining that his life was a mess. He was disorganized and depressed. He was still alienating friends, business associates, and family, and his ex-wife was taking him to court for not paying child support. He spent a night in jail for this.

The therapist was in a quandary. She realized that Mr. M was out of money, prideful about it, and stuck. Unsure of whether she should see him again, her curiosity won out. But in his next appointment, a week later, he was late. He talked about it. He couldn't decide if this was his doing (he'd left plenty of time) or if it was accidental. Like his cancellation of the first session (his partner had to attend a funeral), he claimed, it was out of his hands. The therapist, feeling impatient but still curious, reminded him that this matched his pattern of letting himself and others down while disconnecting himself from his actions. Mr. M's angry response was palpable as he accused the therapist of not liking him. The therapist had to ask herself why she kept persevering, and she thought that it was some combination of not wanting to give up, pity, hatred, her own masochism, and on some level, her horror at the story of this man's childhood. As provoked as she felt, she had invested years of time, energy, and hope in Mr. M, and seeing him depart affected her deeply.

So the sadomasochistic enactment continued. As before, he made himself unlikable and then blamed others for it. Other times, he dropped the "mess" in the therapist's lap. "What should I do?" he would say. He saw a psychopharmacologist in consultation, but never followed through.

The roadblocks in this treatment were ever present, yet the patient and therapist continued the journey. The sadomasochistic connections continued as the therapist did her best to hold on. By letting the treatment continue, she was forced to reflect on her own conflicted wishes as they informed her decisions in this treatment situation. She wondered about her part in the masochistic and sadistic interactions that had become such a familiar pattern in the work with Mr. M, and she knew that she would have to monitor carefully these and other aspects of her countertransference responses to Mr. M. But she also knew that along the way, as his world began to close in on him, he had begun to experience pain, for perhaps the first time. She would have to separate her own fears and anger from those of Mr. M, distinguishing her past from his.

The therapist must remember that an adult survivor of childhood abuse—of which neglect is one form—will never fully trust another (chapter 5). To realize that there *is* another is in itself a major achievement. The act of differentiating causes great pain, but this pain can lead to growth; undifferentiated pain, by contrast, must be repeated time after time and is therefore stunting.

Negative attention is nevertheless attention. Positive attention cannot be trusted because it will not last. Such reasoning leads wary patients to guard against feelings of closeness. Closeness means danger and is to be avoided. Creating a collaborative atmosphere or a working alliance can take years of steady, patient work, and it may never happen. Therapeutic collaboration may seem like a war zone at times of intense negative transference, but if both are engaged in the analytic process, a collaboration exists. In some cases, meeting regularly is the only sign of an alliance (see Mr. F in chapter 2).

> But with Mr. M, the analytic process was constantly hampered. After six months of weekly sessions, with the usual cancellations, Mr. M took a job in another city. He was excited about making a fresh start in a job that he felt suited him very well. He was aware that his pattern did not predict success, but he experienced this as a step up and a good sign. He bounced a check for his last two sessions and asked the therapist to redeposit it when he called to cancel his last appointment before the therapist's vacation. The therapist left for vacation and there was no goodbye.

It remains to be seen when—or whether—Mr. M will be back.

THE CASE OF MS. C

The case of Ms. C illustrates the formidable roadblock of rage projected onto the therapist.

> Ms. C keeps me from being separate by forbidding me to have my own thoughts about anything. She gets angry when I suggest another way of understanding. On some level, she can see what I mean, but if she lets me pursue my own vision, she allows me to be separate. This feels unsafe, and so we inch toward separateness over years of continuous, steady treatment. Her use of marijuana is multidetermined. The drug relaxes her and gives her a feeling of being tuned in to the world, but it exacerbates the paranoia and she pushes people away. This gives her a feeling of control over her feared "craziness." At the same time as she feels close to merger with the object, she makes distance by projecting onto it her own rage and criticism. This replicates a childhood of wishes for loving and reliable caretakers and fears of loss and abandonment. When she does not use marijuana, she can begin to see her role in pushing others away.

The need to hold on to a familiar past prevents Ms. C from growing. Inch by inch, she tries to trust and connect, but with every gain there is a backward slide. Years are devoted to this struggle. It is like relearning after a stroke. The brain makes new connections; the muscles gain tone. But it all takes time and consistent work within a steady frame.

THE CASE OF MS. S

The use of a "recreational" drug, whether it be cocaine, marijuana, or alcohol, may be seen as self-medication and so should alert the therapist to the presence of severe pain. Telling a patient to stop as a condition of treatment is rarely helpful. Understanding with a patient what the drug means to her, how it alleviates her pain, and what the pain actually is are better approaches that over time lead to a working alliance and avoid a power struggle. When the therapist respects the patient's attempts to negotiate life, and when she can replace her critical tendencies with benign curiosity, the patient is less likely to reject her overtures. If the patient sees the drug as a necessary crutch, the therapeutic journey can begin with an exploration of that. Only when the crutch prohibits travel is it necessarily a roadblock.

A case presented by Dr. K demonstrates that, although a behavioral approach is useful and often necessary in work with substance abusers, there is also need for a psychoanalytic component. High relapse rates underscore the need to target the roots of conflict. Despite the time-limited nature of most community-based drug clinic treatments, such an approach can make a deep impact on patients struggling to work through the traumas of their formative years.

Informed by the theoretical and clinical insight gained from institute training, Dr. K began listening to Ms. S's stories with an ear attuned differently from any other in the patient's past experience. Her psychoanalytic lens enabled her to view Ms. S's constant flights and drug-induced highs as efforts to defend against the loneliness, pain, and rage she could not express in words.

Ms. S was a Native American/African American in her mid-thirties. She entered drug treatment for alcohol and cocaine addiction as a condition of regaining custody of her three youngest children, who had been in foster care with her mother for the past two years after they were taken from Ms. S on the grounds of neglect. Ms. S had begun drinking alcohol and smoking marijuana in adolescence, and she developed a cocaine habit in her mid-twenties; by age thirty, she was inhaling cocaine on an almost daily basis. She had called her mother for help after suffering a "breakdown" and was hospitalized for a short time. She had been in two different treatment programs before coming to the clinic, but had been discharged from both because of what had been described as her "acting out" behavior.

Ms. S had been raised in New York City by her maternal grandmother, seeing her mother only on weekends. Nearby, but a thousand emotional miles away, her mother was raising her three siblings (an older full brother and two younger half-sisters). When Ms. S was ten, she met her father formally for the first time. He had come to visit several times before, but no one had told her that he was, in fact, her father. She immediately became very attached to him, spending weekends and summers with him over the next two years. At age twelve, after she told her mother that she wanted to live with him, she was sent down South to stay for a short time with a relative. Two weeks after her departure, her father, then thirty-four, died of an epileptic seizure caused or aggravated by his alcoholism. Ms. S said that a part of her died with him. When she returned to the city, she moved in with her mother, only to be sexually abused by her stepfather, who was also as-

> saulting her mother on a regular basis. After enduring daily abuse for three months, she "ran away" to her grandmother's but was eventually sent back to live with her mother, who refused to believe that she had been sexually molested.
>
> Ms. S had a history of "running away" from things when they proved too much for her: family, men, jobs, therapy. Her work at the clinic was no exception. She bolted from therapy twice, the first time about six months into treatment following the therapist's absence for a week's vacation and the second time following a brief but inevitable disruption at the time of the World Trade Center disaster.

Dr. K was able to resolve the first treatment break, which was accompanied by an alcohol and cocaine relapse, by a gentle but firm insistence that Ms. S come in to talk about what had happened. Dr. K reported that after examining her own feelings, it became apparent that, in Ms. S's view, Dr. K had assumed the expected role in a sadomasochistic enactment—Ms. S was hoping to be coaxed back following a display of disruptive behavior that she knew would worry and disturb Dr. K.

Ms. S had early on become very attached to Dr. K, who seemed to represent her father in the transference; she became frightened and then enraged by the anticipation of devastating loss. She was reliving the drama by provoking a separation with Dr. K, acting out a memory that she was not able to verbalize.

Dr. K recognized the countertransferential feelings of worry, anger, and helplessness that ensued when Ms. S abruptly left treatment. This enabled her to interpret Ms. S's flight and use of drugs as "an attempt to avoid the rage she was experiencing and to defend against further loss." Dr. K also noted:

> At the time, Ms. S largely resisted this attempt to engage her in an exploration of the anger she was projecting, but she did agree to return to treatment. "I don't see it," she said with a sheepish, satisfied grin, "but if you think it will help, I'll give you another chance."

It is not unusual for a patient with a history of abuse to deny feelings of rage, which may be expressed in self-injury or in frustrating the therapist. The object representation internalized as part of the self is impossible to give up. The best the therapist can do is to modify the attachment by providing a new object with whom to identify.

Ms. S's addiction masked the losses and the subsequent depression she had experienced in her formative years. Drug or alcohol abuse is essentially a passive response by the ego to conflict and loss; it provides an illusion, albeit short lived, of power and control. Cocaine and alcohol highs defended Ms. S against the dangers of closeness, separation, and rage (Hall, 1998). By facilitating identification with a neglectful, narcissistic mother and an absent, alcoholic father who surrendered to their own emotions, drug use also represented an attempt to recapture the lost objects and thereby ward off depression. This is an example of how masochistic behavior and the symptom of drug abuse may be indicators of buried rage—an unverbalized, acted-out anger that often ends the treatment.

The second break was complicated by the fact that Ms. S had witnessed the 9/11 terrorist attack from a bus on her way to work in the downtown financial center. The sight of its horrors had retraumatized her, and she isolated herself in her apartment, located in the same downtown area, for approximately two weeks before calling to say she had decided to hospitalize herself for symptoms of post-traumatic stress. Dr. K, who hadn't been able to reach Ms. S during the intervening weeks because of the shutdown of phone service in the area, supported her decision and told her that she would be waiting for her when she got out. In the past, Ms. S had welcomed the "rest" of a psychiatric hospital stay, but this time she checked herself out after a few days, feeling, she said, that she didn't "belong there anymore." She returned to treatment the next day.

The world-shattering events of 9/11 seemed to have shifted her perspective, and Ms. S became more reflective about the quality and meaning of her life and more responsive to Dr. K's attempts to direct her anger into the transference, toward a new object that could contain and not be destroyed by her rage (Hall, 1998). Thus began a new chapter in the treatment process. For the first time, Ms. S was able to acknowledge her anger at Dr. K for not being there in her time of crisis, for not protecting her in her time of desperate need. Reflecting some measure of self–object differentiation, she also acknowledged that her fantasy of rescue was, given the na-

> ture and magnitude of the event, a wish that could not realistically have been fulfilled. In subsequent sessions, she began to voice the longing that she felt for her mother's unconditional love and the deep disappointment she experienced, over and over, as a result of her mother's inability to empathize with her needs.

Other smaller breaks also occurred during the treatment.

> One occurred after Dr. K's absence over an extended holiday weekend. Ms. S did not appear or call the entire next week. When she did come back, she initially denied any anger toward Dr. K, but with some encouragement she was eventually able to talk about feeling abandoned and alone, even though, she felt obligated to point out, Dr. K was "entitled to a day off once in a while." She was able to verbalize feelings of wanting to hurt Dr. K by "picking up" (using cocaine) and disappearing for a while, "to get even." She reluctantly described a fantasy she had been nursing of confronting the therapist with bitter accusations of blame for her relapse and being greeted with the therapist's extreme contrition for having caused her so much pain. Her discomfort at revealing her feelings seemed to ease with Dr. K's acknowledgment of how very difficult it must have been for her to put her true feelings into words and how much progress it revealed. She was then able to go on to talk about how an incident with her mother over the weekend had triggered her anger, and how alone and "little" she had felt. This time she had not resorted to drug use to mask her rage, believing, she said, that she would only have ended up hurting herself.

Dr. K saw these illustrations of Ms. S's acting out in the treatment as a reaction to her feelings of abandonment by her two narcissistic parents, her sense of loss, and the lack of individuation that was the result. Dr. K noted: "Like so many others addicted to drugs and alcohol, Ms. S entered treatment lacking a stable self-image and a sufficiently self-observing ego, and treatment was an effort to engage her in a self-reflective process that would enable her to put words to her thoughts and emotions and, over time, strengthen her ego capacity to self-regulate. While working with abused, addicted individuals is almost always an uphill battle, it can be gratifying when even small advances in the treatment occur."

THE CASE OF MS. L

This next case illustrates how a serious stalemate, encountered three years into treatment, can be overcome by a deeper attention to the transference. Ms. L had been in once-a-week treatment for three years. She was a successful businesswoman, but lived a lonely life with no friends and no outside interests. She was obese, although she had lost weight at different times during treatment. Both therapist and patient were growing bored and impatient; they had lost hope and interest and were feeling restless and angry. A typical stalemate. The patient would fall asleep at times. She complained that therapy was going nowhere. Was she right? What was keeping it frozen?

The consultant on the case felt that the stalemate in an otherwise productive treatment was the result of neglect of the transference. The patient was attached to her therapist, and although she had been threatening to end the treatment, she continued to attend sessions regularly and on time. The patient appeared to be conflicted about going deeper, and the consultant thought that the therapist might be as well. Ambivalence about holding on and letting go was preventing movement of any sort. In short, the consultant felt that a transference/countertransference enactment existed.

A process recording yields clues: references to a new doorman in the therapist's building—who seems friendly and better looking than the last one—suggest the wish for a flirtation.

Ms. L: He's so good looking and I think he remembers me from last week. I wonder what he thinks about me and why I come here.

The consultant suggests to the therapist that she listen for other variations on the theme of being remembered and curiosity in general, and that she reflect with her patient on the transference meaning. In this case, the therapist introduced the idea of transference by saying, "The doorman is the person you see right before you see me. Sometimes feelings about others also refer to me."

It evolves that the patient is feeling curious about the therapist, but has sensed the therapist's lack of interest (both projective identification and induced countertransference, or the therapist's own personal transference) and is worried. She wonders if the therapist is still interested in her.

Ms. L: I have been thinking that you're bored with me. I'm feeling so unattractive and I can't imagine that you remember what I say from session to session.

Using the reference to the doorman, the therapist has opened a door to the transference/countertransference aspect of the treatment.

Therapist: Lately, our work feels flat—like we're on a plateau. And although it feels safe, it can also feel boring. You seem to doze at times, and I find myself doodling.

Ms. L admits to feeling disappointed and blames herself for feeling stuck. She has just turned forty and wants more out of therapy.

Therapist: I think coming here more often will help you get things rolling. How would you feel about that?
Ms. L: Well, something's gotta give—but what if it stays boring?
Therapist: If you say what comes to mind as it comes to mind, no one will be bored.
Ms. L: Nothing interesting—I just go blank.
Therapist: The mind is never blank, but such a feeling might mean that there are thoughts about me going on.
Ms. L: Well, I did notice the last patient—she was crying and I thought maybe you hurt her feelings.
Therapist: Hmm.
Ms. L: She looks like my old neighbor in high school—the most popular girl in town—I envied her to death. [Ms. L describes the neighbor and the hour goes quickly.]

This vignette shows how the doorman comment was useful when brought into the treatment. Some might see it as resistant and looking outside for distraction, and maybe this is true on one level. But the therapist used the information to deepen the work by thinking of the transference meaning. The here and now doorman/therapist who seems interested and curious (as is the patient) leads to mention of the therapist's last patient and to the past. Future work about envy, attraction to men, and feelings about the therapist will be made easier with more frequent sessions. A dying treatment is brought to life. The journey continues and the stalemate is overcome—for now.

STAYING THE COURSE

I have heard therapists express the belief that certain clinic patients, such as drug abusers, seem to make little or no progress in treatment. Yet having worked with and supervised many such cases, I cannot so easily dismiss the potential of psychotherapy. Therapists may become disillusioned when patients won't do the work—when they sit silently or barely interact. But when a patient keeps appointments regularly, it is a sure sign that he or she is taking in something soothing or comforting, whether or not this is ever acknowledged. Some therapists sit tight, waiting for a sign of connection, as with Mr. F and his therapist Ms. O sitting by the side of the road in chapter 2. Others lose interest completely or, sensing the patient's despair, want to distance themselves from it. But the patient is usually doing the best she can, and if we therapists remember this, our staying power will increase. Staying can be life saving.

❖ CHAPTER 9 ❖

Light at the End of the Tunnel

> The aim of psychoanalysis is to end it so new life can begin.
>
> —Jean Laplanche

> As an analyst I know, at each beginning, that analysis ends with renunciations, mourning, and internal change on both sides. I have chosen to accept that I must be "killed" as well as mourned by my analysands in order for them to achieve the freedom to grow.
>
> —Shelley Orgel

I have heard this phrase, "light at the end of the tunnel," so many times in my work I thought it fitting to use it as this chapter's title. It is always exciting and saddening when a patient reports seeing this light, because it signifies both loss and rebirth. All the past losses of patient and therapist are revisited during the final phase of treatment. Mourning is experienced on both sides of the couch. Labor pains herald the end of the journey and the new liberation of both parties in the therapeutic dyad.

Not unlike the separation/individuation stages of development, the termination phase of treatment includes positive and negative feelings, happy and unhappy moments, anxiety and elation. The ability to let go is a prerequisite in an analyst, and this is why her own analysis is so important. Through the treatment, in patient and therapist, exhaustion, hate, and envy of each other are mixed with warmth, empathy, and regard. By the end of the work, pride and love have taken over. Ideally, both therapist and patient have grown in immeasurable ways, and neither will ever be the same as when they started the journey. Letting go and saying goodbye involve deep emotions. For some time after the end of treatment, both parties continue the mourning process, but on a less-intense level. As psychotherapists, we know that treatment that ends prematurely evokes depression and sadness, in part because of the lost chance to experience reparation and gratitude. But this does not mean that patients who don't *finish* therapy have not gained from it. In fact, endings are not always as we would wish. Mrs. W, in twice-weekly psychotherapy for four years, did not return after the therapist's summer vacation. She wrote a note saying that financial difficulties prevented her from continuing. The therapist, Mr. F, called her, and when he could not reach her, he wrote her back suggesting they meet once more to talk in person. There was no response, and he felt Mrs. W was making it clear that she wanted her decision respected. Mr. F had mixed feelings. He was proud of the work that they had done and he was sorry that his patient chose this abrupt way of ending. His intuition told him that saying goodbye, or even making a different arrangement regarding the fee, was not what Mrs. W wanted. She was also expressing her anger about the summer separation in a vehement way. Her inability to control the therapist after four years was intolerable, and ending in this manner must have made her feel very powerful. Mr. F did feel powerless, sad, and angry, but was also able to think of the strides they had made.

The end of treatment is implied when the patient makes her very first contact with the therapist, even though it may be a long time before the end comes into view. When the therapist first hears from the patient, she focuses on the first meeting. She assesses the patient's capacity for insight, for access to affect, for the ability to reflect and to wonder. She thinks about whether a connection has been made, whether the patient can do the work—or what kind of work the patient seems able to do—and whether the patient will end the work in a way acceptable to both parties. The patient assesses how trustworthy she finds the therapist, and the therapist is concerned primarily with tuning in to the patient and creating a safe and productive therapeutic environment. Thinking about how, if, and when the treatment will end seems absurd in a way, because both parties are consciously involved in connecting and forming a working alliance. When someone asks you to dance, do you think about the last step?

As the therapeutic partners begin their dance, however, they are subliminally aware that the music will eventually stop. Although the thoughts of saying goodbye may not reach consciousness early on, they are always present. The end of each session is preparation for the last goodbye. Even though for a long time the partners meet again after each break, whether it be an evening, a weekend, or a month's vacation, the fact of a final separation is a reality often and even usually ignored or denied. How could this not be so? There is much work to do, and beginnings demand all the attention. But the brief recurrent breaks are separations that must be noticed, as they prepare the dyad for the final one.

When a therapist has not come to grips with her own separation anxiety, her countertransference may make the initial phase of treatment longer and more difficult than necessary. Combined with the patient's own fears, issues of separation may become too heavy a burden, causing premature endings or interminable cases. In their efforts to connect, both parties may overlook the reasons that they have come together.

> Mary's therapist was trying to make Mary comfortable by being flexible about fee schedule and time changes. She lowered her standard fee—something we all do at times—but she also agreed to see Mary according to Mary's timetable. There was no safety structure, no continuity, no consistency, and Mary quit before paying her first bill.

Actually, the whole of a treatment can be seen as a prelude to saying goodbye. This is the essence of transference. The whole picture is lit by the wish to avoid separation and to be the chosen one in the oedipal triad. The pressure to repeat the past in the present is an example of how we cling to these wishes and to the past.

As psychoanalytic work has become longer, and as the transference relationship has become its focus, the idea that there will be an end sounds foreign. With the analyst as new object (Loewald, 1960), the main purpose in analytic work is to analyze the transference so that the patient can grow beyond the pressure to repeat the past in the present. The problem with the analyst as new object is that the new object eventually is made into the old object. The therapist's hardest task is to resist the pull of the patient's transference by monitoring her countertransference. Her main job, after all, is to analyze both.

Frequently, therapy takes over life; sometimes it seems that life gets lived in treatment. How long the patient should stay in treatment is a complex question and one that needs to be looked at with each individual patient. The process of ending an analysis is the most important part of it, and it must be addressed especially carefully by those who supervise and train other therapists. There is always more to analyze—one could continue forever—but the ability to separate is never tested if analysis goes on indefinitely. Only the therapeutic duo can decide when it is time to stop, and the decision is never perfect. Many patients return to treatment as needed after termination. Some patients return to the original therapist; others seek treatment with a different analyst. The main point is that going back to treatment after a period of consolidation and mourning is not unusual. Freud recommended that the analyst return to analysis every five years.

One important indicator of readiness to end treatment is improved object relationships and more comfortable compromise formations. Life outside therapy, as measured by work, love, expression of creativity, and the ability to experience pleasure, will have been enhanced. Character change, though hard to achieve, does occur, particularly with sadomasochistic characters. As the analyst monitors the progressions and regressions in treatment, she must also think about what the end will look like with each particular patient.

Endings are just as important as beginnings, and they too have a form. Patient and therapist do not usually become close friends after treatment. There is often a wish that this could be so—in both parties—but although the therapeutic sessions are over, on some level the therapeutic relationship remains, and if preserved it can be useful in future times of crisis.

Some therapists taper off a treatment before ending it. But cutting down slowly rather than ending within the original framework of *x* sessions a week deprives the dyad of an undiluted ending. Drawn-out goodbyes tend to lose their potency. What are the signs of readiness for terminating psychoanalytically based treatment?

- Resolution of intense transference manifestations
- Recognition and working through of envy and rage

- Ability to see the therapist as an independent person with a life of her own
- Improved capacity for empathy
- Structural change (improved ego strength, a more benevolent superego, sublimation of instinctual wishes)
- Recognition and understanding of core fantasies
- Relaxation of constricting defenses
- Improved conflict resolution

Once both parties recognize the light at the end of the tunnel, there is a tendency both to rejoice and to bemoan. This may show in some of the following ways:

- Regression to earlier phases of life or of treatment
- Recurrence of symptoms and acting out
- Depression or sadness
- Resurgence of rapprochement and envy issues
- Planning for the future

Sometimes, signs of improvement seem to disappear when talk of terminating begins. Once again, there are struggles against separation and anger about the termination.

- How can you leave me?
- How can you let me go?
- You never really cared!
- I'll show you what will happen!
- You must be getting ready to retire.
- You're sick and not telling me.
- You're bored with this.
- You're tired of me.
- You'll never have a patient as rewarding as I am.

The therapist, for her part, feels sadness, envy, disappointment, joy, and pride, and she anticipates a loss of income. These combine to make this period of treatment bittersweet for her as well. As acting out recurs, old symptoms flare up, and gains disappear, both patient and therapist begin to wonder if maybe they are thinking of ending too soon.

Saying goodbye is not easy after years of intimacy, and the process is unique for each dyad.

Ideally, setting a date to end therapy is a mutual decision. Somewhere in the middle (or even the beginning) phase of treatment the questions "When does this end?" "How do we stop?" and "When will I know?" come up. The therapist can say something like: "Everyone is different—but as we go along we'll look at that question. Usually, when we feel that you have worked through what has stood in your way, we'll be able to decide on how long the ending phase should be. I usually recommend setting a date that gives us from three months to a year to wrap things up and say goodbye." The most important work often gets done in the termination phase of treatment. Some analysts believe that when the patient is ready to leave, she should leave—without a termination phase. My experience has shown that saying goodbye over a period of time often allows new material to emerge. After some years of work, the idea of ending often comes up. This is not necessarily resistance—it is more like a dawning realization that the work has been done and that change has occurred. There are references to ending or saying goodbye in the patient's material, most often in dreams. Such indications are not always music to the therapist's ears. The therapist may be enjoying the work, and she may on an unconscious level have her own difficulties with separation. Therapists who are having trouble filling their practices may look for reasons to continue treatment. Usually, though, the therapist is heartened by the patient's messages of readiness to think about ending. The subject of ending may occupy the therapeutic stage on and off for long periods of time—it is not a subject to be rushed through.

This is the ideal situation, however, and not the only one. Every therapist has had the experience of premature endings. Some patients end before they begin (see Miss B in chapter 3). Others do some work and quit, such as Nancy:

> Nancy maintained a steady negative transference to her first therapist. She had a need to distance others that played out in all areas of her life. Envy and rage made friendships and love relationships impossible. She acted out her needs for closeness with promiscuous sex and avoided her depression with daily amphetamine use. Her one goal was to get married, but her relationships were short-lived. The treatment went downhill steadily, yet neither party seemed able to stop it. After two years, Nancy finally quit, blaming the therapist for their failure.
>
> Nancy's next therapist was a woman who silently agreed with Nancy's negative assessment of her previous treatment. She found Nancy to be verbal, interesting, and talented. Nancy was in a hurry to straighten her life out and to find a mate. They agreed to begin psychoanalysis. Work proceeded, and Nancy developed an idealizing transference. Accepting the idealization as indication of a narcissistic disorder, the therapist listened and occasionally reflected back Nancy's material. Nancy seemed to accept this empathic listening well for several months, but then she began to complain that nothing was happening in her life. She lost a job and a prospective suitor. She began coming late. Nothing the therapist said made any impression; in fact, Nancy disparaged interpretations. The therapist was aware of a negative countertransference and felt that Nancy was provoking her into a battle. If she said something like "You want me to know how very angry you are," Nancy would respond with, "You're goddamned right I do!" Treatment continued for two years, but after the second summer break Nancy did not return.

The therapist was relieved, but she also blamed herself, thinking that her relative inexperience might have been a factor. Several years later, she heard a case presented in a seminar that sounded exactly like Nancy. The presenter was the fourth therapist, and the case was not going well. The point here is that sometimes the patient doesn't respond, no matter what. In chapter 7, Dr. R made the point that going through a series of therapists often holds a patient together, even though they may never know it. Therapists have different reactions to what looks like failure with a patient. Anger, sadness, sorrow, and relief are some of them, and there are also tendencies to blame oneself, one's method, or the patient. But sometimes a patient cannot tolerate closeness. Nancy called her first therapist's tape ten years after she had quit: "I can't believe you're still there, still alive. I'm not leaving my name but I'm sure you recognize my voice. My God, you're still in practice. I suppose this would be called acting out, and I hate to ruin your image of yourself, but you wasted my money. I'm doing great." The attachment was still there.

The following vignette shows how therapy can prepare a person for a life change:

> Mr. D, age twenty-five, began therapy after his girlfriend recommended it. She felt that, for their relationship to succeed, they both had to be in therapy, not she alone. He agreed, as he knew he had problems. Mr. D had moved here from Japan when he was seven. His father had been a failure in business and was completely self-involved. His mother was much younger than his father, pretty, and seductively close to her son. He had a seductive older sister as well. Mr. D became the adult male of the family way before he was ready. He negotiated and took charge of a family lawsuit when he was thirteen. He spoke English better than his parents and had to translate to them the bad news that they lost most of their money. Mother and sister went to work, and the father did, too, for several years. Mr. D went to a prestigious college on scholarship, but he graduated with difficulty. He was extremely bright, but had trouble studying. Family pressures on him to excel and become gainfully employed contributed to anxiety, procrastination, and depression. However, Mr. D was resilient. He made friends, kept old friends, played tennis, and had a good sense of humor.
>
> When he began treatment, he was contemplating marriage. His family was still needy, his fiancé expected him to excel in business, and he felt he needed to face his anxiety about commitment. Treatment enabled Mr. D to work through many issues. His apparent oedipal victory and the guilt it evoked were the major themes. Mr. D resented not having had a real adolescence or even childhood, but he compensated in the playful side of his personality. As the beloved baby of the family, he had been cherished by two beautiful women. This played into his guilt, but it also gave him the confidence to succeed. Sexual inhibition diminished. Therapy over five years gave him insight and the ability to assert himself at work and with his fiancé/wife. In the transference, the therapist was one of the women—mother, sister, wife—who demanded of him, expected from him, and were supposed to adore him. Shyness, inhibition, and seduction were acted out and understood. Mr. D was a loving and competent husband, and when his

child was born, he became an adoring and competent father. His time in treatment (four times a week) had been well spent. A termination date was set, and treatment ended six months later. Mr. D and the therapist said goodbye with mixed feelings of pride, sadness, and joy, along with the knowledge that both had grown and would retain places in each other's hearts. In this apparent happily-ever-after story, it was the hard work and motivation to succeed that enabled Mr. D to grow and deal with conflict.

The following vignette illustrates how delayed mourning can occur in psychoanalytic work.

Dr. V married a woman who was remote and at times volatile. He complained that she never talked to him, and that when he pushed her she withdrew even more. Dr. V's mother had died when he was twelve. The long illness that eventually killed her had made her tired and emotionally unavailable. Dr. V had not dared to express his rage about this, fearing to displease and upset his ailing mother. Dr. V's death wishes about his mother made him feel unsafe about being close to anyone. A remote wife, who kept her distance, guaranteed safety. His work as a surgeon satisfied his rescue fantasies and assuaged some of his guilt, but married life for Dr. V was a repetition of the past with his mother, and to cling to his marriage was to cling to her.

After years of treatment, Dr. V began to get in touch with his deep disappointment and his vengeful fantasies. In the transference, he slowly mourned his mother and their relationship. As he saw that his anger harmed no one, it was safe for him to become disappointed in the therapist. He tried to make her feel useless, and a long period of negativity developed. The therapist was not destructible, and she returned after separations ready to continue the work. Dr. V gradually allowed himself to feel close. Transference distortions diminished. His own capacity for nurturing grew, and his wife felt a lessening of tension in him. Things improved across the board, and with improvement both patient and therapist began to see light at the end of the tunnel.

References to endings entered the material. In one dream, the end of a baseball game that had gone twelve innings (Dr. V had been twelve when his mother died) was understood to represent the therapy. One year after this dream, Dr. V completed his treatment.

Some of the outcomes of psychoanalytic work in my experience have been:

- The original oedipal defeat is softened and a new love is accepted
- Self and object representations are modified
- Separation/individuation is reworked
- Object constancy is improved
- Grandiosity is tamed
- Paranoid fears are recognized as projections
- Sadistic fantasies are uncovered
- Masochism diminishes as rage is owned
- True differentiation is accomplished

The most difficult part of the therapeutic process is knowing when the dyadic work is completed. Some treatments never end—they just fade away. Some endings are premature. The patient relocates, or new commitments come up that make time an issue. The therapist feels satisfied (or dissatisfied) with the work, wants to retire, becomes ill, or is preoccupied with the illness of another. Ideally, a mutual decision to separate after the long journey together is desirable. The clinical phrase *planned termination* is an unfortunate one for the kind of intimate work that it implies; perhaps *agreement to finish work together* is more realistic. But there comes a time when patient and therapist say goodbye to each other.

Yet because object constancy is firmer, and because the method of psychoanalytic work becomes internalized along with aspects of the analyst, the journey never really ends. Self-analysis is possible: when transference manifestations occur with others, they can be understood; dreams make more sense; fears that crop up can be tolerated based on the analytic work that has already been done. The energy that had previously been spent pleasing, disappointing, hating, needing, killing, envying, destroying, and rescuing is freed. New ambitions, new relationships and commitments, generative activities take the place of pursuits once based on neurotic needs. To varying degrees, envy has evolved into admiration and sarcasm into humor, and this and the ability to love in its deepest, most unselfish sense all make for a fulfilling life.

Both the patient's life and the therapist's have been enriched by the journey, and both parties have grown over the years of travel.

As I realize that I have reached the end of the tunnel with this book, I feel as a patient feels at the end of psychoanalytic work: worried that I haven't done it well enough, fearful that I've left something out, sad that I won't any longer have it to occupy me every day, proud that I've done this work, and hopeful that others will appreciate my endeavor.

References

Abraham, K. (1919). A particular form of neurotic resistance against the psychoanalytic method. In *Selected papers on psychoanalysis* (pp. 303–311). New York: Bruner/Mazel.

Adams-Silvan, A. (1994). "That darkness—Is about to pass." *Psychoanalytic Study of the Child* 49:328–348.

Ardow, J. A. (1969). Fantasy, memory, and reality testing. *Psychoanalytic Quarterly* 38:28–51.

Asch, S. (1988). The analytic concepts of masochism: A reevaluation. In R. A. Glick, and D. I. Meyers (Eds.), *Masochism: Current psychoanalytic perspectives* (pp. 93–115). Hillsdale, NJ: Analytic Press.

Bach, S. (1971). Notes on some imaginary companions. *Psychoanalytic Study of the Child* 26:159–171.

Bak, R. (1968). The phallic woman. *Psychoanalytic Study of the Child* 23:15–36.

Bergmann, M., and Hartman, F. (1976). *The Evolution of Psychoanalytic Technique*. New York: Basic.

Berliner, B. (1958). The role of object relations in moral masochism. *Psychoanalytic Quarterly* 27:38–56.

Bernstein, S. (1983). Treatment preparatory to psychoanalysis. *Journal of the American Psychoanalytic Association* 31:363–390.

Bird, B. (1957). A specific peculiarity of acting out. *Journal of the American Psychoanalytic Association* 5:630.

Bird, B. (1972). Transference, the hardest part of analysis. *Journal of the American Psychoanalytic Association* 20:267–301.

Brenner, I. (2001). *Dissociation of trauma: Theory, phenomenology, and technique*. Madison, CT: International Universities Press.

Camelio, B. (2002). Personal communication.

Carpy, D. (1989). Tolerating the countertransference: A mutative process. *International Journal of Psychoanalysis* 70: 287–294.

Coen, S. (1988). In R. A. Glick and D. I. Meyers (Eds.), *Masochism: Current psychoanalytic perspectives* (pp. 43–59). Hillsdale, NJ: Analytic Press.

Etchegoyen, R. H. (1991). *The fundamentals of psychoanalytic technique*. London: Karnac.

Fairbairn, W. R. D. (1958). On the nature and aims of psychoanalytic treatment. *International Journal of Psychoanalysis* 39:374–385.

Farber, S. (2000). *When the body is the target: Self-harm, pain, and traumatic attachments*. Northvale, NJ: Jason Aronson.

Fonagy, P. (2000). Attachment and borderline personality disorder. *Journal of the American Psychoanalytic Association* 48:1129–1146.

Freud, A. (1936). *The ego and the mechanisms of defense*. London: Hogarth.

Freud, S. (1914). Remembering, repeating and working-through (Further recommendations on the technique of psychoanalysis, II). *Standard Edition* 12. London: Hogarth.

Freud, S. (1916). Some character types met with in psycho-analytic work. *Standard Edition* 14:309–333. London: Hogarth.

Freud, S. (1923). The Ego and the Id. *Standard Edition* 19:3–66. London: Hogarth.

Gabbard, G. (2000). Hatred and its rewards: A discussion. *Psychoanalytic Inquiry* 20, 3:409–420.

Gabbard, G., et al. (2000). On gratitude and gratification. *Journal of the American Psychoanalytic Association* 48:697–714.

Gill, M. M., and Muslim, H. (1976). Early interpretation of the transference. *Journal of the American Psychoanalytic Association* 24:779–794.

Greenacre, P. (1956). Re-evaluation of the process of working through. *International Journal of Psychoanalysis* 37:449–454.

Greenacre, P. (1966). Problems of overidealization of the analyst and of analysis. *Psychoanalytic Study of the Child* 21:195–312.

Greenacre, P. (1969). *Trauma, Growth, and Personality*. New York: International Universities Press.

Greenacre, P. (1970). Notes on the influence and contribution of ego psychology to the practice of psychoanalysis. In *Emotional Growth*, Vol. 2 (pp.776–806). New York: International Universities Press.

Hall, J. (1998). *Deepening the treatment*. New York: Jason Aronson.

Heimann, P. (1950). On countertransference. *International Journal of Psychoanalysis* 31:81–84.

Jacobs, T. (1991). *The use of the self: Countertransference and communication in the analytic situation*. Madison, CT: International Universities Press.

Joseph, B. (1985). Transference, the total situation. *International Journal of Psychoanalysis* 66:447–454.

Kempe, C. H., Silverman, F. N., Steele, B. F., Droegemuller, W., and Silver, H. K. (1962). The battered child syndrome. *Journal of the American Medical Association* 181:17–24.

Kernberg, O. (1975). *Borderline conditions and pathological narcissism*. New York: Jason Aronson.

Klein, M. (1932). Die psychoanalyse des kindes [The psychoanalysis of children]. Wein: Internationaler Psychoanalytischer Verlag.

Klein, M. (1948). *Contributions to psychoanalysis*. London: Hogarth.

Kohut, H. (1971). *The analysis of the self*. New York: International Universities Press.

Kris, E. (1956). The recovery of childhood memories in psychoanalysis. *Psychoanalytic Study of the Child* 11:54–88.

Langs, R. J. (1976). The therapeutic interaction, Vols. 1 and 2. New York: Jason Aronson.

Laplanche, J. (1998). Time and the other. *Essays on Otherness*. London: Routledge.

Loewald, H. (1951). The ego and reality. *International Journal of Psychoanalysis* 32:10–18.

Loewald, H. (1960). The therapeutic action of psychoanalysis. *International Journal of Psychoanalysis* 41:16–33.

Loewald, H. (1979). The waning of the Oedipus complex. *Journal of the American Psychoanalytic Association* 27:751–775.

Mahler, M., Pine, F., and Bergman, A. (1975). *The psychological birth of the human infant: Symbiosis and individuation*. New York: Basic.

McLaughlin, J., and Johan, M. (1992). Enactment in psychoanalysis. *Journal of the American Psychoanalytic Association* 40:827–841.

Modell, A. (1976). "The holding environment" and the therapeutic action of psychoanalysis. *Journal of the American Psychoanalytic Association* 24:285–307.

Nason, J. (1995). The psychotherapy of rage. *Journal of Contemporary Psychoanalysis* 21:167.

Ogden, T. (1989). *The primitive edge of experience*. New York: Jason Aronson.

Orgel, S. (2000). Letting go: Some thoughts about termination. *Journal of the American Psychoanalytic Association* 48:719–738.

Pine, F. (1988). The four psychologies and their place in clinical work. *Journal of the American Psychoanalytic Association* 36:571–596.

Racker, H. (1968). *Transference and Countertransference*. London: Karnac.

Reich, A. (1951). On countertransference. *International Journal of Psychoanalysis* 32:25–51.

Reich, A. (1960). Further remarks on countertransference. *International Journal of Psychoanalysis* 41:389–395.

Reich, W. (1933–34). *Character Analysis*. New York: Touchstone, 1974.

Renick, O. (1993). Analytic interactions. Conceptualizing technique in the light of the analyst's irreducible subjectivity. *Psychoanalytic Quarterly* 64:555–571.

Richards, A. K. (2003). A fresh look at perversion. *Journal of the American Psychoanalytic Association* 51:1199–1218.

Rothstein, A. (1994). A perspective on doing a consultation and making the recommendation of analysis to a prospective analysand. *Psychoanalytic Quarterly* 68:680–695.

Rothstein, A. (1995). *Psychoanalytic technique and the creation of analytic patients*. Madison, CT: International Universities Press.

Sandler, J. (1960). The background of safety. In J. Sandler (Ed.), *From Safety to Superego*. New York: Guilford, 1987.

Sandler, J. (1976). Countertransference and role-responsiveness. *International Journal of Psychoanalysis* 3:43–47.

Sandler, J., Dare, C., and Holder, A. (1992). *The patient and the analyst*. Madison, CT: International Universities Press.

Sandler, J., and Rosenblatt, B. (1962). The concept of representational world. *Psychoanalytic Study of the Child* 17:128–145.

Sandler, J., and Sandler, A. (1998). *Internal objects revisited*. London: Karnac.

Schafer, R. (1983). *The analytic attitude*. New York: Basic.

Schafer, R. (1988). Those wrecked by success. In R. A. Glick and D. I. Meyers (Eds.), *Masochism: current psychoanalytic perspectives* (pp. 81–91). Hillsdale, N.J.: Analytic Press.

Schwaber, E. (1985). *Transference in psychotherapy: Clinical management*. Madison, CT.: International Universities Press.

Sexton, A. (1976). *45 Mercy Street*. L. G. Sexton and L. Conant Jr. (Eds.). Boston: Houghton Mifflin.

Sharpe, E. (1947). The psycho-analyst. *International Journal of Psychoanalysis* 28:1–6.

Shengold, L. (1989). *Soul murder: The effects of childhood abuse and deprivation*. New Haven, CT: Yale University Press.

Shengold, L. (1999). *Soul murder revisited*. New Haven, CT: Yale University Press.

Shengold, L. (2000). *Is there life without Mother?* Hillsdale, NJ: Analytic Press.

Smirnoff, V. M. (1969). The masochistic contract. *International Journal of Psychoanalysis* 50:665–672.

Smith, H. (1999). Countertransference, conflictual listening and the analytic object relationship. *Journal of the American Psychoanalytic Association* 48:95–126.

Steele, B. (1994). Psychoanalysis and the maltreatment of children. *Journal of the American Psychoanalytic Association* 42:1001–1025.

Strachey, J. (1934). The nature of the therapeutic action of psychoanalysis. *International Journal of Psychoanalysis* 15:127–151.

Sterba, R. (1934). The fate of the ego in analytic therapy. *International Journal of Psychoanalysis* 15:117–126.

Tyson, P., and Tyson, R. (1990). *Psychoanalytic theories of development*. New Haven, CT: Yale University Press.

Valenstein, A. (1973). On attachment to painful feelings and the negative therapeutic reaction. *Psychoanalytic Study of the Child* 28:365–392.

Wallerstein, R. (1983). One psychoanalysis or many? *International Journal of Psychoanalysis* 60:5–21.

Wegner, P. (2000). Passion, enactment, and breakdown in the psychoanalysis of a young woman. *Journal of the American Psychoanalytic Association* 48:811–838.

Westen, D., and Gabbard, G. (2002). Developments in cognitive neuroscience II: Implications for theories of transference. *Journal of the American Psychoanalytic Association* 50:99–134.

Wheelis, A. (1956). The vocational hazards of psychoanalysis. *International Journal of Psychoanalysis* 37:171–184.

Winnicott, D. W. (1969). The youth of an object and relating through identifications. In *Playing and Reality* (pp. 86–94). New York: Basic.

Winnicott, D. W. (1971). *Playing and Reality*. New York: Basic.

❖ ❖ ❖

Index

❖ ❖ ❖

About the Author

Jane S. Hall, M.S.W., is a graduate of the Hunter College School of Social Work, the Institute for the Study of Psychotherapy, and the New York Freudian Society, of which she is a member. She is also a member of the International Psychoanalytical Association, and is a founder of the New York School for Psychotherapy and Psychoanalysis. Her publications include *Deepening the Treatment* (Jason Aronson, 1998). A training and supervising analyst who has taught, lectured, and consulted on how to deepen psychoanalytic work for the past twenty-five years, Hall is in private practice in New York City.